BLACKJACK FOR BLOOD

Revised Edition

BLACKJACK FOR BLOOD

A Complete Handbook

and

Winning System

for

Casino Blackjack

Bryce Carlson, B.A., M.B.A.

This book is dedicated to

my son Sean,

my wife Diane,

my mother Virginia,

and to the loving memory of

my father Jade.

Some Good News
        and Some Bad News...

The Bad News:

According to the casinos,
you've got about as much chance
as a lamb in a slaughterhouse.

The Good News:

The day of the lamb has come.[1]

---

1. Thorp, <u>Beat the Dealer</u>, rev. ed. p. 74.

ACKNOWLEDGMENTS

I could not have written this book, nor would my Blackjack career have existed, without the contributions of the talented players and researchers who have come before me. If I have seen beyond the mountain into the valley of truth, it is because I have stood upon the shoulders of giants.[1]

And foremost among these giants is Ed Thorp to whom I, and every other pro Blackjack player, owe a huge debt for his masterful work Beat the Dealer;[2] this is the foundation for everything we have built.

Julian Braun[3] also deserves high praise for his detailed computer studies, which provided the first really accurate playing strategies.

And, of course, no acknowledgment would be complete without mention of the late Lawrence Revere.[4] He could be crusty; he could be crude, and he played both sides of the street--but he taught me how to play, and he showed me how to win.

These are the masters emeritus in the Blackjack Hall of Fame. Their works form the basis for the theory, analysis, and practice of scientific Twenty-One.

----

1. Apologies to Isaac Newton for the use (or abuse) of his words.

2. Edward O. Thorp, Beat the Dealer (New York: Random House, 1962).

3. Julian H. Braun, The Development and Analysis of Winning Strategies for the Casino Game of Blackjack (Chicago: Braun, 1974).

4. Lawrence Revere, Playing Blackjack as a Business (New Jersey: Lyle Stuart, 1969).

Thanks, also, to the many friends and colleagues[5] whose insights, experiences, and suggestions have helped make this a far better work than it otherwise might have been.

And, I guess I also owe a debt to the pit bosses and casino managers who have made my Blackjack career so challenging; dealing with these pit bulls is not only one of the most difficult aspects of professional play, it is also one of the most rewarding.

Lastly, a special thanks to Mons M., and Mlle K., for reasons they alone know, but without whose help my Blackjack career might well have ended late one night in a small town in the south of France.

----

5. In particular, I am indebted to fellow Blackjack experts Donald Schlesinger and Stanford Wong, as well as senior copy editor Lorraine Slattery, for their thorough and thoughtful reviews of the manuscript.

PREFACE

My purpose in writing this book is to provide the reader with a comprehensive strategy for obtaining a winning edge at Blackjack, as it is commonly played in the casinos of Nevada and elsewhere, and also to entertain the reader with some sense of the glamour, excitement and drama that are a part of the world of the professional gambler.

For a Twenty-One game plan to be effective, it must address three fundamental and very different issues. First, it must show the player how to bet his money properly and how to play the hands accurately; without this you have nothing. Second, it must instruct the player on how to deal effectively with casino personnel; if the casino bosses won't allow you to play, it doesn't matter how well you play, you are out of business. And third, a professional approach to the game requires the ability to deal with yourself, to maintain control under pressure, and in situations loaded with stress. This may surprise you, but many fine players have lost everything because they were just unable to handle the stress of serious play. You may play wonderfully, and know every nuance of handling the casino bosses, but if you can't keep your own emotions under control, you are lost. It's just that simple.

If this is all beginning to sound like it might involve a little effort, well, there is good reason for that--it does involve some work! But if the time and effort necessary to master Twenty-One are viewed in perspective, they pale compared to the fantastic rewards the game offers to those who come prepared. And the most satisfying of these rewards is not monetary, although there is a whole lot of money to be made playing Twenty-One. To me, and I think to most expert players, the real satisfaction comes from the mastery of the game itself: to know you are a world class player, one of a handful of the very best, at a game played around the world, is very, very gratifying.

There have been many books, booklets, systems, and strategies written about the game of casino Twenty-One, and they vary in value from the worthless to the priceless, and in cost from two dollars to two thousand(!) dollars. From a purely theoretical standpoint, the best of these works have generally been written by highly trained mathematicians and statisticians working in research laboratories with access to the latest in high speed digital computers. Several excellent Twenty-One strategies have been developed by these talented men, and their works have had a profound impact on the game. Unfortunately, however, because they have been researchers, and not professional Blackjack players, their works have often lacked the practical insights necessary for survival in the casino environment. It is one thing to play Blackjack on a computer, in the sterile atmosphere of a research laboratory. It is a very different thing to play Blackjack in a casino, with your own money at stake, with a paranoid pit boss hawking your every move, a rock band blasting away in the background, and a pretty cocktail waitress jiggling her maracas in your face. Believe me, it makes a difference. Other works, written by active professional players, have handled the practical aspects somewhat better, but they have often been marred by serious mathematical inaccuracies and misconceptions.

Nowhere, to my knowledge, was a work to be found that dealt completely and accurately with all aspects of this fascinating game. That is what I have set out to do in this book; the results achieved by you, my readers, in actual casino play, will be the measure of my success.

TABLE OF CONTENTS

TABLE OF CONTENTS
(continued)

TABLE OF CONTENTS
(continued)

TABLE OF CONTENTS
(continued)

TABLE OF CONTENTS
(continued)

TABLE OF CONTENTS
(continued)

CHAPTER ONE

The Good Life

I awoke to soft strains of Polynesian music and the soothing voice of a kimono-clad JAL stewardess welcoming me to Honolulu, Hawaii. As I looked out the window, I caught a glimpse of Diamond Head silhouetted against the evening sky. And though I have been to the Islands many times, the sight of Diamond Head, guarding the entrance to this island paradise like some majestic, eternal sphinx, always fills me with wonder for the majesty and beauty of nature.

Two weeks in Hawaii. A few days enjoying the night life of Honolulu, and then on to the golden sands and warm tropical waters of Maui, the trophy marlin off Kona on the Big Island, and, finally, the quiet beauty of Kauai. The Garden Isle. A place to relax, unwind, be lulled to sleep by the rhythm of the pounding surf. A place to remember that it is good to be young, and good to be alive.

The professional Twenty-One circuit is international. And some of the best games are to be found outside of Nevada and Atlantic City. In the winter the Islands are delightful, and though Hawaii offers no casino-style gambling, it is the gateway to the Orient. And in the Orient, particularly in South Korea and Malaysia, some of the best Blackjack games in the world are to be found. For example, the Walker Hill hotel/casino in Seoul City offers excellent rules, fine playing conditions, and a warm hospitality seemingly unique to the Far East.

After a couple of weeks of "work" in the casinos of South Korea, Malaysia, Macao, and elsewhere in the Orient, I like to lay over in the Islands, kick back for a week or two, spend some of my winnings enjoying life--and plan my next adventure.

In the spring, the Caribbean beckons. Aruba, Curacao, Nassau, and Paradise Island are a few of my favorites. In addition to their great natural beauty, with miles of brilliant alabaster beaches caressed by the clear emerald sea, hundreds of secluded turquoise lagoons, and an ideal climate, they all offer Twenty-One in hotel/casino resorts of the most opulent splendor. And while the rules in some of these casinos are not the best, the playing conditions are ideal, and winning is both easy and enjoyable.

1

Later in the year, when the autumn breeze cools the blistered desert sands, and the setting sun paints scarlet across the evening sky, my thoughts turn to Las Vegas. Founded by East Coast mobsters with the intent of creating a year-round gambling mecca in the desert near Southern California, the Las Vegas "Strip" stands today as both a monument to the vision of Benjamin "Bugsy" Siegel and a testimonial to the power and greed of those who came after him.

On a clear night the desert sky is aglow with the lights of Las Vegas for fifty miles in any direction. Up close, fantastic neon and metallic marquees blind the eye, as vision is reduced to a swirl of colors and iridescent lights. Amid the glitter, enormous palaces, each one seemingly more grandiose and more garish than the last, fight for attention among the masses of humanity that choke the "Strip." After a while, all is a blur of brilliant color, gaudy streetwalkers, spinning roulette wheels, crystal chandeliers, and people lost in an almost hypnotic orgy of frenetic self-indulgence. In this surreal atmosphere money loses all meaning. Soon five dollars is a "nickel," twenty-five is a "quarter," and a hundred-dollar bill is just a "buck."

People come to Las Vegas to forget the burdens of their workaday world, to enjoy a weekend fling, lose themselves in fantasy and, as they say, to let 'er rip. And so they do. I have seen normally rational people blow thousands at the tables in a few frenzied hours, drunk on the crazy magic of the place--only to come crashing back to reality the next day, their faces masks of shock and despair.

In the midst of all this insanity, I go about the business of making a living playing Twenty-One. I enjoy Las Vegas to the fullest, including the top-name shows, the gourmet dining, and the elegant accommodations, but I avoid the traps. I hit and I split. I make my money, and then I move on. Although, in general, the playing conditions in Las Vegas are among the poorest in the world, there are, nevertheless, plenty of good games for those who know where to look, and for those who know how to play.

And so it goes. Atlantic City, the Caribbean, London, the French Riviera, the Far East, Lake Tahoe, Reno, Las Vegas. I jet around the world first class, dine on nothing but the finest cuisine, stay in the most luxurious resort hotels, play, at my leisure, in elegant casinos of world renown, and return home with a fat profit barely dented by travel expenses.

This is the life of a world-class Blackjack player, as I know it and as I live it. And although the pro tour is an exclusive club, and not everyone can join, if you have the talent, and if you will put in the time to master the material that follows, an exciting and rewarding lifestyle, one that most people only dream about, can be yours for the taking. But whether your goal is to be a professional, or just to improve your game, I think you will find your effort rewarded as we explore together the fascinating world of Twenty-One.

CHAPTER TWO

The Rules of the Game

Your first step on the road to winning Blackjack is a thorough understanding of the rules of the game and the effect of these rules on your prospects for successful play. So, even if you have played a considerable amount of Twenty-One, I strongly advise you to study this chapter carefully.

The Object of the Game

The player's goal is to beat the dealer. To do this, he must obtain a total that is greater than the dealer's but does not exceed 21.

The Number of Players

The game has a dealer and from one to seven players. Some Blackjack tables can accommodate only five or six players, but seven is the usual number.

The Pack

The number of decks used varies widely, from one ordinary 52-card pack, to multiples of this, all the way up to six or eight decks! As we shall see later, the more decks in play, the worse it generally is for the player.

In northern Nevada the rules are usually tough, but the vast majority of games are single-deck. In Las Vegas, on the other hand, the rules are usually better, but multiple-deck games predominate. In Atlantic City, virtually all games use six or eight decks, and the rest of the world, with rare exceptions, is strictly four-, six-, and eight-deck games.

Betting

The layout has betting spaces, usually a circle or similar marking, for each of the players. Before the deal begins, the players place their wagers in these spaces. Once play is under way, the bets may not be changed (except for doubling down, splitting, and insurance, to be explained later). The *minimum* bet varies from a low of $1 to as much as $500, with $2, $5, and $25 minimums the most common. The *maximum* bet varies from $25 to $2,000 or even higher, with $500 the most common.

The Deal

The dealer shuffles the cards and offers them to a player to be cut. He then places the top card in the discard tray or "burns" it to the bottom of the deck(s). The deal begins with the player to the dealer's extreme left and proceeds in a clockwise direction until the dealer has dealt two cards to himself and two cards to each of the players. He deals one of his cards face up and the other face down; the players' cards are either both face up or both face down, depending on the casino. As the dealer must play by fixed rules, it does not matter if he sees the players' cards.

The Value of the Cards

The Ace counts either 1 or 11, as the player chooses. The 10,J,Q,K all count 10, and the other cards count their face value. If a hand contains an Ace, and if counting the Ace as 11 does not result in the total exceeding 21, the hand is said to be "soft." Soft hands, therefore, have two values, the soft total counting the Ace as 11, and the "hard" total counting the Ace as 1. (Ace,7), for instance, has a value of either soft 18 or hard 8. Other hands have only a hard total.

Naturals

If the player's or dealer's first two cards consist of an Ace and a 10-value card, the hand is called a "blackjack," or a "natural." If the player has a natural, and the dealer does not, the player wins the hand and is paid at odds of 3 to 2. If the dealer has a natural, and the player does not, the dealer wins the hand at even money, and collects the player's bet. If both the dealer and the player have blackjack, the hand is a "push," and no money changes hands.

Insurance

If the dealer receives an Ace as his up card, he offers the players an additional side bet known as "insurance" before he checks his down card to see if he has a natural. Any player wishing to take insurance places an amount equal (at most) to half his original bet in the space marked "INSURANCE." If the dealer has a natural, the insurance bet wins and is paid at odds of 2 to 1 (saving the player's original bet--hence the name "insurance"). If the dealer does not have a natural, the insurance bet is lost, and play continues as usual.

Although almost universally offered, one or two casinos in the Reno area do not allow insurance. And in London and elsewhere in the U.K. it is only allowed if the player holds a natural.

The Draw

After the players have received their initial two cards, they may, if they choose, draw one or more additional cards. The draw begins with the player to the dealer's extreme left, and proceeds in a clockwise direction. A player drawing additional cards receives them face up, one at a time, until he is satisfied with his hand, or until his total exceeds hard 21. In the latter case, the hand is "busted," and the dealer collects the player's bet and places his cards in the discard tray. After the players have acted on their hands, the dealer turns up his down card. If his total is 16 or less, the dealer must draw additional cards until his total is 17 or more. If the dealer is dealt an Ace, and if counting the Ace as 11 would bring the dealer's total to 17 or more, without exceeding 21, the dealer must count the Ace as 11, and stand. About half of the casinos in the world have modified this rule for soft hands; in these casinos the dealer must draw to soft 17, and stand on soft 18 or more. This variation results in a small overall gain for the house.

6

Splitting

If the player's first two cards have the same numerical value, he may, if he chooses, treat them as the first cards of two separate hands. This is called "splitting" a pair. To accomplish the split, the player turns his two cards face up on the table, places his original bet by one of the cards, and an equal amount by the other. The dealer then deals a second card to the first split, and the hand is completed in the usual way. A second card is then dealt to the other split, and play on this hand proceeds as usual. If Aces are split, however, the player receives only one card, face down, on each Ace. In addition, if the player receives a 10-value card on one or both of the split Aces, the hand is not a blackjack but counts as ordinary 21. The same is true if a player splits a pair of 10-valued cards and draws an Ace; the hand is not a natural.

If a player, in splitting a pair, draws another card of the same value, most casinos will allow him to split again, up to a total of four split hands.

Doubling Down

After looking at his initial two cards, a player may, if he desires, double his bet and draw one additional card. This option is known as "doubling down."

Some casinos restrict doubling down to hands with certain totals. In the Bahamas and Puerto Rico, for example, doubling down is limited to totals of 9, 10, or 11, and in northern Nevada the player may usually only double on 10 or 11. In Las Vegas and Monte Carlo, on the other hand, a player may double down on any first two cards. Doubling down is usually not permitted on hands formed as a result of splitting.

Late Surrender

After receiving his initial two cards, a player may, if the dealer does not have a natural, toss in his hand and forfeit half his bet to the dealer. This option is known as "surrender." A player may not surrender a hand that has been drawn to, and a player may not surrender a hand formed as a result of splitting.

Most casinos do not offer late surrender; it is currently limited to about half a dozen clubs in Las Vegas and Atlantic City.

Asian Surrender

In this version, a player may surrender his unbusted hand any time during his turn, even if he has drawn additional cards, unless the dealer is showing an Ace. However, as with late surrender, a player may not surrender a hand created by splitting a pair.

This rule is found only in the Far East, particularly in South Korea, and on the Philippine Islands.

Early Surrender

In this version, the player may surrender only his first two cards, as in late surrender, but he may do so before the dealer checks for a natural. This rule is highly favorable to the player, because it allows him to sometimes save half his bet against a dealer's blackjack.

This rule is rarely found. At one time it was available in all the casinos in Atlantic City, but it was abandoned when the New Jersey courts ruled it was illegal for the casinos to bar card counters from play at Twenty-One. It is now limited to an occasional club in Las Vegas and Reno.

The Settlement

After all the players and the dealer have acted on their hands, the dealer compares his total with that of the players.

If the dealer busts, all hands that have not busted win, and are paid even money.

If the dealer does not bust, all hands that have not busted, and have a higher total than the dealer's hand, win and are paid at even money. Those hands with a lower total than the dealer's hand lose the amount wagered. If both the dealer and player have the same total, not exceeding 21, the hand is a "push," and no money changes hands.

Of course, any players who have busted lose their wagers regardless of the dealer's final total.

Customs

There are numerous customs and procedures that vary widely among the casinos. And while not strictly part of the rules, these practices can have a decided effect on the player's prospects for winning.

Two of these customs are of particular importance to the expert player. They are shuffling and barring.

Shuffling:

All casinos reserve the right to shuffle the cards, at their discretion, between hands. However, the dealer may not shuffle during play of a hand, unless the deck is exhausted. Because expert play is most effective near the end of the deck(s), early shuffling can seriously decrease the player's rate of winning. For this reason, it is important to avoid those casinos with unfavorable shuffling practices. We will have more to say on this subject in later chapters.

Barring:

If a casino deals an honest game, with reasonable rules, there is only one reliable way to prevent an expert player from winning; this is simply to bar him from play at the Blackjack tables. Although this is an extreme action, of questionable legality, many casinos, nevertheless, do routinely exclude suspected experts from playing Twenty-One. In fact, several Las Vegas casinos are currently facing multimillion dollar lawsuits for just such barrings. When these suits eventually work their way into federal courts, outside Nevada jurisdiction, the general consensus is that such practices will be abolished throughout the United States. In the meantime, it is important to avoid being detected as an expert player. Much of this book is devoted to just this subject. As for myself, I find this little game of cat and mouse at least half the fun!

TABLE 2.1 - RULES VARIATIONS

This table lists all of the more common rules variations and their effect on the player's advantage when he is playing the Basic Strategy of Chapter Four.

Most players don't have a clue as to what their overall expectation is in any given game of Blackjack. When these players encounter a new rules variation, they just shrug and hope for the best, not knowing how much the new rule affects their chances for success.

That sort of attitude pays for all the bright lights in Las Vegas, but it does not contribute toward winning play. A professional must be able to size up any game immediately and know what his approximate advantage is. Table 2.1 gives you the information you need to do just that.

As an example, suppose you want to know what your expectation is in Reno, using the Basic Strategy of Chapter Four. The rules in Reno generally allow you to double down on 10 and 11 only, and the dealer hits soft 17. Looking at Table 2.1, we see that when doubling down is restricted to 10 and 11 the change in advantage is -.28%. Looking further down the table, we see that when the dealer hits soft 17, the Basic Strategy player is hurt by -.20%. So starting from the assumed single-deck, Las Vegas Strip rules, and an advantage of +.01%, against Reno rules our expectation falls to (+.01% -.28% -.20%) = -.47%.

This is valuable information. In later chapters when we discuss win rates and the theory of Gambler's Ruin its importance will be even more apparent.

Table 2.1

RULES VARIATIONS
AND
THEIR EFFECT ON THE PLAYER'S ADVANTAGE

Basic Strategy

RULES VARIATIONS	CHANGE IN ADVANTAGE(%) [1]
TWO DECKS	-.35
FOUR DECKS	-.51
SIX DECKS	-.56
EIGHT DECKS	-.58
INFINITE DECKS	-.67
DOUBLE DOWN 11 ONLY	-.79
DOUBLE DOWN 10, & 11 ONLY	-.28
DOUBLE DOWN 9, 10, & 11 ONLY	-.14
DOUBLE DOWN ON THREE OR MORE CARDS	+.22
DOUBLE DOWN AFTER SPLITTING	+.14
NO RESPLITTING, ONE DECK	-.02
NO RESPLITTING, TWO DECKS	-.04
NO RESPLITTING, FOUR DECKS	-.05
NO RESPLITTING, SIX OR EIGHT DECKS	-.06
NO RESPLITTING, INFINITE DECKS	-.08
RESPLITTING OF ACES, ONE DECK	+.03
RESPLITTING OF ACES, TWO DECKS	+.04
RESPLITTING OF ACES, FOUR DECKS	+.05
RESPLITTING OF ACES, SIX OR EIGHT DECKS	+.06
RESPLITTING OF ACES, INFINITE DECKS	+.08
NO SPLITTING OF ACES	-.16
NO SPLITTING OF PAIRS	-.45
UNLIMITED DRAW TO SPLIT ACES	+.14
LATE SURRENDER, ONE DECK	+.02
LATE SURRENDER, INFINITE DECKS	+.09
ASIAN SURRENDER	+.14
EARLY SURRENDER	+.61
PLAYER'S 21 TIES DEALER'S NATURAL [2]	+.20
DEALER TAKES NO HOLE CARD [3]	.00
DEALER TAKES NO HOLE CARD [4]	-.13
DEALER HITS SOFT 17	-.20

----

1. CHANGE IS FROM SINGLE DECK, LAS VEGAS STRIP RULES.

2. PLAYER'S 21, IN ANY NUMBER OF CARDS, TIES DEALER'S NATURAL WITH 10 UP.

3. IF PLAYER DOUBLES OR SPLITS, HE LOSES ONLY HIS ORIGINAL BET TO DEALER'S NATURAL.

4. IF PLAYER DOUBLES OR SPLITS, HE LOSES HIS ENTIRE BET TO DEALER'S NATURAL.

FIGURE 2.1 - PLAYER'S ADVANTAGE VS. NUMBER OF DECKS

This is an interesting graph; it shows how the player's expectation declines as the number of decks in play increases.

The biggest change, about -.35%, comes when we go from single deck to double deck. As the number of decks increases beyond two, the decline in expectation levels off, eventually approaching nearly -.7% in an infinite-deck game.

Another intriguing fact is that Figure 2.1 is approximated closely by a graph defined by the equation $C_d = (C_{inf} - (C_{inf}/d))$,[1] where C_d is the change in expectation for d number of decks, and C_{inf} is the change in expectation for an infinite number of decks. For example, if we consider six decks, the above equation looks like this: $C_6 = (-.67 - (-.67/6))$, which reduces to -.558, which is in very close agreement to the value of -.56 listed in Table 2.1.

There are several reasons why the player's expectation is hurt by multiple-deck games, but the two most important concern naturals and doubling down. In a six-deck game, for example, the player will receive about 1.61% fewer blackjacks than he will in a single-deck game, and when he doubles down on 11, his chances of catching a 10 are reduced by 3.23%.

This increase in the casino's edge is one reason many clubs have gone over to multiple-deck games. Another, more important, reason for this trend is that multiple decks run flatter with respect to relative deviations from normal deck composition, thus reducing the advantage to be gained by counting cards. Fortunately, the players have countermeasures of their own that go a long way toward neutralizing the inherent problems with multiple decks. We'll have a lot more to say about this later on.

----

1. Compare Peter A. Griffin, <u>The Theory of Blackjack</u>, rev. ed. p. 115.

Figure 2.1

PLAYER'S ADVANTAGE[1]
VS.
NUMBER OF DECKS

Basic Strategy

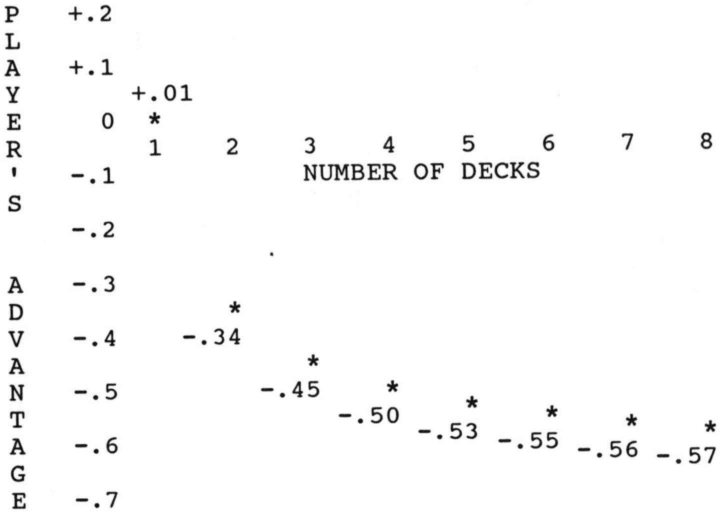

```
P    +.2
L
A    +.1
Y        +.01
E     0  *
R        1    2    3    4    5    6    7    8
'    -.1           NUMBER OF DECKS
S
     -.2

A    -.3
D           *
V    -.4  -.34
A              *
N    -.5    -.45   *
T                -.50  *
A    -.6            -.53  *    *    *
G                        -.55 -.56 -.57
E    -.7
```

---
1. LAS VEGAS STRIP RULES.

CHAPTER THREE

An Introduction to the Theory
of Casino Twenty-One

Of all the many games of chance offered in a modern casino, Twenty-One is unique in having no fixed percentage working against the player. The other games banked by the casino, such as Craps and Roulette, for example, are what mathematicians term "independent trials processes." Each toss of the dice or spin of the wheel is a separate, independent event, in no way influenced by previous tosses or spins. For this reason, the odds never change; and since the casinos have been careful to structure these games so the percentage always favors the house, there is no system, betting scheme, or playing strategy capable of overcoming the casino edge. The longer one plays at such games, the more opportunity the unfavorable odds have to express themselves, and the greater the likelihood of a serious loss.

The odds during play at Twenty-One, on the other hand, are constantly changing and are subject to what are termed "conditional probabilities." Don't let that term scare you; the idea is really very simple. As cards are dealt out of the deck(s) to complete a round of play, the odds (conditional probabilities) of drawing specific cards change, both during the current round and for future rounds, until the cards are reshuffled. As an example, suppose that on the first round after the shuffle, all four Aces appear in a single-deck game; this means that on subsequent rounds dealt before the next shuffle, no Aces can appear. Therefore, the chance of the player getting a blackjack is exactly zero. This differs markedly from the 4.8% chance the player has of getting a blackjack on the first round of play after a shuffle. And since blackjacks greatly favor the player, it is obvious their absence shifts the odds in favor of the house. If, on the other hand, no Aces had appeared on the first round, the chance of the player getting a blackjack on subsequent rounds dealt before the reshuffle would be greatly increased, and the odds would shift in the player's favor.

It is this unique feature of Twenty-One, the constantly changing basic odds, combined with the opportunities afforded the player to exercise skillful play, that makes it possible to beat the game and, in effect, turn the tables on the house.

Why, you may wonder, would the casinos be so foolish as to bank a game that can be beaten with skillful play? That's a fair question. The primary reason is that when the game was first introduced in the casinos, during the early 1930s, no one imagined it was vulnerable to defeat. The casinos knew the basis for the house advantage lay in the fact that if the player busted, he lost his wager, even if the dealer, in playing out his hand, were also to bust. In fact, this "double bust" rule was so strong for the house, it was necessary to offer the player a number of bonuses and playing options just to reduce the house advantage to a level the players would tolerate. The most important of the bonuses, the 3 to 2 payoff on untied player blackjacks, reduced the house advantage by 2.3%. The double down and pair splitting options, *with typical play*, took about another 1.2% off the casino edge. And various other minor bonuses (rarely encountered nowadays), such as a $5 bonus for a player natural consisting of the Ace of Spades and either the Jack of Spades or Jack of Clubs (hence the name "Blackjack"), reduced the house edge by another .1% or so, depending on the amount of the player's average wager. In total, these features, *with typical play*, reduced the house edge by about 3.6%. And still, in spite of all this, the casino win consistently amounted to about 25% of the players' total buy-ins, suggesting the players, as a whole, were losing at a rate of between three and four percent of their action!

As tables were full, and profits were excellent, with no players winning consistently, it is little wonder the casinos assumed the game was completely secure and would go on "getting the money" indefinitely.

But this is where the plot begins to thicken. For, about this time, a small team of mathematicians, headed by Roger Baldwin and William Cantey, working at the Army's research laboratory at Aberdeen Proving Grounds in Maryland, began to grow weary of developing ever more efficient ways of blasting large rocks into very small rocks and started looking around for new worlds to conquer. Since both Baldwin and Cantey had been bitten by the Blackjack bug and had been consistently picked clean on their infrequent sojourns into casinoland, it seemed natural that a deeper look into this intriguing little game was in order.

When they began their analysis, the Baldwin team reasoned that proper use of the playing options afforded the player, such as when to hit and when to stand, when to double down, and when to split a pair, should decrease the overall house advantage significantly. They had no idea by how much, but it was obvious the average player, who lost at a rate of between three and four percent, was not using these options anywhere near optimally. Unfortunately, computers were not yet in general use, even in government think tanks, so Baldwin & Co. had to use desk calculators. This unpleasant fact turned a tough job into mission improbable, and our heroes labored for months and months, hovering over their calculators for endless hours, far into the night, in dimly lit little rooms, until finally one night Baldwin looked up from his labors and croaked, "I've got it!" Of course, by this time, Baldwin and his friends were so hunched over from the long hours spent at their desks they looked like they had been studying posture with Quasimodo; but it was worth it because, for the first time, the proper playing strategy for casino Twenty-One had been discovered! This strategy has come to be called the Basic Strategy, and it provides the player with the correct play for any possible hand, when the only information he considers is the dealer's up card, and the cards that comprise his own hand.

When they published their results in the September, 1956, issue of the <u>Journal of the American Statistical Association</u>, the Baldwin team claimed their strategy reduced the house advantage to a meager .62%. Further research, using high speed digital computers, has shown that with the rules assumed in the Baldwin study the actual advantage was .1% *for the players!* In other words, when you are playing Basic Strategy on the Las Vegas Strip, in a single-deck game, the house has no advantage whatsoever. For all practical purposes the game is dead even. This result has been verified countless times in major research laboratories around the world. IBM, General Dynamics, Sperry Rand, the Jet Propulsion Laboratory, the Massachusetts Institute of Technology, and the Atomic Energy Commission are among the highly respected laboratories that have verified the power and accuracy of Basic Strategy.

If you are to become a world-class player, or even just a good player, it is absolutely essential that you master Basic Strategy--and I do mean master. You must be able to play it quickly, accurately, automatically, and without conscious thought. The reason Basic Strategy is so important is because even when you progress to a more powerful winning system, you will still play Basic Strategy over 75% of the time. And also because when you pick up your hand, you will immediately know what you are probably going to do and therefore avoid making any foolish mistakes.

In spite of the fact that the Baldwin strategy showed the player how to confront the casinos on essentially even terms, it had very little impact and went virtually unnoticed outside of academic circles. One person who did notice, however, was an associate professor of mathematics and statistics at the University of California at Los Angeles (UCLA) named Edward O. Thorp. Thorp took a long, hard look at Baldwin's results, then submerged himself in deepest thought. By the time he finally surfaced, he had reached some startling conclusions, conclusions that were to revolutionize the game of Twenty-One, and shake the casino gambling industry to its very foundation. Thorp had perceived that Blackjack could be beaten! And beaten badly.

He began his analysis with two facts. First, he knew from Baldwin's work that a player using Basic Strategy was playing about even with the house, overall. But he also knew that the conditional probabilities were constantly changing, sometimes favoring the player and sometimes favoring the house. To be sure, the favorable swings were just canceled out by the unfavorable swings, and overall the results averaged out just as Baldwin had said. But what if the favorable situations could be identified, and "large" bets made at these opportune times, and "small" bets made when the deck(s) favored the house? The net effect should be that the player would win more on his "large," favorable bets than he would lose on his "small," unfavorable bets--for a substantial net win! Thorp also reasoned that, although Basic Strategy was the best way to play Blackjack on the average, it was obvious that as cards were dealt during play, and the composition of the undealt pack changed, the player could sometimes improve upon Basic Strategy, and thereby add to his advantage, by varying his play depending on the current composition of the undealt pack.

To test his ideas, Thorp wrote a program, in Fortran, for an IBM 704 computer that, using direct probability theory, allowed him to analyze any arbitrary set of cards. He called this program the "Arbitrary Subsets Program." He found that when "small" cards (2,3,4,5,6,7) were removed from a complete deck, the odds were shifted in favor of the player and, conversely, when "large" cards (10,J,Q,K,Ace) were removed, the odds favored the house. The density of the "intermediate" cards (8,9) was found to have little significance.

The reason a deck depleted of "little" cards favors the player is because when drawing to a "stiff" (hard 12,13,14,15,16) a relative excess of "large" cards increases the likelihood of busting the hand; since the dealer hits all stiffs and the player does not, the dealer will bust many more hands than the player. In addition, when the player doubles down, he generally hopes to catch a "large" card; with a deck depleted of "small" cards, his chance of doing so increases. Finally, when the deck is rich in "large" cards, the chance of a blackjack increases, and since untied player blackjacks pay 3 to 2, and dealer blackjacks pay only even money, a blackjack will help the player more (50% more) than it will help the dealer.

Using all this information and more, Thorp developed a powerful winning system that involved keeping track of the relative density of the 10s (10,J,Q,K) versus the other cards. He called this system the Ten Count; it was the first scientifically derived "count" system ever devised.

In 1962 Thorp published the Ten Count, together with Basic Strategy and other valuable information, in his classic book Beat the Dealer. The book was an instant sensation. Within 30 days of publication it had shot to the top of the New York Times Non-Fiction Best Seller List. And after the media picked up the story, people who didn't know a Blackjack table from a picnic table were suddenly fighting each other for the last copy at the local book store. For here was a book, written by a respected mathematician from a prominent university, that contained the secret formula for making free money! Or so some thought.

But if the man in the street were overreacting a bit, it was nothing compared to the hysteria that seized the casino industry. Their sweet little game had turned on them! Suddenly, they had nightmares of thousands of trained counters swooping down on them like swarms of merciless locusts, devouring every hundred dollar bill in sight. The tension in the casinos was electric! Finally, their paranoia totally out of control, the Las Vegas casinos snapped! On April Fool's Day 1964, the casinos on the Las Vegas Strip changed the rules of Blackjack. The first (and only) time the rules of a major casino game had ever been significantly altered. And the changes were drastic. Doubling down was restricted to two-card totals of 11 only, and a pair of Aces could no longer be split. The effect on the average player was disastrous, and play at the Twenty-One tables all but vanished. After a few weeks, when it became obvious the players would never buy the new rules, they were quietly scuttled, and play resumed as before.

In the aftermath of this bizarre incident, two important facts emerged. First, before the rules changes, play at the Blackjack tables had increased dramatically as new players, drawn in by Thorp's book, discovered Twenty-One for the first time. And second, at the time of the rules changes there were not 10 counters in the entire State who played well enough and were well enough financed to pose any kind of a threat to the casinos at all. But how, you may ask, could this be so? After all, Thorp's system did work. The answer lay in human nature. Tens of thousands of people had bought Beat the Dealer, hoping to find a simple rule for riches they could memorize on the taxi ride to the casino. What they found instead was a scholarly textbook crammed with tables, charts, formulas, ratios, and all manner of forbidding esoterica. Though not difficult to understand, the Ten Count did require a lot of work and practice to learn to play well, and this is not what the people were looking for. They preferred instead to continue in their old uninformed ways: hitting all stiffs, standing on all stiffs, always splitting, never splitting, playing hunches, betting bunches, and watching their money disappear.

It has now been over 20 years since <u>Beat the Dealer</u> burst on the scene, and despite the fact that several other fine books detailing powerful winning systems have also appeared, there has been far from any invasion of killer counters to overwhelm the casinos. Basic play has improved slightly, as players have picked up a pointer or two, but for every expert player turned out by books on counting, there are a multitude who think they can win but who have learned just about enough to lose. So let me warn you now. Lady Luck has a heart of stone. If you treat her with respect and court her favor with care, she will reward you with riches. If you do not, she will wipe you out. It is just that simple.

I want you to be a winner, and this book contains everything you need to know to become a winning player. It includes all the knowledge and insight I have gained in over 15 years on the pro tour, as well as the results of many, many hours of theoretical analysis and computer simulations. Everything I know about Twenty-One is here. The rest is up to you.

CHAPTER FOUR

Basic Strategy

If you study people at play in the casinos, as I have done, you will soon realize that to most players Blackjack is a guessing game. To many of these people every hand is a mystery and an adventure. Sometimes they will stand with 12 or 13 against the dealer's 5 or 6; sometimes they will not. Sometimes they will hit 15 or 16 when the dealer is showing an Ace; at other times they will hesitate, sigh in resignation, then slowly slide their cards under their bet. And not only do they often have no idea what they are doing, some of them seem to have an absolutely perverse genius for doing the wrong thing. Example: I was playing with one other player late one night at the Playboy Club Casino in Nassau, the Bahamas. The shoe was absolutely gangbusters with 10s and Aces, so I had placed a maximum (for me) bet of $400. The other player, a heavy-set man in his late forties, had bet a quarter ($25). The dealer gave herself a 6, and to my considerable delight I hooked a 7 and a 3, for a total of 10. Naturally, I shoved out another $400, and doubled down. Eight-hundred dollars was now riding on the outcome of this hand. With casual confidence I did not look at the down card the dealer gave me but turned instead to see what my portly companion was going to do. His hole cards were (A,5) so it was obvious he had to take a hit. He looked at his hand, squinted through his glasses at the dealer's 6, then turned to me and said, "No way I'm taking her bust card," and signaled he was standing pat. Now I've seen a lot, but this play was breaking some strange new ground; nevertheless, I played it straight and gave no response. The dealer turned up her hole card, a 10, for a total of 16, and promptly hit it with what should have been this guy's card. Naturally, it was the "case" 5, giving the dealer 21. As she raked in my $800 the dealer flipped over my double-down card, the King of Spades, for a total of 20. "Very close," she purred. "Too bad this isn't Horseshoes." *Yeah, or hand grenades,* I thought to myself, as I glared at the flustered form to my left.

Of course bad plays by other players do not change your overall expectation. Sometimes such plays will help you, and sometimes they will hurt you; overall, they will have no mathematical effect. In the above example, for instance, the dealer's hit card could just as easily have been a 10 as a 5. But this story, a true

21

one, does illustrate the ignorance, the superstition, and the incompetence that are so characteristic of typical casino play.

Perhaps, I should be more respectful of unskilled players. After all, these are the sacrificial lambs that provide the casinos with the millions of dollars in excess profits that subsidize the winnings of professionals like me. If it were not for these losers, there could be no winners. And I am grateful, but what I respect are winners, and in the game of Blackjack, as in the game of life, winning is tough. It requires determination, preparation, and plenty of perspiration.

The Basic Strategy of this chapter is the cornerstone of winning play. Everything that comes later will be built upon this rock. Basic Strategy, in itself, will not give you an edge over the house, but it will virtually eliminate the advantage the casinos usually enjoy. Depending on the number of decks in play, and the exact rules in force, your long-run expectation will range from about +.2% to -.6%. And Basic Strategy does not involve card counting. It is simply the correct way to play when the only information you consider is the dealer's up card and the cards that comprise your own hand.

Understand one important fact: there is absolutely no room for guesswork or sloppy play in Blackjack. The best players, using the strongest counting systems available, and making use of every possible legal angle, have an edge over the house of just under +2%. This is a narrow edge. If you make mistakes, whether out of misinformation or because you allow fatigue, alcohol, stress, or superstition to affect your play, you will have no advantage whatsoever; you will be just another loser throwing good money after bad money.

Basic Strategy and the counting strategies that follow in later chapters are scientifically derived systems that have been proven accurate and powerful, both in the laboratory and in actual casino play. This is something you must accept without reservation. If you cannot do this, if you insist on playing hunches or allowing unsound ideas to influence your play, then this is not the book for you. I wish you luck; you're going to need it, and I suggest you play seldom and small. But if you are ready to be a winner, and if you are willing to pay the price, then now is the time, and this is the place.

I know from my work with students that it usually takes about 15 hours of intense study to master Basic Strategy, but whether it takes you five hours or 50 hours, it is absolutely essential that you do master the material. Before you can go any further, you must be able to play Basic Strategy perfectly, rapidly, and without conscious thought.

The practice charts at the end of this chapter are designed to make this learning process as quick and painless as possible. Another useful technique is to make flash cards for each individual playing decision. Do not keep the flash cards in any special order, just shuffle them randomly before each use. In this way you'll avoid becoming dependent on any particular sequence to recall correct plays. And do not attempt to learn Basic Strategy by dealing hands to yourself. You'll be tempted to do this because it is more fun to play Blackjack than to study Blackjack. But some hands have such a low incidence of occurrence that you will never learn to play them right. With a single deck, for instance, the player will hold (9,9) versus the dealer's 9 on the average once in every 5,525 hands. Friends, that's a lot of Twenty-One.

Basic Strategy varies slightly depending on the rules in force and the number of decks in play. The strategy that follows assumes a single-deck game and Las Vegas Strip rules (double down on any *first* two cards, resplit all pairs except Aces, and the dealer stands on soft 17). Use of this strategy in multiple-deck games, or where the rules differ, will result in very small errors that gain a few hundredths of a percent for the house. Although errors of this magnitude are trivial, for the sake of accuracy and completeness the proper modifications for the most common rules and dealing variations are included at the end of this chapter. After you have completely mastered Basic Strategy, you may wish to learn these additional fine points.

STANDING VS. DRAWING (Hard Hands)

Most of the gain from proper playing strategy comes from knowing when to stand and when to draw. This is true for the count strategies as well as for Basic Strategy. And considering the gross errors most players make in this regard, you might suppose the proper strategy is complicated or difficult to understand. Well, nothing could be further from the truth. In fact, Table 4.1 is so simple and intuitively logical, it's a wonder experienced players don't come close just by instinct alone.

If you are like most players, you will find it easier to memorize the strategy tables if you understand the reasons why various plays are made. Of course the exact reasons are often hidden in the arcane recesses of probability theory and may not be readily apparent, but reasonable inferences can often be drawn that will help you gain insight and develop a better understanding of the game. So whenever it seems useful, I will offer perspectives intended to clarify the concepts that need to be learned.

As you look at Table 4.1, the first thing to note is that you never stand with a total less than hard 12. This is reasonable; if a hand totals less than 12, it may be helped by drawing a card, but it cannot be hurt (busted). The next thing to notice is that the player stands with much lower totals if the dealer is showing a "bust" card (2,3,4,5,6) than if he is showing a strong card (7,8,9,10,Ace). The reasoning here is also very simple and can best be understood by assuming the dealer always has a 10 (10,J,Q,K) in the hole. Of course the dealer won't always have a 10 in the hole, but because there are 16 10s in a complete single deck, and only four each of every other card, the dealer will have a 10 in the hole four times as often as he will have any other given card. So, with an assumed 10 in the hole and bust card showing, the dealer is a good bet to break the hand. If the player then is holding a "stiff" (12,13,14,15,16) himself, it seems reasonable that the proper play is to stand and hope the dealer busts when he draws to complete his hand. This, of course, with two exceptions, is precisely what Basic Strategy recommends. An explanation for these two exceptions (12 vs. 2 or 3) is left for the reader as an exercise in logical thought. (Hint: the only card that will bust a 12 is a 10).

Of course when the dealer is showing power (7,8,9,10,Ace), the situation changes completely. Now with the presumed 10 in the hole, the dealer is likely to be "pat" with a total of at least 17 and perhaps as much as 20 or 21. So unless the player is pat as well, he can probably kiss the hand goodbye. Holding hard 12 through 16, the player is faced with three disagreeable options. He can stand and hope the dealer is somehow stiff himself and busts when he draws. He can draw, hoping to improve the hand, but knowing he stands a good chance of busting, or he can grab his bet, and as many loose checks as possible, and make a break straight for the door. This last play, though it stands the best chance of saving the bet, is decidedly <u>not</u> recommended; for should it fail, it may lead to a rather lively back-room "discussion" with an oversized Sicilian no-neck with hair on his thumbs and brass knuckles on his fists. Given the choice between standing, drawing, and bloodshed, computer studies have conclusively shown the best thing to do is to draw and keep on drawing until the hand is either busted or totals at least hard 17. This will result in a savings for the player of between three and 25 percent, depending on the player's total and the dealer's up card. Holding (10,3) vs. 10, for example, the player's disadvantage if he draws is 39%. If he stands, his disadvantage is about 51%. So hitting rather than standing, in this case, saves about 12% for the player.

Notice there is one exception to this rule of always hitting a stiff when the dealer is showing a strong card: Basic Strategy says to stand holding (7,7) vs. 10. Why? I was tempted to leave this as an exercise, but perhaps it would be instructive if we analyze it together.

The first thing to realize is that when holding 14 the player's fondest wish, should he hit, is to draw a 7 for a total of 21. Normally the player has four chances (the four 7s in a complete single deck) in 49 cards (52, minus the dealer's up card and the player's two hole cards) of doing this. This works out to a probability of about 8.2%. Now consider what happens when the player's 14 consists of (7,7): his likelihood of hooking a 7 drops to only 2 chances in 49 cards, a mere 4.1% long shot.

The second thing to realize is that when drawing to (7,7) the player is more likely to bust than he is with any other two-card 14. The reason for this is as follows: there are four different two-card hands that total hard 14. They are (10,4) (9,5) (8,6) and of course (7,7). Notice also that to bust 14 the player must draw at least an 8. Now every two-card 14, except (7,7), depletes the undealt deck of one of these bust cards. In the case of (10,4) it is the 10. With (9,5) it is the 9, and with (8,6) it is the 8. Since (7,7) does not deplete the undealt pack of any bust cards, it follows that the player's chance of busting increases significantly.

So the player drawing to (7,7) has a greater chance of breaking than he would with any other two-card 14, and even if he doesn't break his chances of drawing to 21 are vastly reduced. Even after averaging these two factors with all the other considerations, direct probability analysis has conclusively demonstrated that the player holding (7,7) vs. 10 should stand. And pray.

It is interesting to note that in spite of the above analysis, when the game is dealt with more than one deck, the correct play is to hit (7,7) vs. 10. Think about that. Can you understand why?

You may be wondering why we are spending so much time on these kinds of exercises. Are they really that important? After all, as we noted earlier, they are just approximations and not really accurate in any rigorous sense. So why bother? I'll tell you why. Playing Blackjack in a casino for real money, your money, is hairy business. The stresses and distractions are countless. Noise, fatigue, losing, winning(!), fast dealers, bad players, and paranoid pit bosses are just a few of the disruptive influences you're going to have to deal with. Add to this the burden of keeping an accurate count, adding up your hand correctly, verifying the dealer's total, and recalling instantly any one of hundreds of different strategy decisions, and you have some idea of the difficulty involved. The only way it can be done is to reduce everything possible to an automatic, nonthinking reflex; this will free up your mind for the important decisions that have to be made. And the more you understand about the game and the better your feel for the various plays, the easier this process will be and the more accurate and enjoyable your play will become. So the time invested now will pay big dividends later on.

Table 4.1

STANDING VS. DRAWING
Hard Hands

Basic Strategy

PLAYER	DEALER'S UP CARD									
HAND	2	3	4	5	6	7	8	9	10	A
17	S	S	S	S	S	S	S	S	S	S
16	S	S	S	S	S	H	H	H	H	H
15	S	S	S	S	S	H	H	H	H	H
14	S	S	S	S	S	H	H	H	H[1]	H
13	S	S	S	S	S	H	H	H	H	H
12	H	H	S	S	S	H	H	H	H	H

LEGEND: S=STAND
         H=HIT

----
1. STAND (7,7) VS. 10.

STANDING VS. DRAWING (Soft Hands)

Soft hands are really a cinch to play. Disregarding doubling down for the moment, the whole thing reduces to simply always standing with soft 18 or more and always hitting soft 17 or less, and, as usual, we have a couple of exceptions: hit soft 18 when the dealer is showing a 9 or 10.

We hit soft totals of less than 17 because it's impossible to hurt such hands with a one card draw; this is because all final totals of 16 or less are equivalent: they win if the dealer breaks, otherwise they lose. With soft 17, although the player has an outside chance of pushing the dealer (about 14.6%), his chances of improving the hand by hitting far outweigh the risk of ending up with a lower total.

The most important reason we hit soft 18 against a 9 or 10 is because the dealer's average total in such situations is greater than 18. In fact, with a 9 up, the dealer will achieve a total of 19 or better about 54% of the time. And with the 10 showing, the dealer's total will exceed 18 about 52% of the time, and that's not including blackjacks! Another important reason for hitting is that the player will improve his hand often enough to more than compensate for those times he hurts the hand by busting or ending up with a lower total. In fact, computer studies have shown that the player gains about 9.2% by hitting soft 18 when the dealer is showing a 9, and about 4.5% when the dealer is showing a 10.

Although Table 4.2 says to stand with soft 18 against an Ace, this decision is virtually a toss up. If the dealer stands on soft 17, *and* the game is dealt with a single deck, it is just barely better to stand on soft 18 rather than hit. But if the dealer hits soft 17, or the game is dealt with more than one deck, then it is definitely better to hit soft 18 rather than stand. So for the sake of simplicity, and at virtually no loss, you may wish to change Table 4.2 to read hit soft 18 against an Ace. If you do, you'll get no argument from me.

We will have a lot more to say about handling soft hands in our discussion on doubling down.

Table 4.2

STANDING VS. DRAWING
Soft Hands

Basic Strategy

PLAYER	DEALER'S UP CARD									
HAND	2	3	4	5	6	7	8	9	10	A
A,8	S	S	S	S	S	S	S	S	S	S
A,7	S	S	S	S	S	S	S	H	H	S
A,6	H	H	H	H	H	H	H	H	H	H

NOTE: DOUBLING DOWN NOT CONSIDERED.

LEGEND: S=STAND
        H=HIT

DOUBLING DOWN (Hard Hands)

Doubling down was originally introduced by the casinos as a way to stimulate play by making the game more interesting and by reducing the house edge to a more acceptable level. Many players, including some experts who should know better, do not believe this; they assume the double down option was put in as just one more way of fleecing the player. And while it is certainly true that the vast majority of players handle this option pretty badly, it is also true that most players do benefit, at least to some degree, from its presence. For example, a common strategy followed by many unskilled players is to always double down on 10 or 11, and never double with any other total. This unsound practice will result in a gain, for the player, of about 1.3%. In Las Vegas and Monte Carlo, where you can double on any first two cards, a player using Basic Strategy for doubling down will gain about 1.7%. So, in this case, even unskilled play achieves about three-quarters of the available gain from doubling down. And, in fact, most of the commonly seen doubling strategies do provide a significant gain.

As far as Basic Strategy is concerned, however, there is only one valid reason for doubling down: if doubling down results in a positive expectation for the hand, and if that expectation, expressed as a percentage of the original bet, is larger than what could be obtained by following any other playing option (hitting, for instance), then, and only then, should the player double down. In other words, only double down when it will get you the most money. That's all there is to it. Sound and simple.

Consider, for example, a player holding (4,4) vs. the dealer's 6 in a single-deck Las Vegas game. Should the player double down, should he hit, or should he split? As it turns out, this decision is extremely close. Research has shown that if the player doubles down he will have an advantage of about 19% of his original bet. If he hits his advantage will be about 17%, and if he decides to split his edge will be about 18% of the original bet. In other words, if the player had bet $100 on this hand, if he doubles down, he could expect, on the average, to save his $200 ($100 doubled) and win an additional $19 besides. If he decides instead to just hit until he has a total of 12 or more, he figures to win about $17, and if he splits his 4s, his average expected win would be around $18. So, as it happens, it is just barely worthwhile for the Basic Strategy player to double down with (4,4) vs. 6.

As you look at Table 4.3, you will note that the closer the player's first two cards are to 11 without exceeding it, the more likely he is to double down. This is reasonable because, as we mentioned earlier, the player's most likely draw is a 10. So starting with 11, the player stands a good chance (almost 33%) of ending up with an unbeatable 21 if he doubles down. Beginning with 10, he stands the same chance of achieving a powerful 20 and an outside chance (about 8%) of catching an Ace for a total of 21. As the player's original total drops below 10, however, the opportunities for profitable doubling diminish rapidly. With 9, for example, it pays to double only if the dealer is showing a bust card, and with 8 doubling is just barely profitable even when the dealer is showing a 5 or 6. With totals below hard 8, you are throwing your money away if you double down. Nevertheless, you will occasionally see people in the casinos double down with hard totals of 7, 6, or even 5! When you see these plays you can be sure you are looking at one or the other of two breed of fool. You are either watching a totally unskilled player practice his moves for Loser of the Year, or you are watching an amateur counter make a play that may be mathematically sound but looks so bad that the unfavorable impact on the casino bosses far outweighs any theoretical gain. Further observation will quickly determine which is the case.

If you play in the casinos long enough, you will see just about every outrageous move possible. And doubling down with hard totals of 12 or more is no exception. Even though it is virtually <u>never</u> correct to double on totals above hard 11, you will nevertheless sometimes see this play. To give you an idea of just how costly this can be, consider the player who doubles down with (7,5) against the dealer's 6. This play loses for the player at the rate of 36%! This means that a player doubling a $100 bet would, on the average, figure to lose $36 to the dealer every time he made this play! There may be more pleasant forms of financial suicide, but doubling on 12 is surely one of the fastest.

I remember a bizarre incident that occurred a few years ago at a large and famous casino on the Las Vegas Strip that shows what can happen when a player doubles down on a breaking hand. I was playing at a single-deck $100 minimum game early one Sunday morning. The other two players at the table were really high rollers, and their wild play and radical bets were making things easy for me by drawing off all the heat. Although they were obviously very poor players, with that kind of money in action, the bosses were taking no chances. One of the players, a small man with a full beard practically obscuring his face, had been drinking and losing steadily for hours. Suddenly, out of apparent frustration, he decided to just chuck it all and go for broke. Whipping out a thick wad of $100 bills, he promptly proceeded to bet three holes, $2,000 per hole. The dealer's eyes widened and he immediately shuffled the deck. Simultaneously, the wary pit bosses exchanged puzzled looks and descended on the game like a pack of hungry wolves. The other player and I backed out, joining the rapidly growing gallery so we could watch this fascinating development without distraction. All eyes were riveted on the drama about to unfold. The dealer, obviously "sweating" from all the heat, practically shuffled the spots off the cards, and then after the cut began to deal very slowly and very carefully. The last thing he wanted to do was make a mistake. As he dealt his up card, the 5 of Clubs, I saw his jaw muscles tighten visibly. Our fearless champion picked up his first hand, a pat 20, smiled and slid the hand under his bet. Hand two was also pat with a total of 19. Hand three, however, was a little more interesting; it consisted of a pair of 7s. The right move was to split the 7s; the next best play was to stand on the 14, and hope the dealer busted. Our hero did neither; instead he shoved out another $2,000 and doubled down! Incredulous, the dealer could hardly conceal his contempt as he dealt out the double card face down. The dealer then flipped up his hole card, the 3 of Spades, and promptly hit it with an Ace, for a total of 19. As he paid out $2,000 to the player's winning 20 and indicated a push on the second hand, you could almost hear him thinking, *No sweat, we'll get it back with interest on that crazy double down.* I was thinking the same thing. Then the dealer turned up the double-down card. It was the 7 of Hearts, for a total of 21. For a moment no one spoke, no one moved. Not a sound. Then a deep restless rumble, at first more felt than heard, suddenly exploded from the crowd into a roaring cheer that crashed through the casino, assaulting the ear and overwhelming the mind. Total pandemonium. The bosses in the pit were in shock. They stood there, frozen, their great stone faces staring in disbelief. Strangely, our bearded friend seemed to be taking this all in stride. Bleary eyed and almost incoherent moments before, he now appeared cold sober and well under control. No sooner was the hand paid than he scooped up his cash and over $6,000 in checks and headed straight for the door. Surprisingly, the other player had also disappeared. The bosses looked uneasy. Blind luck was one thing, but this, they sensed, was something more.

About this time the phone connecting the pit to the "eye in the sky" began to ring. The shift boss picked it up and began a short conversation. After a few words he looked up and fixed two hard evil eyes on the dealer at our table. Hanging up, he walked over and whispered something in the dealer's ear. The dealer's face blanched, and he looked like he was going to be sick. Removing his dealing apron, he left the table and walked shakily out of the pit. Next the shift boss fanned the deck, face up, across the felt, and began to sort out the 7s. One, two, three, four, five...FIVE?! In a single-deck game? The joint, as they say, had been had! The whole thing had been a setup, one great elaborate con. The crazy bets, the wild plays, the drinking. Everything. Our boy had waited hours to make his move, and then when everything was just right--WHAM!

To this day I'm still not sure exactly how this caper went down. But I do know there are people haunting the clubs who can do more things with a deck of cards than a monkey can do with a coconut.

Among old Vegas hands, this incident is considered something of a classic, and I count myself lucky to have been there to see it. But like I say, if you hang out in these joints long enough, you see it all.

Table 4.3

DOUBLING DOWN
Hard Hands

Basic Strategy

PLAYER	DEALER'S UP CARD									
HAND	2	3	4	5	6	7	8	9	10	A
11	D	D	D	D	D	D	D	D	D	D
10	D	D	D	D	D	D	D	D	H	H
9	D	D	D	D	D	H	H	H	H	H
8	H	H	H	D¹	D²	H	H	H	H	H

LEGEND: H=HIT
        D=DOUBLE

----
1. EXCEPT (6,2) VS. 5.

2. EXCEPT (6,2) VS. 6.

DOUBLING DOWN (Soft Hands)

Compared to doubling down with hard hands, the potential gain from soft doubling is fairly modest. Average players, if they double at all with soft hands, generally make so many mistakes they don't benefit at all; even Basic Strategy players profit by only about .14%. In addition to this, many casinos essentially prohibit soft doubling by limiting doubling down to hard totals of 9, 10, and 11. Most of these casinos will allow you to double on (Ace,8), but if you catch a Deuce, the total is 11, not 21. In light of all this, you may be inclined to consider soft doubling relatively unimportant and not worthy of serious study. Many beginning students do share this view, but believe me, this is not the way it is. Remember, Blackjack is a tough game to beat, and the only way to survive and prosper is to fight for <u>every</u> possible edge. So whenever soft doubling is available it is essential that you use it to maximum advantage. Fortunately, as you can see from Table 4.4, as far as Basic Strategy is concerned, this is not very hard to do; for of all the strategy options available, soft doubling is probably the easiest to learn.

In fact, the most difficult thing about soft doubling is not remembering when to do it, but understanding why to do it. Everyone can readily understand the logic behind doubling with 11 in the hopes of catching a 10. But what is the idea behind doubling down with, say, (Ace,2)? Or risking the ruination of a pretty good hand like 18 by doubling down on (Ace,7)? These are good questions. And the answers are not as simple and intuitive as they are with hard doubling.

In general terms, the conceptual difference between hard and soft doubling boils down to one of emphasis rather than one of kind. When we hard double, for instance, we generally expect to win the hand by achieving a higher total than the dealer. Of course sometimes we will end up with a low total and win anyway because the dealer busts, but the primary emphasis in hard doubling is attaining a powerful hand. With soft doubling, on the other hand, the emphasis is reversed. Doubling down with (Ace,2) vs. 6, for example, we might get lucky and draw an 8 for an unbeatable 21, but that is not the primary reason for making this play. What we are really banking on is that the dealer will break and it won't make any difference what total we end up with. It is for this reason that soft doubling, unlike hard doubling, is only done when the dealer is showing a bust card and is therefore likely to break as he draws to complete his hand.

To make this comparison more understandable, let's consider a concrete example. Basic Strategy says to double down with hard 11 vs. the dealer's 6. Suppose we make this play 1,000 times in an infinite deck game. What would be the expected result? Computer studies have shown that, on the average, we would end up with a total of 21, 308 times, a total of 20, 19, 18, or 17, 77 times each, and a total of 16 or less 384 times. The dealer, by contrast, would achieve a total of 21 only about 98 times in 1,000 trials, a total of 20 about 101 times, a total of 19 or 18 about 106 times each, a total of 17 about 167 times, and he would be expected to bust about 422 times.

Of course we would win outright the 422 times the dealer busted, and of the 578 times the dealer achieved a total of 17 or higher, we would expect to beat him 211 times (and tie 67 times).

So, in 1,000 trials, doubling down with hard 11 vs. the dealer's 6, we would figure to win about 633 times. And of these 633 wins, 211 of them, a full one-third, would be the result of outdrawing the dealer.

Now consider what happens when instead of hard 11, we double down with (Ace,2), (Ace,3), (Ace,4), or (Ace,5) vs. the dealer's 6. Naturally, assuming an infinite deck game, the dealer's probabilities remain the same. But look at what happens to the player's chances. In the 1,000 trials, we will draw to a total of 21 only about 77 times. The same is true of totals of 20, 19, 18, and 17: we will achieve these totals only about 77 times each in 1,000 trials. But we will reach a total of 16 or less 615 times!

As before, we win automatically the 422 times the dealer busts. But now of the 578 trials when the dealer makes a hand, we only win 100 times (and tie 45 times).

So in 1,000 trials we now figure to win 522 times. Of these 522 wins, only 100, less than one-fifth, are the result of outdrawing the dealer.

The implications are obvious: with hard doubling, though wins through dealer busts are important, the emphasis is on outdrawing the dealer; with soft doubling, though wins through outdrawing the dealer are important, the emphasis is clearly on the dealer breaking.

Soft doubling with hands like (Ace,7) or (Ace,8) differs from ordinary soft doubling in that we are much more likely to end up with a pat hand than usual. But this is offset by the fact that we started out with a fairly good hand, and drawing a card by doubling down may very well mess it up. So the emphasis remains on the dealer breaking, and this, as with all soft doubling, is only done when the dealer is a very good bet to break his hand.

Table 4.4

DOUBLING DOWN
Soft Hands

Basic Strategy

PLAYER	DEALER'S UP CARD									
HAND	2	3	4	5	6	7	8	9	10	A
A,8	S	S	S	S	**D**	S	S	S	S	S
A,7	S	**D**	**D**	**D**	**D**	S	S	H	H	S
A,6	**D**	**D**	**D**	**D**	**D**	H	H	H	H	H
A,5	H	H	**D**	**D**	**D**	H	H	H	H	H
A,4	H	H	**D**	**D**	**D**	H	H	H	H	H
A,3	H	H	**D**	**D**	**D**	H	H	H	H	H
A,2	H	H	**D**	**D**	**D**	H	H	H	H	H

LEGEND: S=STAND
        H=HIT
        D=DOUBLE

SPLITTING PAIRS

Knowing when to split and, just as importantly, when not to split is an essential element of successful play, for used properly pair splitting is a very powerful weapon in the player's arsenal. In fact, when played in accordance with the Basic Strategy, this option is worth nearly a full .5% to the player. Unfortunately, when played in accordance with the basic tragedy that describes most casino play, pair splitting is worth little, if anything, to the player and may, for some perversely gifted losers, even add to the casino's edge.

Most players mishandle pair splitting this badly because they have little, if any, real understanding of what they are trying to accomplish when they split a pair. They just merrily spill their checks all over the layout as they eagerly split almost every pair that comes their way. So, before you get down to the nitty-gritty of memorizing Table 4.5, let's take a look at the ideas behind this valuable strategy.

Basically, pair splitting can be broken down into two categories: offensive splitting and defensive splitting. Offensive splitting occurs when we are presented with a pair that if split would result in an advantage for the player, and, of course, this advantage must be greater than that afforded by any other available playing option. The great advantage of offensive splitting is that it allows the player to double his bet in a favorable situation. Defensive splitting occurs when we receive a pair and no matter how we play the hand the house will have the edge, but if we split, in spite of the fact that we must double our bet, our expected loss will be minimized.

A hand that is often seen in actual play, and that clearly illustrates the ideas of offensive and defensive splitting, is a pair of 8s. If splitting were not allowed, this hand would be a big loser no matter what the dealer's up card. Against a 5, for example, if the player can't split his next best move is to stand and hope the dealer busts; this will result in a house edge of almost 17%. Against other up cards things get steadily worse, until with a 10 up the player is at a whopping disadvantage of over 51%!

Fortunately, thanks to the splitting option, things don't have to be this grim. In fact, when the dealer is showing a 2, 3, 4, 5, 6, or 7, the player can get the upper hand by aggressively splitting the hand, thus turning a big loser into an even bigger winner. Against the dealer's 5, for instance, instead of a 17% disadvantage, splitting the 8s will result in an advantage for the player of over 31%! This is offensive splitting at its very best.

Against the dealer's 8, 9, 10, or Ace, however, things are not so rosy, for now no matter what we do, including splitting, the house will have the best of it. So our goal here is not to win money but to get out of the hand as cheaply as possible. This is where defensive splitting comes into play. Splitting (8,8) against the dealer's 10, for example, reduces the house edge to only about 45% of our original bet instead of the 51% mentioned before. This may not sound like much of a savings, but money saved is money earned and it is just such defensive plays as this that will keep your losses on bad hands small enough so that your wins on good hands will put you at least even (for now) with the house.

Table 4.5

PAIR SPLITTING

Basic Strategy

PLAYER			DEALER'S		UP	CARD			
HAND	2	3	4	5	6	7	8	9	10	A
A,A	P	P	P	P	P	P	P	P	P	P
10,10	S	S	S	S	S	S	S	S	S	S
9,9	P	P	P	P	P	S	P	P	S	S
8,8	P	P	P	P	P	P	P	P	P	P
7,7	P	P	P	P	P	P	H	H	S	H
6,6	P	P	P	P	P	H	H	H	H	H
5,5	D	D	D	D	D	D	D	D	H	H
4,4	H	H	H	D	D	H	H	H	H	H
3,3	H	H	P	P	P	P	H	H	H	H
2,2	H	P	P	P	P	P	H	H	H	H

LEGEND: S=STAND
           H=HIT
           D=DOUBLE
           P=SPLIT

SURRENDER

As we saw in the chapter on rules, there are three variations to the surrender theme. And though they differ in some respects, all three share the same basic idea: if the player doesn't like his hand, he can toss it in--providing he is willing to forfeit half his bet to the house.

Although ignored by most players, even when available, those who do use this option almost invariably surrender far too often. This is because they disregard, or more likely don't understand, the simple logic involved: if you have to give up 50% of your bet, you only want to do this when the house edge against you is greater than 50%. This should be obvious, yet you would be surprised at the hands some players surrender. It often seems these people toss in any hand they think they have less than an even chance of winning. This, of course, is absurd, not to mention expensive, but I have seen it so often I know it is true. Perhaps some players really do confuse a 50% disadvantage, which means the player figures to win one hand in four, with a 50% chance of losing, which means the player figures to win one hand in two. Others probably have no idea what the odds are and just toss in any hand they think is lost. But whatever the reasons, the result is the same: sloppy play, once again, turns a valuable playing strategy into a money maker for the house. And surrender is valuable. For although late surrender and Asian surrender yield only nominal gains when played with Basic Strategy alone, they are both very important when used in conjunction with the sophisticated card counting techniques of later chapters. And early surrender should always yield big savings for the player, with or without card counting.

Another important benefit is the stabilizing influence surrender has on your bankroll. This occurs because surrendering flattens the fluctuations that would normally occur if all hands were played to completion. So, even though most casinos don't offer it, the profit potential when you can surrender makes it well worth your while to master Table 4.6.

For some curious reason many of the casinos that offer surrender do not advertise this fact. Caesars Palace and Bally's Grand in Las Vegas, for example, have offered surrender for years, yet if you go into these casinos you will find no indication that surrender is available. The same is true of a number of other clubs, both in Nevada and elsewhere, so whenever you are in doubt, ask the dealer if you can play surrender. And when it is available, use it!

Table 4.6

SURRENDER

Basic Strategy

LATE SURRENDER   ASIAN SURRENDER

PLAYER	DEALER'S UP CARD		
HAND	9	10	A
16	H	**Sr**	**Sr**
15	H	**Sr**	H

PLAYER	DEALER'S UP CARD		
HAND	9	10	A
16	**Sr**[1]	**Sr**	H
15	**Sr**[2]	**Sr**	H

NOTE: DO NOT SURRENDER (8,8).   NOTE: DO NOT SURRENDER (8,8).

EARLY SURRENDER[3]

PLAYER	DEALER'S UP CARD		
HAND	9	10	A
17	S	S	**Sr**
16	H	**Sr**	**Sr**
15	H	**Sr**	**Sr**
14	H	**Sr**	**Sr**
13	H	H	**Sr**
12	H	H	**Sr**
7	H	H	**Sr**
6	H	H	**Sr**
5	H	H	**Sr**

LEGEND: S=STAND
        H=HIT
        Sr=SURRENDER

NOTE: DO NOT SURRENDER SOFT HANDS.

----
1. **ONLY** IF 16 CONSISTS OF THREE OR MORE CARDS, EXAMPLE: (9,5,2).

2. **ONLY** IF 15 CONSISTS OF THREE OR MORE CARDS, EXAMPLE: (9,4,2).

3. EARLY SURRENDER ALL PAIRS THAT TOTAL THE INDICATED VALUES, EXAMPLE: (8,8) VS. 10 OR ACE.

43

INSURANCE

Insurance is a side bet that has been grafted onto the game because it makes a lot of money for the house and because it entertains the players by giving them the illusion of protection against the dealer's blackjacks.

Insurance is normally a very bad bet, so unless you are counting cards you never take insurance. Never.

Let's consider a couple of examples to drive this point home. If the dealer has an Ace up, his chances of having a blackjack are about 31.4%, in a single-deck game. If insurance were a "fair" proposition, that is, one with no edge for either side, the payoff would be 2.19 to 1. But insurance does not pay 2.19 to 1; it pays 2 to 1. So the noncounting player who always takes insurance stands to lose at a rate of about 5.9% of his insurance bet.

Or consider this: most dealers will tell you that it is a *must* play to take insurance whenever you have a blackjack. The reasoning goes something like this: if the dealer doesn't have a natural, the insurance bet is lost but the player's blackjack wins at time and a half, for a net win of one unit. Or, if the dealer does have a natural, the blackjacks tie but the insurance bet wins at 2 to 1; again, with a net win of one unit. So, the argument goes, it makes sense to take insurance whenever you have a blackjack, because you will win one unit no matter what happens. Right--and wrong. Right, you will win one unit. Wrong, it does not make sense to take insurance just because you are holding a blackjack. Let's take another look to see why.

In a single-deck game, if you have a blackjack and the dealer has an Ace up, he will have a blackjack himself about 30.6% of the time. We already know that if you take insurance you will win one unit, but what happens if you don't take insurance. Well, obviously, the blackjacks tie 30.6% of the time, and no money changes hands. But 69.4% of the time the dealer will not have blackjack, and you will win one and a half units. Overall, this works out to an average win of 1.04 units each time you have a blackjack against the dealer's Ace. So, in other words, if you take insurance when you have a blackjack, you are giving away, on the average, nearly 4% of your profit back to the house. Believe me, this game is tough enough without looking for ways to shortchange yourself on blackjacks.

So, for now, stay away from insurance. Later on, when we get into sophisticated counting systems, you will see that insurance *can* be a money maker when the deck is right (the number of 10s in the remaining deck greater than half the number of non-10s), but remember, if you're not counting cards it's a sucker bet all the way.

TABLE 4.7 - BASIC STRATEGY, SINGLE-DECK

This table consolidates all of the information in Tables 4.1 through 4.5, and most of Table 4.6. After you have generally learned Basic Strategy from these tables, you will find using Table 4.7 very helpful in visualizing the inherent patterns in Basic Strategy. Recognizing these patterns is a big help in memorizing the strategy.

Some casinos will allow you to double down on hands formed as a result of splitting pairs; in these clubs make the following changes to Table 4.5 and Table 4.7:

PAIR	WHEN TO SPLIT
7,7	AGAINST 2 - 8
6,6	AGAINST 2 - 7
4,4	AGAINST 4,5,6
3,3	AGAINST 2 - 7
2,2	AGAINST 2 - 7

Asian and early surrender are not included in Table 4.7. This is because these are fairly uncommon rules variations, and unless you know you are going to be playing in clubs that allow these options, you are better off saving your mental energies for more useful pursuits. Late surrender, however, is included in Table 4.7.

Table 4.7

BASIC STRATEGY

Single-Deck

PLAYER HAND	|	DEALER'S UP CARD								
	2	3	4	5	6	7	8	9	10	A
17	S	S	S	S	S	S	S	S	S	S
16	S	S	S	S	S	H	H	H	Sr	Sr
15	S	S	S	S	S	H	H	H	Sr	H
14	S	S	S	S	S	H	H	H	H[1]	H
13	S	S	S	S	S	H	H	H	H	H
12	H	H	S	S	S	H	H	H	H	H
11	D	D	D	D	D	D	D	D	D	D
10	D	D	D	D	D	D	D	D	H	H
9	D	D	D	D[2]	D[3]	H	H	H	H	H
8	H	H	H	D[2]	D[3]	H	H	H	H	H
A,8	S	S	S	S	D	S	S	S	S	S
A,7	S	D	D	D	D	S	S	H	H	S[4]
A,6	D	D	D	D	D	H	H	H	H	H
A,5	H	H	D	D	D	H	H	H	H	H
A,4	H	H	D	D	D	H	H	H	H	H
A,3	H	H	D	D	D	H	H	H	H	H
A,2	H	H	D	D	D	H	H	H	H	H
A,A	P	P	P	P	P	P	P	P	P	P
10,10	S	S	S	S	S	S	S	S	S	S
9,9	P	P	P	P	P	S	P	P	S	S
8,8	P	P	P	P	P	P	P	P	P	P
7,7	P	P	P	P	P	P	H	H	S	H
6,6	P	P	P	P	P	H	H	H	H	H
5,5	D	D	D	D	D	D	D	D	H	H
4,4	H	H	H	D	D	H	H	H	H	H
3,3	H	H	P	P	P	P	H	H	H	H
2,2	H	P	P	P	P	P	H	H	H	H

NOTES: WITH HARD HANDS, AND WITH (A,2) THROUGH (A,6), IF YOU'RE NOT ALLOWED TO DOUBLE, THEN HIT.

WITH (A,7) AND (A,8), IF YOU'RE NOT ALLOWED TO DOUBLE, THEN STAND.

IF YOU CAN'T LATE SURRENDER, THEN HIT.

----

1. STAND (7,7) VS. 10.

2. HIT (6,2) VS. 5.

3. HIT (6,2) VS. 6.

4. HIT IF DEALER HITS SOFT 17.

TABLE 4.8 - BASIC STRATEGY, MULTIPLE-DECK

This is the strategy you will use when you are playing against three or more decks. There are fifteen changes from Table 4.7. When you play against two decks, use the single-deck strategy of Table 4.7, but make the following corrections:

```
HIT 7,7      AGAINST    10
HIT A,7      AGAINST    ACE
HIT 8        AGAINST    5 OR 6
STAND A,8    AGAINST    6
```

In casinos that allow you to double down after splitting, make the following changes to Table 4.8:

```
PAIR         WHEN TO SPLIT

6,6          AGAINST 2 - 6
4,4          AGAINST 5 OR 6
3,3          AGAINST 2 - 7
2,2          AGAINST 2 - 7
```

The changes to Basic Strategy for multiple decks should be considered refinements and should not be learned until you have mastered the single-deck strategy.

Table 4.8

BASIC STRATEGY

Multiple-Deck

PLAYER HAND	2	3	4	5	6	7	8	9	10	A
17	S	S	S	S	S	S	S	S	S	S
16	S	S	S	S	S	H	H	**Sr**	Sr	Sr
15	S	S	S	S	S	H	H	H	Sr	H
14	S	S	S	S	S	H	H	H	H	H
13	S	S	S	S	S	H	H	H	H	H
12	H	H	S	S	S	H	H	H	H	H
11	D	D	D	D	D	D	D	D	D	**H**
10	D	D	D	D	D	D	D	D	H	H
9	**H**	D	D	D	D	H	H	H	H	H
8	H	H	H	**H**	**H**	H	H	H	H	H
A,8	S	S	S	S	**S**	S	S	S	S	S
A,7	S	D	D	D	D	S	S	H	H	**H**
A,6	**H**	D	D	D	D	H	H	H	H	H
A,5	H	H	D	D	D	H	H	H	H	H
A,4	H	H	D	D	D	H	H	H	H	H
A,3	H	H	**H**	D	D	H	H	H	H	H
A,2	H	H	**H**	D	D	H	H	H	H	H
A,A	P	P	P	P	P	P	P	P	P	P
10,10	S	S	S	S	S	S	S	S	S	S
9,9	P	P	P	P	P	S	P	P	S	S
8,8	P	P	P	P	P	P	P	P	P	P
7,7	P	P	P	P	P	P	H	H	**H**	H
6,6	**H**	P	P	P	P	H	H	H	H	H
5,5	D	D	D	D	D	D	D	D	H	H
4,4	H	H	H	**H**	**H**	H	H	H	H	H
3,3	H	H	P	P	P	P	H	H	H	H
2,2	H	**H**	P	P	P	P	H	H	H	H

NOTES: WITH HARD HANDS, AND WITH (A,2) THROUGH (A,6), IF YOU'RE NOT ALLOWED TO DOUBLE, THEN HIT.

WITH (A,7), IF YOU'RE NOT ALLOWED TO DOUBLE, THEN STAND.

IF YOU CAN'T LATE SURRENDER, THEN HIT.

CHANGES FROM TABLE 4.7 ARE IN BOLDFACE.

TABLE 4.9 - BASIC STRATEGY, ATLANTIC CITY

This is the strategy you will use when you are playing in Atlantic City. It is essentially the Multiple-Deck Basic Strategy of Table 4.8, modified for those casinos where doubling down after splitting is allowed, but surrender is not allowed.

In contrast to Las Vegas and Reno, all the casinos in Atlantic City play by virtually the same rules. At this time they all use six or eight decks,[1] and about the only difference, from casino to casino, is a slight variation in how far into the pack they will deal before shuffling.

Atlantic City is not currently a good place for an *individual* card counter to invest his time and money. Even with the relatively good Atlantic City rules, six or eight decks, dealt down about two-thirds before shuffling, will not yield an acceptable rate of return. Fortunately, the conditions in Atlantic City are just about ideal for *team* play, and if you plan to play for serious money, I suggest you study the section on team play carefully; it is essential for really successful results in the Atlantic City casinos.

Atlantic City is still in transition, and it will be years before this area fully matures. Because Atlantic City is central to a population of over forty million, and because the New Jersey State Casino Control Commission has mandated near-uniform rules, the casinos have been able to put across a very conservative game. As the number of casinos increases, however, and as Indian reservations and other areas continue to open up to casino-style gambling, Atlantic City will have to become more competitive and liberal if it expects to keep the crowds coming and the profits growing. This is good news for card counters, because it means that conditions in Atlantic City will probably get better in the coming years. The most likely changes are either a return to some form of early surrender, or the introduction and spread of double-deck games.

----

1. Occasionally a club will experiment with some four-deck games.

Table 4.9

BASIC STRATEGY

Atlantic City[1]

PLAYER	DEALER'S UP CARD									
HAND	2	3	4	5	6	7	8	9	10	A
17	S	S	S	S	S	S	S	S	S	S
16	S	S	S	S	S	H	H	H	H	H
15	S	S	S	S	S	H	H	H	H	H
14	S	S	S	S	S	H	H	H	H	H
13	S	S	S	S	S	H	H	H	H	H
12	H	H	S	S	S	H	H	H	H	H
11	D	D	D	D	D	D	D	D	D	H
10	D	D	D	D	D	D	D	D	H	H
9	H	D	D	D	D	H	H	H	H	H
8	H	H	H	H	H	H	H	H	H	H
A,8	S	S	S	S	S	S	S	S	S	S
A,7	S	D	D	D	D	S	S	H	H	H
A,6	H	D	D	D	D	H	H	H	H	H
A,5	H	H	D	D	D	H	H	H	H	H
A,4	H	H	D	D	D	H	H	H	H	H
A,3	H	H	H	D	D	H	H	H	H	H
A,2	H	H	H	D	D	H	H	H	H	H
A,A	P	P	P	P	P	P	P	P	P	P
10,10	S	S	S	S	S	S	S	S	S	S
9,9	P	P	P	P	P	S	P	P	S	S
8,8	P	P	P	P	P	P	P	P	P	P
7,7	P	P	P	P	P	P	H	H	H	H
6,6	P	P	P	P	P	H	H	H	H	H
5,5	D	D	D	D	D	D	D	D	H	H
4,4	H	H	H	P	P	H	H	H	H	H
3,3	P	P	P	P	P	P	H	H	H	H
2,2	P	P	P	P	P	P	H	H	H	H

----

1. RULES: MULTIPLE DECKS, DOUBLE ANY TWO CARDS, INCLUDING AFTER SPLITS, DEALER STANDS ON SOFT 17, NO RESPLITTING OF PAIRS.

TABLE 4.10 - PLAYER'S ADVANTAGE, BASIC STRATEGY

For a Blackjack player, the information in this chart is priceless. It gives the player's average advantage with any possible hand, against any dealer up card.

This is a reference chart, so don't do anything crazy like try to memorize it, rather use it to build your feel and understanding of the game.

Even good players can learn a lot from Table 4.10. For example, the typical counter would guess from his experience that a player holding 18 against the dealer's 8 would be little better than even money to win this hand. Not so! As Table 4.10 shows, 18 vs. 8 gives nearly a full 10% advantage to the player.

And Table 4.10 is full of little surprises and riddles. Notice, for instance, that hands 13 through 16, against 2 through 6, respectively, have very similar expectations; from our discussion of Basic Strategy, can you see why? Notice also, that even though the expectations are similar, there are small differences. Can you guess why this is so?[1]

Another result many inexperienced players find hard to accept is that 17 is a loser against <u>any</u> up card. They make this mistake because they wrongly assume that when the dealer is showing a 5 or 6, he is such a sure bet to bust, that any pat hand will have the edge.

We could go on and on, but I think you get the idea. A thorough familiarity with Table 4.10 goes hand in hand with Basic Strategy as we build toward a complete mastery of the game.

----

1. The reason the expectations are similar is because against 2 through 6 the player stands with 13 through 16, and all hands less than 17 are equivalent.

The reason for the small differences is because the dealer's draw is influenced by the cards that comprise the player's hand.

Table 4.10

PLAYER'S ADVANTAGE[1]

Basic Strategy

PLAYER				DEALER'S	UP	CARD				
HAND	2	3	4	5	6	7	8	9	10	A
19	38.5	38.4	40.4	44.8	48.4	61.0	57.7	26.4	10.3	30.8
18	11.9	14.4	16.4	20.2	26.8	38.9	9.6	-19.6	-15.5	-8.2
17	-15.4	-11.9	-6.8	-4.3	-1.1	-12.2	-39.7	-41.5	-40.8	-46.4
16	-29.3	-25.0	-19.4	-14.6	-17.9	-37.6	-42.5	-48.0	-50.8	-50.6
15	-28.7	-24.3	-19.0	-14.1	-16.2	-35.9	-41.3	-47.0	-50.0	-49.1
14	-29.6	-24.5	-19.1	-13.6	-15.7	-34.4	-36.1	-41.9	-45.0	-44.6
13	-29.0	-24.8	-18.8	-13.7	-15.6	-28.7	-34.7	-37.6	-41.0	-40.4
12	-25.0	-22.3	-18.6	-13.8	-15.5	-22.7	-29.3	-36.4	-36.4	-36.0
11	54.2	59.2	65.4	72.2	72.3	47.9	34.1	22.4	16.2	21.4
10	43.1	49.5	56.2	63.3	65.0	45.1	31.5	16.6	3.2	8.6
9	11.4	19.3	28.6	37.7	39.3	19.4	11.1	-5.2	-14.4	-7.7
8	-1.5	2.2	8.4	14.1	16.4	9.2	-5.6	-21.3	-25.1	-22.1
7	-11.1	-7.1	-1.2	5.2	6.4	-6.9	-22.3	-29.4	-34.0	-33.8
2,4	-15.1	-10.6	-5.5	0.9	1.4	-16.4	-23.4	-30.5	-30.9	-33.5
2,3	-13.1	-9.8	-4.1	2.2	1.9	-11.9	-18.1	-26.3	-30.8	-29.2
A,10	150.0	150.0	150.0	150.0	150.0	150.0	150.0	150.0	150.0	150.0
A,9	65.6	64.4	65.4	68.2	69.4	77.3	78.5	76.6	55.5	68.1
A,8	40.2	42.0	41.6	46.1	48.3	61.5	60.8	28.8	6.4	29.0
A,7	13.6	18.9	31.3	34.9	38.5	41.2	12.1	-8.7	-13.9	-10.1
A,6	1.3	7.4	15.5	28.0	26.7	6.0	-6.5	-13.5	-18.9	-20.0
A,5	-3.2	-0.2	6.3	14.8	21.7	-2.4	-8.4	-16.7	-22.3	-20.6
A,4	-1.2	2.3	8.5	17.5	20.1	3.4	-3.6	-11.3	-17.0	-15.4
A,3	1.7	4.4	10.9	20.4	22.2	6.0	3.5	-6.0	-12.4	-10.1
A,2	3.9	7.1	11.5	21.2	23.0	10.7	3.9	-1.4	-8.9	-6.8
A,A	56.6	61.3	66.9	73.2	75.8	54.1	40.7	29.0	19.4	22.4
10,10	62.7	63.6	64.5	67.4	69.7	76.5	78.3	74.4	58.3	65.0
9,9	18.8	24.2	32.0	41.5	43.7	40.1	20.7	-9.3	-13.3	-5.5
8,8	6.4	13.2	21.5	31.2	35.6	25.9	-5.9	-38.3	-44.7	-36.3
7,7	-10.5	-2.0	10.3	20.0	22.0	-5.6	-37.8	-47.5	-51.0	-49.5
6,6	-16.5	-6.9	4.7	17.2	15.1	-22.6	-32.2	-38.6	-38.7	-38.6
4,4	-1.3	2.9	9.8	19.7	19.3	11.1	-5.5	-20.4	-24.1	-20.9
3,3	-11.6	-3.1	10.2	22.8	22.0	-6.8	-23.1	-31.0	-34.4	-33.4
2,2	-4.7	2.4	11.2	23.9	24.0	-0.6	-14.1	-22.3	-27.6	-25.9

----
1. SINGLE DECK, LAS VEGAS STRIP RULES WITH DOUBLE AFTER SPLITS.

PRACTICE CHARTS 4.1 AND 4.2 - BASIC STRATEGY

Practice Charts 4.1 and 4.2 are designed to drill you in Basic Strategy until you know it stone cold.

When you think you know Tables 4.1 through 4.6, and Tables 4.7, 4.8, and 4.9 thoroughly, you are ready for these practice drills.

With the exception of blackjacks, which you already know how to play, these charts list every possible initial hand against every dealer up card. There are 540 such combinations, and they are all here.

To conserve space, a condensed notation has been used; for example, (9,Ace) vs. 10 is denoted as 9A T.

I have found that many students learn faster if they begin with Practice Chart 4.1, which lists the hands in order, rather than starting immediately with Practice Chart 4.2, which lists the same hands in a random fashion. So, I suggest you use Chart 4.1 to "fix" Basic Strategy in your mind, running through the hands in order, from start to finish, until you get to the point that you can respond quickly, accurately, and without conscious thought.

Once you do get Basic Strategy fixed in your mind, you are ready for the random drills of Practice Chart 4.2. And it is absolutely essential that you do these drills until you can start anywhere in this chart, go through it in any order, and instantly know the correct answers. When you can do this, you *know* Basic Strategy.

I am stressing the importance of learning Basic Strategy without any dependence on order, because that is how the hands are dealt to you: in a purely random, unpredictable fashion. And if your knowledge of Basic Strategy is dependent upon a particular sequence, you are going to have some problems. For example, a couple of years ago I had a student who after a few hours of training and practice claimed to have mastered the Basic Strategy. I tested him, and sure enough, he rattled off the strategy tables, from memory, without a glitch. Then I sat him down at my Blackjack table and began to deal some hands; he played perfectly, but it took him somewhere between 10 and 30 seconds to play each hand. Curious, I asked him why he played so slowly. He told me that he had all the strategy tables memorized, in order, and that before he could recall a play, he had to mentally flash through every cell, of every table, until he came to the hand in question! I smiled, handed him a copy of Practice Chart 4.2, and sent him back to the drawing boards.

This may sound extreme, and it is, but it is surprising how many people become dependent upon some sequence or order to recall correct plays. This is all right in the initial learning phase, when you are just trying to fix the strategy in your mind; but when you get down to really mastering the material, it has got to be in a totally random, arbitrary manner.

Practice Chart 4.1

BASIC STRATEGY

	2	3	4	5	6	7	8	9	T	A
22	22 2	22 3	22 4	22 5	22 6	22 7	22 8	22 9	22 T	22 A
23	23 2	23 3	23 4	23 5	23 6	23 7	23 8	23 9	23 T	23 A
24	24 2	24 3	24 4	24 5	24 6	24 7	24 8	24 9	24 T	24 A
25	25 2	25 3	25 4	25 5	25 6	25 7	25 8	25 9	25 T	25 A
26	26 2	26 3	26 4	26 5	26 6	26 7	26 8	26 9	26 T	26 A
27	27 2	27 3	27 4	27 5	27 6	27 7	27 8	27 9	27 T	27 A
28	28 2	28 3	28 4	28 5	28 6	28 7	28 8	28 9	28 T	28 A
29	29 2	29 3	29 4	29 5	29 6	29 7	29 8	29 9	29 T	29 A
2T	2T 2	2T 3	2T 4	2T 5	2T 6	2T 7	2T 8	2T 9	2T T	2T A
2A	2A 2	2A 3	2A 4	2A 5	2A 6	2A 7	2A 8	2A 9	2A T	2A A
33	33 2	33 3	33 4	33 5	33 6	33 7	33 8	33 9	33 T	33 A
34	34 2	34 3	34 4	34 5	34 6	34 7	34 8	34 9	34 T	34 A
35	35 2	35 3	35 4	35 5	35 6	35 7	35 8	35 9	35 T	35 A
36	36 2	36 3	36 4	36 5	36 6	36 7	36 8	36 9	36 T	36 A
37	37 2	37 3	37 4	37 5	37 6	37 7	37 8	37 9	37 T	37 A
38	38 2	38 3	38 4	38 5	38 6	38 7	38 8	38 9	38 T	38 A
39	39 2	39 3	39 4	39 5	39 6	39 7	39 8	39 9	39 T	39 A
3T	3T 2	3T 3	3T 4	3T 5	3T 6	3T 7	3T 8	3T 9	3T T	3T A
3A	3A 2	3A 3	3A 4	3A 5	3A 6	3A 7	3A 8	3A 9	3A T	3A A
44	44 2	44 3	44 4	44 5	44 6	44 7	44 8	44 9	44 T	44 A
45	45 2	45 3	45 4	45 5	45 6	45 7	45 8	45 9	45 T	45 A
46	46 2	46 3	46 4	46 5	46 6	46 7	46 8	46 9	46 T	46 A
47	47 2	47 3	47 4	47 5	47 6	47 7	47 8	47 9	47 T	47 A
48	48 2	48 3	48 4	48 5	48 6	48 7	48 8	48 9	48 T	48 A
49	49 2	49 3	49 4	49 5	49 6	49 7	49 8	49 9	49 T	49 A
4T	4T 2	4T 3	4T 4	4T 5	4T 6	4T 7	4T 8	4T 9	4T T	4T A
4A	4A 2	4A 3	4A 4	4A 5	4A 6	4A 7	4A 8	4A 9	4A T	4A A
55	55 2	55 3	55 4	55 5	55 6	55 7	55 8	55 9	55 T	55 A
56	56 2	56 3	56 4	56 5	56 6	56 7	56 8	56 9	56 T	56 A
57	57 2	57 3	57 4	57 5	57 6	57 7	57 8	57 9	57 T	57 A
58	58 2	58 3	58 4	58 5	58 6	58 7	58 8	58 9	58 T	58 A
59	59 2	59 3	59 4	59 5	59 6	59 7	59 8	59 9	59 T	59 A
5T	5T 2	5T 3	5T 4	5T 5	5T 6	5T 7	5T 8	5T 9	5T T	5T A
5A	5A 2	5A 3	5A 4	5A 5	5A 6	5A 7	5A 8	5A 9	5A T	5A A
66	66 2	66 3	66 4	66 5	66 6	66 7	66 8	66 9	66 T	66 A
67	67 2	67 3	67 4	67 5	67 6	67 7	67 8	67 9	67 T	67 A
68	68 2	68 3	68 4	68 5	68 6	68 7	68 8	68 9	68 T	68 A
69	69 2	69 3	69 4	69 5	69 6	69 7	69 8	69 9	69 T	69 A
6T	6T 2	6T 3	6T 4	6T 5	6T 6	6T 7	6T 8	6T 9	6T T	6T A
6A	6A 2	6A 3	6A 4	6A 5	6A 6	6A 7	6A 8	6A 9	6A T	6A A
77	77 2	77 3	77 4	77 5	77 6	77 7	77 8	77 9	77 T	77 A
78	78 2	78 3	78 4	78 5	78 6	78 7	78 8	78 9	78 T	78 A
79	79 2	79 3	79 4	79 5	79 6	79 7	79 8	79 9	79 T	79 A
7T	7T 2	7T 3	7T 4	7T 5	7T 6	7T 7	7T 8	7T 9	7T T	7T A
7A	7A 2	7A 3	7A 4	7A 5	7A 6	7A 7	7A 8	7A 9	7A T	7A A
88	88 2	88 3	88 4	88 5	88 6	88 7	88 8	88 9	88 T	88 A
89	89 2	89 3	89 4	89 5	89 6	89 7	89 8	89 9	89 T	89 A
8T	8T 2	8T 3	8T 4	8T 5	8T 6	8T 7	8T 8	8T 9	8T T	8T A
8A	8A 2	8A 3	8A 4	8A 5	8A 6	8A 7	8A 8	8A 9	8A T	8A A
99	99 2	99 3	99 4	99 5	99 6	99 7	99 8	99 9	99 T	99 A
9T	9T 2	9T 3	9T 4	9T 5	9T 6	9T 7	9T 8	9T 9	9T T	9T A
9A	9A 2	9A 3	9A 4	9A 5	9A 6	9A 7	9A 8	9A 9	9A T	9A A
TT	TT 2	TT 3	TT 4	TT 5	TT 6	TT 7	TT 8	TT 9	TT T	TT A
AA	AA 2	AA 3	AA 4	AA 5	AA 6	AA 7	AA 8	AA 9	AA T	AA A

Practice Chart 4.2

BASIC STRATEGY

```
55 A    59 6    33 7    8T T    69 5    47 2    79 A    9T A    28 8    69 A
A7 2    4T 4    88 8    27 6    A7 T    67 7    33 4    A7 9    23 5    22 4
99 T    78 3    3T 5    89 2    25 7    TT 8    2T 6    TT 5    AA 7    47 6
TT 7    35 3    37 2    69 7    23 A    47 A    35 9    35 6    23 8    36 A
58 9    46 9    58 A    A8 A    TT A    33 8    25 5    6T 4    36 4    A5 7
AA 6    8T A    39 3    25 8    25 2    AA A    5T T    78 T    A2 8    A7 6
57 5    22 6    AA 2    78 9    48 7    44 9    28 6    68 6    A8 2    27 T
46 8    AA 5    89 4    33 2    A5 4    46 3    22 T    5T 5    A7 5    A2 9
9T 9    89 8    46 4    27 4    6T 2    33 A    23 7    26 3    25 A    89 7
66 7    29 T    99 A    39 6    TT 4    A3 A    A9 6    44 5    A2 4    79 5
59 2    55 4    34 5    26 2    88 A    37 7    25 6    28 A    5T 6    68 3
27 5    77 4    89 T    39 7    37 5    6T 6    66 5    68 2    29 A    34 7
57 8    39 8    33 6    77 7    A6 4    35 8    56 4    2T T    36 8    77 5
55 9    4T 8    29 9    44 3    7T 9    38 4    8T 9    55 6    36 T    TT T
69 9    48 6    A7 8    68 A    78 6    8T 5    39 A    59 A    4T 7    A5 A
58 3    66 3    5T 8    3T 7    39 T    58 6    69 8    TT 9    A3 2    49 A
66 9    38 5    7T A    48 5    A4 9    A6 A    49 3    67 5    99 4    2T 5
TT 3    88 3    28 7    34 A    57 3    7T 7    A3 T    A7 7    58 7    9T 7
49 5    7T 8    A4 5    A2 3    7T 5    A2 5    45 7    A6 T    28 4    A9 3
5T 7    58 4    A5 3    67 4    25 T    5T 4    79 8    23 4    A4 2    46 T
4T 2    29 3    26 A    46 7    27 2    67 8    78 4    47 4    A5 8    25 9
33 3    68 9    2T 3    A3 7    A9 7    A8 4    48 9    3T 8    45 A    23 6
88 5    58 5    A9 8    56 7    39 5    34 4    22 A    45 5    39 2    AA T
66 6    4T 5    39 4    37 3    24 7    8T 6    TT 6    A4 A    29 5    69 4
9T 4    46 2    A5 2    49 7    A7 3    68 4    39 9    26 8    68 5    79 4
77 6    24 3    24 A    7T 3    99 6    22 2    7T T    77 A    34 6    6T 3
78 A    56 T    58 8    38 7    6T 7    4T 6    24 4    66 2    79 3    56 2
79 2    4T T    7T 4    29 4    77 2    3T T    45 9    35 A    8T 4    58 2
45 3    5T 2    28 2    8T 8    6T 5    89 5    7T 2    24 6    9T 2    TT 2
46 6    23 2    59 9    47 7    2T 4    99 2    AA 8    3T 2    36 5    69 6
47 5    88 4    29 2    24 9    88 6    35 4    99 7    8T 3    49 6    79 7
78 5    3T 4    47 3    59 5    26 5    57 4    29 6    4T 3    49 4    3T 3
36 9    57 6    99 5    A9 2    26 7    A2 A    6T 8    79 6    9T 8    56 3
48 4    45 4    45 2    28 9    4T 9    67 6    25 3    99 8    8T 7    A7 A
5T 9    77 8    A9 A    89 9    49 8    45 6    67 2    27 8    99 3    88 9
36 6    3T 6    69 3    22 3    77 3    55 3    28 T    38 3    79 9    A2 2
22 8    2T A    A8 7    A6 7    A8 6    78 8    36 3    66 8    A5 9    44 7
78 2    88 2    27 A    55 5    44 6    A3 9    26 9    28 5    A5 6    A3 6
A4 3    45 T    2T 8    69 2    A8 9    2T 7    A9 4    37 6    57 T    33 T
55 7    27 3    9T 5    24 2    37 A    A7 4    A4 4    56 8    59 7    A9 5
46 5    A5 5    3T A    37 4    59 3    67 3    34 2    23 T    A6 6    44 T
A4 7    22 5    49 T    59 T    A9 9    67 9    47 8    36 7    24 5    59 4
66 4    A8 3    35 2    A2 6    2T 9    33 9    68 7    A9 T    AA 9    A3 5
36 2    5T 3    22 7    55 8    35 5    44 A    7T 6    37 8    57 7    26 6
A8 5    A6 5    2T 2    38 6    22 9    44 2    24 T    46 A    34 T    6T 9
88 7    A4 6    9T 6    A3 4    48 3    38 2    35 T    A8 T    48 8    68 8
57 2    AA 3    A3 3    A4 T    29 7    45 8    89 6    A6 3    66 T    3T 9
69 T    56 6    38 T    A6 8    56 9    37 T    58 T    9T 3    A2 T    89 3
56 5    78 7    35 7    79 T    37 9    27 7    56 A    27 9    59 8    67 A
99 9    34 8    44 8    A3 8    48 T    66 A    29 8    55 T    24 8    9T T
38 8    4T A    47 9    57 9    77 T    6T T    49 9    A8 8    5T A    49 2
8T 2    38 9    48 A    AA 4    A6 2    A6 9    38 A    47 T    48 2    34 9
77 9    67 T    23 3    88 T    23 9    34 3    44 4    89 A    26 4    26 T
25 4    6T A    68 T    55 2    57 A    33 5    28 3    A4 8    A5 T    A2 7
```

A WORD TO THE WISE

Before we wrap this chapter up and get on with the really exciting stuff, I want you to think about this: even though I have spent absolutely countless hours on the research and writing of this book, I am under no illusions. I know that many of my readers, despite all my efforts, will end up losers. Some will be short on talent, some will be short on patience; in the end most will be short on cash. I am telling you this to alert you, not depress you. It is all here. Everything you need to be a winner. But it won't do you any good if it stays here. To win with this book, you must master this book, and Basic Strategy is where it all begins. This is your foundation; build it carefully and build it well. And remember, there are *no* short cuts! So don't turn another page until you have learned the strategy tables, mastered the practice charts, and understood every paragraph, every line and every word.

CHAPTER FIVE

The Basic Omega II System

The card counting systems of the early 1960s were generally based on the "Ten Count" method, so-called because it involved counting 10s versus all other cards.

In these systems a player began with two numbers, which represented the total of 10s and others in a complete pack. For example, in a single-deck game, the player began with (36,16), meaning 36 others and 16 10s. Then as cards were dealt out, he kept track by reducing the appropriate number. For instance, if the player picked up his hand and found a blackjack (Ace,10), he would adjust the count to (35,15), if the dealer's up card were a 7, the count would then be (34,15), and so on through the deck.

This running count was used to mentally calculate a ratio of others to 10s, which was used for betting, insurance, and the play of the hands. With the above count, for example, the ratio would be $34/15 = 2.27$.

With a lot of practice, it was possible to get very good at this mental gymnastic of counting backwards, calculating ratios, and mentally comparing the ratios to memorized strategy tables.

But then an ugly thing happened: In an attempt to stop counters, the casinos started dealing more and more multiple-deck games. If counting down one deck was tough, it was child's play compared to say, four decks. Imagine starting with (144,64), instead of (36,16), and coming up with an accurate ratio for, say, (131,53) in the twinkle of an eye. There *had* to be a better way.

And fortunately there was. For about this time several researchers realized that both power and simplicity would be served by using a point count system and counting forward instead of backward. With this technique, it was almost as easy to count down four or six decks as it was a single deck!

The point count concept really is a model of simplicity. Each card is given a value, plus (+) or minus (-), that reflects its relative value in the game. The player then keeps a running cumulative count of the cards as they fall and uses this information to make his betting, insurance, and playing decisions. Simple, accurate--and powerful.

THE OMEGA II COUNT

All modern count systems use some variation on this point count theme. And the system you will learn in this chapter, the Basic Omega II System, uses the most accurate and powerful level 2 count ever devised.[1]

This will be your first winning Blackjack system. It is both powerful and easy to use. From its power, you will gain the confidence that comes from winning play, and from its simplicity, you will gain the satisfaction that comes from masterful play.

The count you will use is as follows:

The Omega II Count

	2	3	4	5	6	7	8	9	10	A
VALUE:	+1	+1	+2	+2	+2	+1	0	-1	-2	0

To understand why this count was chosen, a little Blackjack theory is in order. We count cards in Blackjack to enable us to do three things more accurately than would otherwise be possible: 1) Bet our money, 2) Take insurance, 3) Play our hands. Unfortunately, the ideal count for any one of these tasks is not ideal for the other two. For example, the following count is perfect for insurance:

Insurance Count

	2	3	4	5	6	7	8	9	10	A
VALUE:	+4	+4	+4	+4	+4	+4	+4	+4	-9	+4

A careful examination of this count will reveal that it is really our old friend the Ten Count in disguise. And since both the Ten Count and insurance are a function of the ratio of others to 10s, it follows that this count is ideal for insurance purposes.

----

1. The level of an integer count is defined by the largest absolute value assigned in the count. For example, a level 2 count, such as the Omega II Count, has no value greater than +2, or less than -2.

But now consider betting. What is the best count for this purpose? Computer studies have given the following count as just about ideal for betting:

Betting Count

	2	3	4	5	6	7	8	9	10	A
VALUE:	+5	+5	+7	+10	+5	+4	0	-2	-6.5	-8

And finally, lets take a look at a nearly optimal count for deciding on the play of the hands:

Playing Count

	2	3	4	5	6	7	8	9	10	A
VALUE:	+3	+4	+6	+8	+6	+5	+2	-2	-8.5	+2

Even though each of these counts has exactly the same number of positive and negative points, practically every card rank has a different value in each count. The Insurance Count, for example, values the Ace as +4, while the Betting Count values it at -8, and the Playing Count gives it a value of +2. It's no wonder then, that a count optimized for one purpose is no where near ideal for the other two.

In the first edition of Beat the Dealer, Thorp suggested the solution to this puzzler was to keep both the Ten Count *and* a second count, like the Betting Count shown above, and use whichever was more appropriate for the task at hand.[2] Sure we will. No problem. And while we're at it, we might as well toss in memorizing the exact order of the deal as well; you just never know what might come in handy. Mathematicians give a lot of advice like this. It's one reason they analyze Blackjack a lot better than they play it.

But, seriously, if keeping multiple counts is out of the question, how *do* we go about achieving any real accuracy with our insurance, betting, and playing decisions?

----

2. Thorp, Beat the Dealer, pp. 164ff.

Well, let's take another look at our three optimal counts; and this time we'll add some additional information as well:

	2	3	4	5	6	7	8	9	10	A	E_i	E_b	E_p
Insurance:	+4	+4	+4	+4	+4	+4	+4	+4	-9	+4	1.00	.72	.62
Betting:	+5	+5	+7	+10	+5	+4	0	-2	-6.5	-8	.72	1.00	.55
Playing:	+3	+4	+6	+8	+6	+5	+2	-2	-8.5	+2	.92	.87	.70

The headings E_i, E_b, and E_p indicate the efficiencies of the various counts for insurance, betting, and the play of the hands, respectively. The term efficiency, as we are using it here, means the ratio of the actual gain achievable by the count to the theoretical gain achievable by a perfect knowledge of the card densities in the remaining deck.[3]

The highest possible efficiency rating is 1.00; this rating indicates the count is essentially perfect for that purpose. The lowest rating is 0.00,[4] which means the count provides no gain whatsoever for that purpose. Intermediate ratings indicate varying degrees of efficiency for the purpose considered.

It is interesting to note that although the Insurance Count has an E_i of 1.00, and the Betting Count has an E_b of 1.00, the Playing Count does not have an E_p of 1.00. In fact, the Playing Count has a higher efficiency rating for insurance and betting than it does for playing!

The reason for this surprising fact is that card counting systems that assign a single value to each card rank, the so-called *single-parameter* systems, simply cannot handle the play of the hands as well as they do insurance and betting. The problem lies primarily with the middle cards, the 7s, 8s, and 9s. Sometimes they behave as small cards, as when drawing to 12, for instance, and sometimes they behave as large cards, as when drawing to 15. The proper way to handle such cards is to give them a value, (+) or (-), that reflects their average value, as we have done in the Omega II Count, and then keep a side count of each of them and

----

3. Compare Peter A. Griffin, <u>The Theory of Blackjack</u>, rev. ed. p. 43.

4. One could even create counts that had *negative* efficiencies, in that their use would result in a loss, not a gain. But we are assuming best use of the count, and if best use is no use, then no use it is!

adjust the main count depending on the situation and the relative excess or shortage of these cards in the remaining deck. With this technique it is possible to bring the playing efficiency (E_p) of an ideal count up to about .95.

The problem with this *multiparameter* approach is that it's not playable in the real world. It's no problem to do it on a computer, but it's a big problem to do it in a casino. Any attempt to keep a side count of several cards will result in losses from counting errors a lot bigger than any theoretical gains.[5]

Given the above analysis and the fundamental differences in our three optimum counts, it is not surprising that the efficiency ratings bear out our claim that a count ideal for one purpose may not be very good for another.

OK, fine, we've confirmed we have a problem. Now what are we going to do about it? Well, for openers, it's obvious we're going to have to make some compromises, but where and how?

Let's start by deciding on the relative importance of insurance, betting, and the play of the hands on our prospects for winning. Insurance, as it turns out, is of secondary importance, contributing well under 10% of our overall gain from counting. As for betting and playing, their relative importance is primarily a function of how freely we can spread our bets and how deeply the casino will deal before shuffling.

With conditions as they exist in the casinos today, computer studies have shown that in single-deck games the play of the hands is slightly more important than betting, and in multiple-deck games betting is somewhat more important than the play of the hands. Overall, for our purposes, the two factors are about equal in importance.

So, as a first step in creating a count that is as close as possible to being all things to all purposes, let's combine our three optimum counts, using a weighted

----

5. I know from experience, however, that it is feasible to keep a side count of *one* extra card. The most profitable card to count this way is the Ace, and the best use of this added information is to adjust the running count for betting purposes only. A little later in this chapter we'll discuss this topic more thoroughly.

average[6] based on their importance,[7] and see what we get:

<u>Weighted Average Optimum Count</u>

2	3	4	5	6	7	8	9	10	A
VALUE: +4.0	+4.47	+6.37	+8.74	+5.42	+4.47	+1.16	−1.68	−7.58	−2.63

Now we're getting somewhere. But notice also, that among the three optimum counts, the biggest discrepancy occurs in the value of the Ace. The other card values, particularly in the Betting and Playing Counts, show a good deal of similarity.

The reason for this remarkable variance in the value of the Ace is due to its "blackjack potential." Blackjacks greatly favor the player because they pay a 50% bonus. That is why the Ace is a big minus card in the Betting Count: as the Aces fall, so do the player's chances for getting a blackjack. But in the Playing Count we are not concerned with blackjacks. What matters here is a card's potential for busting or making a hand when we, or the dealer, draw. Since it is virtually impossible to bust drawing an Ace, and since it seldom does much to make a hand either,[8] it's no surprise that in the Playing Count the Ace has very little value.

----

6. This technique of a weighted average works because Blackjack counts are essentially proportional and linear with respect to their efficiency coefficients for insurance, betting, and the play of the hands.

7. Using a weighting ratio of approximately $1_i : 9_b : 9_p$.

8. This is not strictly true, because when we, or the dealer, are drawing to 8, 9, or 10, there is nothing sweeter than hooking an Ace. But single-parameter (+) (-) card-counting schemes are not capable of taking the *playing* effect of the Ace, when valued as 11, into account. This is because, when valued as 11, the Ace acts like a big (-) card in terms of making a hand of 10 or less, but reverts to a value of 1 and acts like a small (+) card instead of busting a hand of 11 or more.

If this seems confusing, don't worry, even experts have a tough time with the schizophrenic Ace.

This analysis has led many experts, this author included, to the conclusion that the Ace should be valued as zero in the main count, and a that a side count of Aces should be kept to adjust the main count for betting purposes only.

Following this reasoning, let's value the Ace as zero in our Weighted Average Optimum Count, adjust the other values to maintain balance, and see what we come up with:

2	3	4	5	6	7	8	9	10	A
VALUE: +3.7	+4.13	+5.89	+8.08	+5.0	+4.13	+1.07	−1.68	−7.58	0

Hmmm, interesting. We're almost there now. In fact, if you were a computer or other major mutant, you would use this count. For the rest of us, though, we've still got a little work to do.

First off, this count is way too big to be practical, so let's cut it down to size. We're looking for a level 2 count, so let's divide through by a constant that will give us a count in that range. Dividing by say, 3.25, we get:

2	3	4	5	6	7	8	9	10	A
VALUE: +1.14	+1.27	+1.81	+2.48	+1.54	+1.27	+.33	−.52	−2.33	0

That's better. Now, rounding to the nearest whole number, to make the count playable by us mere mortals, and what do we have?

2	3	4	5	6	7	8	9	10	A	E_i	E_b	E_p
VALUE: +1	+1	+2	+2	+2	+1	0	−1	−2	0	.85	.92	.67

You guessed it, the Omega II Count.

Now take a look at the efficiency ratings of Omega II. Notice that, even though each of the optimum counts is still tops in its field, overall the Omega II Count is king.

You may be wondering why we have chosen a level 2 count when a level 1 count is easier to play, and a higher level count may be stronger. Well, an optimal higher level count may offer slightly more power, but the gain is trivial, and the increase in effort is substantial. For example, I played the Revere 14 Count for years, logging over 150,000 hands of big-money play. This was a level 4 count that looked like this:

<u>Revere 14 Count</u>

	2	3	4	5	6	7	8	9	10	A	E_i	E_b	E_p
VALUE:	+2	+2	+3	+4	+2	+1	0	-2	-3	0	.82	.92	.66

In fairness, I have to say that I won a <u>lot</u> of money with this count and averaged a win rate of over +1.9% in mostly single-deck play. That's the good news. The bad news is that this count was a ball buster to use, and to stay sharp I had to practice nearly an hour every single day. Now I use the Omega II Count; I win just as fast, and the only time I practice is just before I go out to play.

Notice also, that the 14 Count's efficiency ratings are slightly *inferior* to those of the Omega II Count. So bigger is not necessarily better.

Level 1 counts also present some problems. To begin with, even the best of them are only about 90% as powerful as the Omega II Count. And even though they are slightly easier to use, counting errors, even small ones, are greatly magnified. For instance, suppose you are counting down a deck, and at some point in the deal the correct running total with a particular level 1 count is +4. Suppose also that this same deal would yield a running total of +8 with an equivalent level 2 count. Now let's say that somewhere along the line you miscounted the 3 of Spades, which has a value of +1 in <u>both</u> our level 1 and level 2 counts, and instead of adding +1 to the count you made a mistake and *subtracted* +1 from the running count. So, in the level 1 count you now have a mistaken running total of +2, and in the level 2 count you have a running total of +6. These kinds of errors are not uncommon in actual play, and as you can see they can be a lot more serious in level 1 counts than they are in level 2 counts. In the above example, for instance, the level 1 count is off by 50% and the level 2 count is "only" off by 25%.

In spite of all this, some experts insist that the simplicity of a good level 1 count is the most important consideration. Others argue that an optimal level 3 or level 4 count will eke out enough additional gain to justify all the extra work needed to play such counts accurately.

As far as I am concerned, level 2 offers just the right balance of power and simplicity.

This chapter contains a fair amount of theory, more than you really need to learn a point count system. There are two reasons for this. First, I want you to be convinced that the Omega II Count is as good as I say it is: there is nothing like knowing you are playing the best to sustain your confidence at the Blackjack tables. And second, in Blackjack, knowledge is power, power is money, and money is the name of the game.

LEARNING THE OMEGA II COUNT

The best way to learn the Omega II Count is through counting drills using a double deck of cards.

Take the two decks of cards and shuffle them together thoroughly. Now practice turning over the cards, one at a time, while keeping the running count. Accuracy is more important than speed, so start slowly and add speed as your proficiency improves.

Eventually, you should be able to go through a double deck, one card at a time, in about 50 seconds. But remember, accuracy is the most important thing, so do <u>not</u> sacrifice accuracy for speed.

It's also a good idea to <u>overtrain</u>, so that when you run into big plus decks you do not get flustered and lose the count. There is nothing more disheartening than to wait out the game for an hour or more, finally get a gangbusters deck, and then lose the count because you are not used to such big numbers. Believe me, this hurts. The way to avert this problem is to occasionally "load" the double deck with most of the small cards near the front; this will give you practice with counts as big or bigger than anything you will see in actual play.

Practice big minus counts using this technique as well. Just load the double deck with most of the 10s near the front; then practice the running count until you can handle these big minus decks as easily as the less extreme ones that occur in normal play.

Once you are good at these counting drills, it's time to start practicing by turning over the cards <u>two</u> at a time, instead of just one at a time. This is important because the dealer will turn over the players' hole cards two at a time, and your count will be faster and more accurate if you count them this way as well. It is much faster to count (3,9) as zero, for instance, than to first add +1, and then add -1.

With practice, you should be able to go through a double deck, two cards at time, in about 30 seconds.

When you are good enough to accurately count down a double deck, one card at a time, in less than a minute, and two cards at a time, in less than 35 seconds, your counting skills are ready for actual casino play.

THE BASIC OMEGA II STRATEGY

A Blackjack system based on counting cards consists of a playing strategy, as well as a count.

The count we have chosen, the Omega II Count, is extremely accurate, and in the chapter on the Advanced Omega II System, we will combine this count with a sophisticated playing strategy to create one of the most powerful Blackjack systems ever devised.

Our goals with the Basic Omega II System of this chapter, however, are a little more modest. Here we are going to team the Omega II Count with a modified version of the Basic Strategy. While not optimal, this system *will* give you a decided edge over the house. For the many players who have no desire to be professionals, but who are just looking for a method that will allow them to enjoy their vacations in casinoland more thoroughly, and return home showing a profit, this simple system is all they will ever need.

But even if your intentions are more ambitious than this, I want you to learn this system first and use it to gain experience in the casinos. You will find that, in the beginning, you will have your hands full keeping an accurate count, betting properly, adding up your cards, and learning how to deal with the casino bosses, without compounding all this by trying to learn and utilize a sophisticated playing strategy.

Later on, when all these things have become second nature, you can learn the Advanced Omega II Strategy.

The Basic Omega II Strategy consists of three separate playing strategies. The first one, in Table 5.1, is called the -6 Strategy. You will use this strategy any time the "true count" (see page 78) is less than or equal to -6. The second strategy is simply the normal Basic Strategy of Chapter Four. This strategy is used any time the true count is greater than -6, but less than +6. For convenience the Basic Strategy is listed in Table 5.2. The third and final strategy, found in Table 5.3, is called the +6 Strategy. You will use this strategy any time the true count is greater than or equal to +6.

A glance at the following graph (Figure 5.1) should clarify any questions you may have as to when a particular strategy is used.

Figure 5.1

STRATEGY DOMAINS

Basic Omega II

```
    -6 Strategy        Basic Strategy        +6 Strategy
<-------------------|-----------------|------------------->
 ...-10  -9  -8  -7  -6        0        +6  +7  +8  +9  +10...
```

The concept behind this multistrategy approach is straightforward. When the true count is within a few points of zero, the normal Basic Strategy is a good approximation to the correct strategy. However, when the true count begins to deviate substantially from zero, the Basic Strategy no longer makes for accurate play, and our strategy must change accordingly. The +6 Strategy and the -6 Strategy adjust our play to more accurately handle these extreme counts.

Later on, when you learn the Advanced Omega II Strategy, you will gain even more power and accuracy in your play.

Borderline Counts

Sometimes the true count will be right on the edge between Basic Strategy and either the +6 or -6 Strategy. In situations like this, unless you're sure the count justifies a change, I advise you to play the hand with Basic Strategy.

You'll never get hurt badly erring on the side of Basic Strategy, and if your count is slightly off this play may save you some money.

This technique also works with more sophisticated strategies such as the Advanced Omega II Strategy, so keep it in mind for use later on.

Some experts (notably Wong) advise that in borderline stand/draw situations it is desirable to draw on minus decks and stand on plus decks, so as to either "eat" up bad (-) cards and perhaps force an early shuffle, or save good (+) cards and maybe get an additional round from a favorable pack.

This is crafty play and it works, but it does require a very accurate true count, so only make this play if you are really sure of your count; otherwise, stick with Basic Strategy in borderline situations.

TABLE 5.1 - THE -6 STRATEGY

When the true count is less than or equal to -6, the deck is very rich in "small" cards (2,3,4,5,6,7) and very lean in 10s and 9s. Obviously the normal Basic Strategy, which assumes full-deck probabilities, will not do a very good job of handling these situations. That's where the -6 Strategy comes in; this strategy is specifically designed to handle these "minus" decks with far more accuracy than is possible with Basic Strategy.

Note that there are 48 changes from Basic Strategy in the -6 Strategy. Basically the changes consist of hitting more often, and doubling down and splitting less often.

We hit more often because with the deck loaded with "little" cards, the dealer is less likely to bust and far more likely than usual to make a good hand. The chances of improving our total are also a lot better with these "minus" decks, so it makes good sense that we hit certain "stiffs" that we would normally stand with if we were using Basic Strategy.

We hard double in fewer situations because the chances of catching the desired 10 are greatly reduced, and because with the dealer busting less often, and making more good hands, there are fewer situations where it pays to double your bet and risk losing twice the money.

Soft doubling is a little trickier. Here we are generally hoping to catch a "small" card, so "minus" decks actually work to our advantage in this respect. However, this small gain is more than offset by the added risk posed by the dealer's likelihood of achieving a strong hand. So, as with hard doubling, there are fewer situations where it pays to double your dough and risk losing twice the bread.

With pair splitting, both you and the dealer are more likely than usual to draw good hands, but because if you both bust, the dealer wins, you have to be more conservative than the dealer in deciding when to hit, and that means he will often beat you on the draw. So there are fewer situations where it pays to split a pair than would occur with a neutral deck.

One more thing, you never take insurance with the -6 Strategy. Insurance, even with a neutral deck, is a bad bet. With the "minus" decks we're considering here, it is suicidal.

Table 5.1

-6 STRATEGY

PLAYER				DEALER'S	UP	CARD				
HAND	2	3	4	5	6	7	8	9	10	A
17	S	S	S	S	S	S	S	S	S	S
16	S	S	S	S	S	H	H	H	**H**	**H**
15	S	S	S	S	S	H	H	H	**H**	H
14	**H**	S	S	S	S	H	H	H	H	H
13	**H**	**H**	**H**	S	S	H	H	H	H	H
12	H	H	**H**	**H**	**H**	H	H	H	H	H
11	D	D	D	D	D	D	D	**H**	**H**	**H**
10	D	D	D	D	D	D	**H**	**H**	H	H
9	**H**	**H**	**H**	D	D	H	H	H	H	H
8	H	H	H	**H**	**H**	H	H	H	H	H
A,8	S	S	S	S	**S**	S	S	S	S	S
A,7	S	**S**	D	D	D	S	S	H	H	**H**
A,6	**H**	**H**	D	D	D	H	H	H	H	H
A,5	H	H	**H**	D	D	H	H	H	H	H
A,4	H	H	**H**	**H**	D	H	H	H	H	H
A,3	H	H	**H**	**H**	D	H	H	H	H	H
A,2	H	H	**H**	**H**	**H**	H	H	H	H	H
A,A	P	P	P	P	P	P	P	P	P	**H**
10,10	S	S	S	S	S	S	S	S	S	S
9,9	**S**	**S**	**S**	P	P	S	P	P	S	S
8,8	P	P	P	P	P	P	P	P	P	P
7,7	P	P	P	P	P	P	H	H	**H**	H
6,6	**H**	**H**	**H**	P	P	H	H	H	H	H
5,5	D	D	D	D	D	D	**H**	**H**	H	H
4,4	H	H	H	**H**	**H**	H	H	H	H	H
3,3	H	H	**H**	P	P	P	H	H	H	H
2,2	H	**H**	**H**	P	P	P	H	H	H	H

NOTES: WITH HARD HANDS, AND WITH (A,3) THROUGH
(A,6), IF YOU'RE NOT ALLOWED TO DOUBLE,
THEN HIT.

WITH (A,7) IF YOU'RE NOT ALLOWED TO DOUBLE,
THEN STAND.

THERE ARE 48 CHANGES FROM TABLE 5.2, AND
THEY ARE IN BOLDFACE.

TABLE 5.2 - BASIC STRATEGY

This strategy is just the normal Basic Strategy of Chapter Four. By now, you should have a master's degree in this strategy. If you don't, now is the time to go back and review this material thoroughly.

This strategy will handle those decks where the true count is greater than -6, but less than +6. Because the count will remain fairly close to neutral most of the time, you will use Basic Strategy far more often than the other two strategies. So be certain you understand it completely and can play it perfectly.

Also, as with the -6 Strategy, you <u>never</u> take insurance with the Basic Strategy.

Table 5.2

BASIC STRATEGY

Single Deck[1]

PLAYER HAND	\multicolumn{10}{c}{DEALER'S UP CARD}

PLAYER HAND	2	3	4	5	6	7	8	9	10	A
17	S	S	S	S	S	S	S	S	S	S
16	S	S	S	S	S	H	H	H	Sr	Sr
15	S	S	S	S	S	H	H	H	Sr	H
14	S	S	S	S	S	H	H	H	H[2]	H
13	S	S	S	S	S	H	H	H	H	H
12	H	H	S	S	S	H	H	H	H	H
11	D	D	D	D	D	D	D	D	D	D
10	D	D	D	D	D	D	D	D	H	H
9	D	D	D	D	D	H	H	H	H	H
8	H	H	H	D[3]	D[4]	H	H	H	H	H
A,8	S	S	S	S	D	S	S	S	S	S
A,7	S	D	D	D	D	S	S	H	H	S[5]
A,6	D	D	D	D	D	H	H	H	H	H
A,5	H	H	D	D	D	H	H	H	H	H
A,4	H	H	D	D	D	H	H	H	H	H
A,3	H	H	D	D	D	H	H	H	H	H
A,2	H	H	D	D	D	H	H	H	H	H
A,A	P	P	P	P	P	P	P	P	P	P
10,10	S	S	S	S	S	S	S	S	S	S
9,9	P	P	P	P	P	S	P	P	S	S
8,8	P	P	P	P	P	P	P	P	P	P
7,7	P	P	P	P	P	P	H	H	S[2]	H
6,6	P	P	P	P	P	H	H	H	H	H
5,5	D	D	D	D	D	D	D	D	H	H
4,4	H	H	H	D	D	H	H	H	H	H
3,3	H	H	P	P	P	P	H	H	H	H
2,2	H	P	P	P	P	P	H	H	H	H

NOTES: WITH HARD HANDS, AND WITH (A,2) THROUGH (A,6), IF YOU'RE NOT ALLOWED TO DOUBLE, THEN HIT.

WITH (A,7) AND (A,8) IF YOU'RE NOT ALLOWED TO DOUBLE, THEN STAND.

IF YOU CAN'T LATE SURRENDER, THEN HIT.

----

1. SEE TABLE 4.8 OF CHAPTER FOUR FOR MULTIPLE-DECK CHANGES.

2. STAND (7,7) VS. 10.

3. HIT (6,2) VS. 5.

4. HIT (6,2) VS. 6.

5. HIT IF DEALER HITS SOFT 17.

TABLE 5.3 - THE +6 STRATEGY

When the true count is greater than or equal to +6, the deck is very rich in 10s and 9s. When this is the case, the player enjoys a big-time advantage. The major reason for this is because with such a 10-packed deck, the dealer will bust on the draw far more often than usual. More blackjacks will be dealt as well, further adding to the player's advantage. Hard doubling also becomes much more profitable with the added likelihood of catching a 10 on the double and the dealer busting with a 10 on the draw. So, all in all, a 10-rich deck is well worth waiting for.

The +6 Strategy is designed to take full advantage of these delightful 10-rich decks. Notice that there are 12 changes from Basic Strategy. These changes primarily call for standing and doubling down more often than usual.

We stand more often with the +6 Strategy because with the deck loaded with 10s and 9s, the dealer is a good bet to bust any hand he draws to. Our chances of busting are higher too, so it makes good sense that we stand with the +6 Strategy more often that we do with Basic Strategy.

The increased likelihood of the dealer busting on the draw is also the primary reason we double down more with the +6 Strategy than we do with Basic Strategy. With hard doubling, there is the added bonus that we are much more likely than usual to hook a 10, so that even if the dealer doesn't bust, he is facing a player with a powerful hand.

And, finally, if you've been chomping at the bit, dying to find an excuse to take insurance, well, this is it. With the deck this "plus," on the average the number of 10s will be greater than half the number of non-10s, so when you are using the +6 Strategy always take insurance.

Table 5.3

+6 STRATEGY

PLAYER HAND	2	3	4	5	6	7	8	9	10	A
17	S	S	S	S	S	S	S	S	S	S
16	S	S	S	S	S	H	H	H	**Sr**[1]	Sr[2]
15	S	S	S	S	S	H	H	H	**Sr**	H
14	S	S	S	S	S	H	H	H	H[3]	H
13	S	S	S	S	S	H	H	H	H	H
12	**S**	**S**	S	S	S	H	H	H	H	H
11	D	D	D	D	D	D	D	D	D	D
10	D	D	D	D	D	D	D	D	H	H
9	D	D	D	D	D	**D**	H	H	H	H
8	H	H	H	**D**	**D**	H	H	H	H	H
A,8	S	S	**D**	**D**	D	S	S	S	S	S
A,7	**D**	D	D	D	D	S	S	H	H	S[4]
A,6	D	D	D	D	D	H	H	H	H	H
A,5	H	**D**	D	D	D	H	H	H	H	H
A,4	H	H	D	D	D	H	H	H	H	H
A,3	H	H	D	D	D	H	H	H	H	H
A,2	H	H	D	D	D	H	H	H	H	H
A,A	P	P	P	P	P	P	P	P	P	P
10,10	S	S	S	S	S	S	S	S	S	S
9,9	P	P	P	P	P	S	P	P	S	S
8,8	P	P	P	P	P	P	P	P	P	P
7,7	P	P	P	P	P	P	H	H	S	H
6,6	P	P	P	P	P	H	H	H	H	H
5,5	D	D	D	D	D	D	D	D	H	H
4,4	H	H	H	D	D	H	H	H	H	H
3,3	H	**P**	P	P	P	P	H	H	H	H
2,2	H	P	P	P	P	P	H	H	H	H

NOTES: WITH HARD HANDS, AND WITH (A,2) THROUGH (A,6), IF YOU'RE NOT ALLOWED TO DOUBLE, THEN HIT.

WITH (A,7) AND (A,8), IF YOU'RE NOT ALLOWED TO DOUBLE, THEN STAND.

THERE ARE 12 CHANGES FROM TABLE 5.2, AND THEY ARE IN BOLDFACE.

----

1. IF YOU CAN'T LATE SURRENDER, STAND 15 OR 16 VS. 10.

2. IF YOU CAN'T LATE SURRENDER, HIT 16 VS. ACE.

3. STAND (7,7) VS. 10.

4. HIT IF DEALER HITS SOFT 17.

LEARNING THE BASIC OMEGA II STRATEGY

The Basic Omega II Strategy is not difficult to learn. You already know the Basic Strategy, and the +6 and -6 Strategies are so similar to the Basic Strategy that they can be learned in just a few hours.

Because the playing decisions called for in the +6 Strategy are made when you have your larger bets out, it is important to master all the changes from Basic Strategy thoroughly in order to maximize your winning opportunities.

The -6 Strategy, on the other hand, is used when you are making minimum bets, so the changes from Basic Strategy here are not as critical to your overall edge. I suggest, therefore, that you start by mastering the stand/draw and hard-doubling changes in the -6 Strategy, playing the other hands with Basic Strategy, and only adding the other strategy changes as you become comfortable and proficient.

The best way to learn the +6 and -6 Strategies is to use the same techniques you used to master the Basic Strategy. After you have generally learned these strategies from Tables 5.1 and 5.3, you should either make up a set of flash cards for each of the strategies or use Practice Charts 4.1 and 4.2 of Chapter Four. Either way, practice until you have completely mastered these two new strategies. Be sure to start with Practice Chart 4.1 (or ordered flash cards) and continue until the playing decisions are firmly "fixed" in your mind; then use Practice Chart 4.2 (or shuffled flash cards) until you have completely mastered both the +6 and -6 Strategies.

When you can go through Practice Chart 4.2 quickly and accurately with the +6 and -6 Strategies, as well as the Basic Strategy, your strategy skills are ready for actual casino play.

THE TRUE COUNT

It's fairly obvious that a given running count is less significant when only a few cards have been dealt than it is later on in the deal. A single deck with a running count of +8, for example, would be far less rich in 10s if only four cards had been dealt, than it would be if only four cards <u>remained</u> to be dealt. In the former case, only one-third of the remaining cards would be 10s, but in the latter case, <u>all</u> of the remaining cards would be 10s, because the last card must always return the count to zero.

So, in deciding how to bet our money, take insurance, and play our hands, we need some way of adjusting or standardizing the running count so that the same adjusted count always means the same thing, regardless of when it occurs in the deal.

The technique we will use to adjust the running count is called the true count, and it works like this:

True Count = (Running Count)/(Remaining Decks)

For instance, in a four-deck game, with a running count of +6 and three decks remaining to be played, the true count is:

True Count = (+6)/(3) = +2

Or in a single-deck game, with a running count of -5 and one-fourth of the deck remaining to be played, the true count is:

True Count = (-5)/(.25) = -20

In effect, what the true count does is adjust the running count to the equivalent running count with one deck remaining to be played. In other words, it standardizes the count on one full deck. This is why the true count is sometimes called the "count per deck."[9]

----

9. Wong, <u>Professional Blackjack</u>, p. 48.

LEARNING TO USE THE TRUE COUNT

When calculating the true count, the degree of accuracy required in estimating the number of remaining decks depends on the size of the unplayed pack. Rounding to the nearest half deck is fine down to about two decks remaining. After that, I suggest you round to the nearest quarter deck.

Use the following table as a guide to the accuracy required in estimating the number of remaining decks:

Decks Remaining	Estimate to Nearest
6 or more	full deck
< 6 but > 2	half deck
2 or less	quarter deck

As an example, say we are playing in a four-deck game; the running count is +11, and there happen to be exactly 2.68 decks remaining. Obviously, at the table, we cannot tell exactly how many decks remain, but with what looks like a little over 2.5 decks left, we estimate decks remaining at 2.5 (rounding to the nearest half deck) and come up with a true count of $+11/2.5 = +4.4$.

In this case the actual true count is $+11/2.68 = +4.1$. And both our estimate and the actual true count give the same result when rounded to the nearest whole number.

Most casinos use a tray to hold the discards. You will find it a lot easier to estimate the size of the remaining pack by looking at the discard tray than by estimating directly from the shoe or the dealer's hand. This method does require the extra step of mentally subtracting the estimate of the number of decks in the tray from the total number of decks in play to arrive at the number of decks remaining. But I know from experience that with practice this step becomes automatic and checking the discard tray is more natural and accurate than straining to try to see what's left in the shoe or in the dealer's hand.

In practice, you'll probably find, as I have, that after a while you'll *know* what the contents of the discard tray mean without actually having to do the subtraction. For example, if I am in a four-deck game, and I see about 2.5 decks in the tray, I know, without having to subtract 2.5 from 4, that I have to divide my running count by 1.5 to arrive at the true count. Stuff like this becomes a no-brainer once you get some experience.

A good way to practice estimating the true count is to count down a double deck, one or two cards at a time, just as you did to get proficient with the Omega II Count. Only this time, stop every quarter deck and mentally calculate the true count. Deal the double deck all the way down to one-quarter deck remaining. When you can do this, quickly and accurately, across the full range of (+) and (-) running counts, your true count skills are ready for actual casino play.

Entering a Game in Progress

Sometimes, especially with multiple decks, you may want to enter a game in progress rather than wait for the shuffle.

The way to calculate the true count in situations like this is to count any cards you see on the table, and consider all unseen cards, including those in the discard tray, as undealt. For example, suppose you enter a four-deck game after about two decks have been dealt out; as you sit down you scan the layout and see about 26 cards with a total running count of, say, +16. This count justifies a maximum bet on the next round (see Table 5.7), and the true count before any additional cards are seen is about +4.6 (+16/3.5). Note, that you divide by the *entire* unseen pack, not just the portion left in the shoe, to calculate the true count.

Some otherwise knowledgeable players do not accept this. In the above example, for instance, they would argue that the reason the cards seen on the table had a running count of +16 is because a lot of minus cards (9s and 10s) had probably already been dealt in previous rounds producing a surplus of small cards in the remaining pack which, naturally, resulted in a number of plus cards then coming out. They would argue that the count is probably not really plus, at all, so they would wait for the shuffle to pick up the count and enter the game.

The error in this analysis is their assumption that the excess of minus cards is in the dealt portion of the unseen pack, only. In the above example, there *is* an excess of minus cards in the unseen pack, but on average these minus cards will be evenly dispersed throughout both the dealt and undealt parts of the unseen pack, resulting in a true count of about +4.6, as shown above.

THE RIGHT WAY TO COUNT

When you are counting cards in a casino, with all its noise and distractions, it is easy to miss some cards, or even to count some cards more than once. To prevent these problems, it is important to get into the habit of always counting the cards in exactly the same way.

I suggest you count the cards in the following order:

Face-Down Games	Face-Up Games
1. The dealer's up card.	1. Starting to your far right (first base) and going clockwise to your far left (third base), count each player's two hole cards.
2. Your hole cards.	
3. Starting to your far right (first base) and going clockwise to your far left (third base), count each hit card, all busted hands, and any hole cards you see.[10]	
	2. The dealer's up card.
	3. Starting as in step 1, above, count each hit card.
4. The dealer's hole card.	4. The dealer's hole card.
5. The dealer's hit card(s), if any.	5. The dealer's hit card(s), if any.
6. The other players' hole cards and double-down cards as the dealer turns them over.	6. Any double-down cards not previously seen as the dealer turns them over.[11]

If you always count this way, you will never miss any cards, and you will never count any cards more than once. An accurate count is the foundation of winning play: without this you have nothing. So practice this counting method, dealing hands to yourself and to several phantom players, until the technique becomes natural, automatic, and easy to use.

----

10. If you count any of the other players' face-down hole cards at this point, use chips or some other memory aid so you don't count them again in step 6.

11. Most clubs that deal a face-up game will deal double-down cards face up as well; however, a few of these clubs deal double cards face down, and you won't be able to see them until the settlement.

BETTING YOUR MONEY

In the good old days, up to about 1964, the conditions in the casinos were just about ideal. In Las Vegas and Reno, for example, virtually all of the games were single deck; most of the clubs dealt down to the last card, and you could spread your bets as wildly as you liked without much risk of an early shuffle or being barred from further play.

In those days the clubs were not managed, as they are today, by MBAs from Harvard and Wharton; instead they were mostly run by street-smart hoods who got their start in the crime syndicates of Chicago, Detroit, and New York.

These guys got most of their education majoring in rackets at the school of hard knocks. So while they could spot just about every grifter scam ever conceived, from marked cards to bogus chips, they were helpless when confronted with a scientific assault on their sweet little Blackjack money machine.

In those days, the handful of players who had developed valid counting schemes had a field day in the casinos. These systems were very crude by today's standards, but back then it didn't take a whole lot to get something on the game.

These early players generally used "end play,"[12] with wild bet swings near the end of the deck, to gain a big advantage over the house. Many of these card counting sharpies absolutely cleaned up, unmolested by casino bosses who refused to believe that the game could be had.

Then came Beat the Dealer, and things began to change.

If the casino bosses were guilty of perhaps underreacting to the threat posed by the early card counters, they more than made up for it by going certifiably berserk in the face of the publicity and media attention that accompanied the introduction of Thorp's classic book on counting.

Within a year, pit bosses who had sneered at the very idea the game could be beaten were barring and shuffling on just about anyone who spread his bets or looked like he might have read a book on Blackjack. These overzealous bozos managed to "86" a remarkable number of their very best customers, while the real

----

12. End play involves counting down the deck until just a few cards remain, usually less than half a dozen, and then making very large bets in favorable situations. With end play and an accurate count, the player can get a big edge over the house, even if his basic playing strategy is not very accurate.

pros went on playing and winning, more or less undisturbed by the panic and chaos in the pits.

Fortunately, as the casinos have slowly begun to realize that books and articles on counting promote the game and produce far more losers than winners, their fears have gradually subsided and the conditions in the clubs have generally improved.

You still have to be careful, though, because if they get on to you they will bar you, shuffle on you, and otherwise harass you. So, it is very important not to look like a counter, and one of the most important elements of this camouflage is in the way you spread your bets.

The tables that follow are designed to give you the maximum bet spread possible without the risk of being detected as a counter. Very few casino bosses can spot a counter by the way he plays his hands. They look, instead, for particular betting patterns to decide who is, and who is not, a counter; and these tables are specifically designed not to fit the pattern the bosses are looking for.

I suggest, however, that you use these tables merely as guides. If you follow them exactly after a while your play is going to start looking too mechanical. So, it's a good idea to occasionally vary your betting pattern, slightly, as well as to sometimes mix different chip colors (denominations) together, in order to enhance the natural look you are striving to project.

Also, when you increase your bet above 2 units, say, from 2 to 4, it is often desirable to spread to *two* hands rather than pile all the chips on just one hand.

This play has two important advantages. First off, it's good camouflage because it looks to the bosses like less of a bet spread than the same amount on one hand.

Second, the fluctuations in your playing stake are reduced somewhat because the two hands are independent except for about a 50% linkage through the dealer's up card.

The only danger is that in some instances "eating" up the extra cards will cause the dealer to shuffle one round earlier than usual. This hurts. In fact, I advise you *not* to make this play if you think it'll cost you a round. In many cases, though, especially with other players at the table, you'll get the same number of rounds whether you spread to two hands or not.

And one more thing, if you increase your bet and the dealer unexpectedly shuffles, do not reduce the bet. Just leave it alone. If the bosses see you reducing your bets based on the shuffle they are likely to assume you are counting.

Bet Spread - Single-Deck Games

Because single-deck games are so easy to beat, the clubs are very sensitive to bet changes. Therefore, when you are playing in a single-deck game with good rules, as in Las Vegas, I suggest you limit your bet spread to 2:1. Bet 1 or 2 units off the top, then spread your bets in the following way:

Table 5.4

SINGLE DECK
Las Vegas Rules

Bet	W/L	Count[13]	Bet < 1/2[14]	Bet > 1/2[15]
1	W	(+)	2	2
1	L	(+)	2	1
1	W	(-)	1	1
1	L	(-)	1	1
2	W	(+)	2	2
2	L	(+)	2	2
2	W	(-)	1	1
2	L	(-)	1	1

For example, say you bet 1 unit; you lose, the count goes plus, and the next hand will come out of the second half of the deck: your next bet is 1 unit. Or suppose you bet 2 units; you lose, the count stays plus, and the next hand will come out of the first half of the deck: your next bet is 2 units.

----

13. In this context, (+) does not mean any plus count; it means a count sufficiently plus to mathematically justify the indicated bet. (-) also is relative; it means a count that is either actually minus, or one that is insufficiently plus to mathematically justify a larger bet. The Betting Indices tables list these critical betting counts.

14. This means the next hand will be dealt from the *first* half of the pack.

15. This means the next hand will be dealt from the *second* half of the pack.

Bet Spread - Double-Deck Games

When you are playing in a double-deck game with good rules, or a single-deck game with bad rules (as in Reno), you have to spread your bets more widely to get an acceptable edge. Fortunately, the clubs are more willing to tolerate an aggressive bet spread in these games than they are in single-deck games with good rules. So when you are playing under these conditions, I suggest you use a 4:1 bet spread. Bet 2 or 4 units off the top, then spread your bets in the following way:

Table 5.5

DOUBLE DECK
Las Vegas Rules

Bet	W/L	Count	Bet < 1/2	Bet > 1/2
1	W	(+)	2	2
1	L	(+)	2	2
1	W	(−)	1	1
1	L	(−)	1	1
2	W	(+)	4	4
2	L	(+)	4	2
2	W	(−)	1	1
2	L	(−)	1	1
4	W	(+)	4	4
4	L	(+)	4	4
4	W	(−)	2	2[16]
4	L	(−)	2	2

Although beating double decks does require a more aggressive bet spread than is necessary with single decks, in other ways double decks are just about ideal. For instance, in double-deck games the number of other players at the table is not that critical to your win rate, and dealers often deal out double decks deeper (percentage-wise) than they do single decks.

----

16. Resist the temptation to cut back to a 1 unit bet in these situations. Such a big drop just looks too suspicious; wait for the next hand to back off to 1 unit.

Bet Spread - Multiple-Deck Games

Although you do have a clear advantage, I do not recommend playing the Basic Omega II System in multiple-deck games. These games are tough to beat, so you need every possible edge you can get. I suggest you get some experience first playing in single- and double-deck games, then when you are ready for multiple decks, learn the Advanced Omega II System of Chapter Seven. Once you know the Basic Omega II System of this chapter, the Advanced Omega II System will be easy to learn. The count is the same, and you will bet your money in the same way. The only difference is in the strategy you will use to play your hands.

If, in spite of all this, you decide to play the Basic Omega II System in multiple-deck games anyway, bear in mind that it takes a big bet spread to beat these games. Fortunately, betting camouflage is not a major issue in multiple-deck games. The clubs generally assume these games are fairly safe and will tolerate wide bet spreads without getting unduly uptight. So, in these games, I suggest you bet 4 units off the top, then spread your bets as shown in Table 5.6.

"Steaming" Minimum Bets

Steaming is an important camouflage technique that works in single-, double-, and multiple-deck games.

The basic idea is to use a *range* of minimum bets that averages out to 1 unit (or slightly less), instead of always betting exactly 1 unit in unfavorable situations.

In addition, and this is key, save your *larger* minimum bets for really minus counts, and make your smaller minimum bets when the count is closer to zero.

For example, suppose you're betting $50 to $200, a 4:1 spread. Say the count is fairly minus, so you bet $50. You win that hand and the count rises somewhat for the next hand (though not enough to justify a 2-unit bet); *reduce* your bet to $25. Now, let's say you lose this hand and the count goes really minus for the next hand--*increase* your bet to $75!

Any boss watching this will assume you are using some worthless progression system that has a curious bias toward bigger bets on very minus counts.

Of course, when the count gets sufficiently plus to justify 2-, 4-, or 8-unit bets, use Bet Spread Tables 5.4, 5.5, or 5.6 to determine your proper bet size.

Steaming is a crafty technique that makes it very difficult for the casino bosses to spot you as a counter. You look like just another loser chasing after his losses.

The Basic Omega II System

Table 5.6

MULTIPLE DECK
Las Vegas Rules

Bet	W/L	Count	Bet < 1/2	Bet > 1/2
1	W	(+)	2	2
1	L	(+)	2	2
1	W	(−)	1	1
1	L	(−)	1	1
2	W	(+)	4	4
2	L	(+)	4	4
2	W	(−)	1	1
2	L	(−)	1	1
4	W	(+)	8	8
4	L	(+)	8	4
4	W	(−)	1	1
4	L	(−)	1	1
8	W	(+)	8	8
8	L	(+)	8	8
8	W	(−)	1	1[17]
8	L	(−)	1	1

Multiple decks *are* a challenge. But there is also something very rewarding about mastering the precision play necessary to beat these games. And contrary to what you might think, because of the reduced level of casino scrutiny, multiple-deck games are actually quite relaxing and enjoyable to play.

----

17. This is aggressive play, and it does not look especially innocent; however, if you expect to beat multiple-deck games, you've got to back off fast with minus counts.

WHEN TO INCREASE YOUR BET

Many books on counting make a big fuss about exactly when to increase your bet to 2 units, 3 units, 4 units, and so on. According to these authors, each of these different betting levels must occur at its own unique count, and the player is therefore expected to memorize a large table of critical betting indices.[18]

This kind of advice is generally given by experts who have never tried, or at least never succeeded in, making their living playing Twenty-One. The last thing you need is another table, crammed with superfluous numbers, to memorize.

Don't misunderstand me. I am not saying that the count at which you increase your bet is not important. It is. What I am saying is that, for a given situation, only *two* index numbers are required. The first index is for bets of 2 units, and the second is for all bets larger than 2 units. In a later chapter, when we discuss the theory of Gambler's Ruin and delve into sophisticated betting schemes such as the Kelly System, we will explore this matter more thoroughly. For now, though, trust me when I say that two indices do the trick nicely, without any significant loss in power or increase in risk.

I have also found, through years of experience, that the running count is much easier to use than the true count for betting purposes. This does involve memorizing a few more indices, but calculating the true count for every bet is tougher than learning a few additional numbers.

The following table lists the betting numbers for increasing your bet above 1 unit. Notice that, because we are betting with the running count rather than the true count, the betting indices are dependent upon the size of the remaining pack.[19]

Notice also that, as might be expected, the betting numbers for games with bad rules (as in Reno) are higher than the betting numbers for games with good rules (as in Las Vegas).

----

18. Thorp, Beat the Dealer, p. 96, par. 4.

19. As a matter of fact, even if we were using the true count, the betting indices would rise slightly with the size of the remaining pack. This is because, even with the same true count, the player's expectation drops slightly as the size of the remaining pack increases.

Table 5.7

THE BETTING INDICES

Las Vegas Rules[20]

REMAINING DECKS

BET SIZES	6	5	4	3	2	1.5	1	.75	.5
Bet = 2 units	+20	+15	+10	+7	+4	+3	+2	+1	0
Bet > 2 units	+27	+21	+15	+11	+7	+5	+3	+2	+1

Reno Rules[21]

REMAINING DECKS

BET SIZES	6	5	4	3	2	1.5	1	.75	.5
Bet = 2 units	+27	+21	+15	+11	+7	+5	+3	+2	+1
Bet > 2 units	+34	+27	+20	+15	+10	+7	+4	+3	+2

All index numbers indicate the *running* count.

As an example, say you are playing in Las Vegas, double deck; your last bet was 2 units; you won that bet, and with just under one deck remaining the running count jumps to +4: bet 4 units. Note, however, if you had lost the 2-unit bet, even though the running count at +4 is high enough to justify a 4-unit bet, for the sake of camouflage you would only bet 2 units, as is shown in Table 5.5.

In multiple-deck games, to moderate swings in your bankroll, I suggest you shade the index numbers up slightly for 8-unit bets--say, by about one running-count point *per* remaining deck.

If you play outside Nevada, use the betting table that more closely approximates the rules you will be playing against.

----

20. Las Vegas Rules are as follows: double down on any *first* two cards, resplit all pairs except Aces, and the dealer may (downtown), or may not (Strip), hit soft 17.

21. Reno Rules are as follows: double down on *first* two cards totaling 10 or 11 only, resplit all pairs except Aces, and the dealer hits soft 17.

ADJUSTING THE RUNNING COUNT

The Omega II Count is very accurate for betting purposes, with an efficiency rating of .92. However, because of the Ace's blackjack potential, a side count of Aces can increase this betting efficiency to .99. In practical terms, this can amount to an increase in your advantage of as much as .2%!

Keeping a side count of Aces is not something you should try while you are still learning and gaining experience. This is strictly an advanced play. When you are ready for it, it will be easy to do and will add to your edge. If you try to force it, however, you will make counting errors that will decrease, if not totally eliminate, your advantage. On top of that, pit bosses are quick to spot the straining behavior of overachieving counters, so don't push it, or you may very well find yourself both down on your luck and down on the street.

After you have logged some hours in casino play, however, and are thoroughly comfortable using the Basic Omega II System, you can improve your betting accuracy somewhat by adding a side count of Aces.

The basic idea here is that although the Ace has little value in the play of the hands, it behaves as a "big" minus card for betting purposes due to its effect on blackjack probabilities.

With normal density, there should be one Ace for every 13 cards. When this is the case or nearly so, the running Omega II Count, even with the Ace valued as zero, is accurate for betting purposes. However, if there is a relative excess or shortage of Aces in the undealt pack, that is, if the density of Aces is significantly greater or less than one Ace for every 13 unplayed cards, then the running Omega II Count can be improved, for betting purposes, by keeping a side count of Aces and adjusting the raw running count accordingly.

The way to do this is simple: keep track of every Ace as it falls by counting on the fingers of your hand under the table. This last part is important; you don't want the bosses to see you keeping track of anything, much less Aces.

In two-deck or multiple-deck games, you count the Aces in sets of four, 1, 2, 3, 4, on your fingers, under the table. Then set a marker indicating four Aces are out. Then, 5, 6, 7, 8, on your fingers, under the table again, and set the marker indicating eight Aces are out, and so on. The way I set the marker is by using my grad-school ring. This ring has a big knobby stone on top, and it is easy to rotate the ring *one-quarter* turn for every set of four Aces. So if, for example, I am playing in a four-deck game, and I have two fingers extended under the table, and my grad-school ring is rotated three-quarters around, I know that 14 Aces have fallen. This technique is harder to explain than it is to do, so don't be concerned if it sounds complicated. It's really not, and with a little practice you shouldn't have much trouble using it. I have tried various other ways of keeping track of Aces, using chips and other devices, but I have found the rotating ring and fingers under the table to be the most natural way to go. So give this method a shot before you try anything else. I think you will find it as easy and natural as I have.

Once you have the side count of Aces, it is used to adjust the running count in the following way: for every "extra" Ace add +2 to the running count; for every Ace "short" add -2 to the running count. "Great," you say. "Now what the hell is an 'extra' Ace, and how do I tell a 'short' Ace from a 'tall' one?" No problem, it works like this: at the beginning of each hand, just before you place your bet, compare the number of Aces that <u>would</u> have been dealt with average distribution[22] (one Ace for every 13 cards) to the actual number your side count indicates <u>have</u> been dealt. If an excess of Aces remain, add +2 to the running count for each "extra" Ace per 13 dealt cards. If an excess of Aces have fallen, add -2 to the running count for each Ace "short" per 13 dealt cards.

Let's take a look at a couple of examples. Say we are playing in a double-deck game. It comes time to bet, and checking the return tray we see that about one deck has been dealt out. We know that with average distribution four Aces would have fallen, but our side count indicates only one Ace is out. So, in this example, we have three "extra" Aces left in the pack. Let's say our raw running count at this point is -1; adding +2 for <u>each</u> of our three "extra" Aces, we end up with an adjusted running count, for betting purposes, of +5 instead of -1. Quite a difference. We now have a count that mathematically justifies a maximum bet, whereas before the Ace adjustment we would have made a minimum bet.

Or let's say we are playing in a single-deck Las Vegas game, and after one round the return tray shows that about one-fourth deck has been dealt. With average distribution one Ace would have fallen, but this time our side count indicates that three Aces have been dealt. In this case the remaining deck is two Aces "short," so if our raw running count is say +3, adding -2 for each of the two "short" Aces results in an adjusted running count of -1, for betting purposes. A

----

22. In this discussion, the term average distribution is used in the colloquial not rigorous statistical sense.

big difference, once again. This time what would have been a dangerously inaccurate maximum bet gets reduced to an accurate, and much safer, minimum bet.

Remember, however, the Ace adjustment is for *betting purposes only*. As soon as you have placed your bet, discard the adjusted count and fall back to the original raw running count. In the first example above, for instance, after placing our bet, we would toss out the +5 adjusted running count, revert back to the original running count of -1, and continue with the play of the hand.

The side count of Aces is a powerful weapon in skilled hands, and when you are ready for it, I want you to use it. But remember, first get the basics down stone cold. Refinements like this will make you money if you use them accurately, but they can hurt you if you force them before you're ready.

Counting by Inference

Another powerful adjustment technique is estimating the count of unseen cards in other players' hands based on the dealer's up card, and the way these hands are played.

If you can accurately adjust the count for unseen cards *before* you play your own hand, you can often significantly increase the power and accuracy of your play. This is money in the bank.

If, for example, you held 9 vs. 7 in a double-deck game with a running count of +9 and about one deck remaining, the true count would also be +9, and you would be prepared to double down. However, if you knew the unseen cards in several other players' hands had a total count of -6, you would adjust the running count (and in this case the true count, as well) to +3 (+9-6) and *not* double down--probably saving yourself from an expensive loss.

The key is accurately estimating the count of unseen cards. This is how to do it: (1) If the dealer's up card is 7, 8, 9, 10, or Ace, and a player stands on his original two cards, count that player's hole cards as -2. (2) Against any up card, if a player draws hit cards totaling hard 10, 11, 12, 13, 14, 15, or 16, and stands, count that player's hole cards as +2. In either (1) or (2), at the settlement, make any necessary corrections to your count as the cards are exposed by the dealer.

As with a side count of Aces, counting by inference is a refinement that will make you money if it's done accurately, but it will hurt you if you make mistakes. So, wait until you're really ready before you add it to your playing arsenal.

THE PLAYER'S ADVANTAGE

The win rate with the Basic Omega II System can vary significantly, depending on such factors as rules, number of decks, shuffle depth, number of players, bet spread, selective shuffling,[23] and accuracy of play.

Under ideal single-deck conditions,[24] for example, the player's advantage is 2.8%; however, under adverse multiple-deck conditions,[25] the player's edge can slip to 0.5%.

If you limit yourself to high quality single- and double-deck games only, and use the rather conservative betting schemes of Tables 5.4 and 5.5, your win rate will be about 1.0% of your total action.

This is a significant, but not overwhelming, edge so it is important that you play only under the best conditions. I suggest you select your games as follows:

Single-Deck Conditions

- Reno rules or better.
- Deal 70% of deck or better.
- Two other players or less.
- Tolerate 2:1 bet spread (4:1 Reno rules).
- No selective shuffling by dealer.

Assuming the above conditions, your advantage in a single-deck game, using the Basic Omega II System and betting according to Table 5.4 (Las Vegas) or Table 5.5 (Reno), is about 1.0%.

----

23. Some dealers have the nasty habit of counting along with you, and shuffling anytime the count really gets good. This practice can wreak havoc with your advantage, so anytime you encounter this tactic get out of the game immediately.

24. Head-to-head play; single deck, dealt to last card; 10:1 bet spread; Las Vegas Strip rules.

25. Full table; 6 decks, shuffled after three decks dealt; 10:1 bet spread; Las Vegas Strip rules.

Double-Deck Conditions

- Las Vegas Strip rules or better.
- Deal 70% of pack or better.
- Full table or less.
- Tolerate 4:1 bet spread.
- No selective shuffling by dealer.

Assuming the above conditions, your advantage in a double-deck game, using the Basic Omega II System and betting according to Table 5.5, is about 1.0%.

Multiple-Deck Conditions

I advise you to master the Advanced Omega II System of Chapter Seven before you tackle multiple-deck games. But if you decide to play in these games with the Basic Omega II System anyway, then follow these guidelines:

- Las Vegas Strip rules, <u>with</u> double down after splits.
- Four decks or less.
- Deal 75% of pack or better.
- Full table or less.
- Tolerate 8:1 bet spread.
- No selective shuffling by dealer.

Assuming the above conditions, your advantage in a four-deck game, using the Basic Omega II System and betting according to Table 5.6, is about .75%.

Hourly Win Rate

To calculate your hourly win rate (W), multiply your average bet (B) times your advantage (E) times the number of hands played per hour (T). In algebraic form it looks like this: $W = (B)(E)(T)$.

Generally, figure your average bet (B) at about half your maximum bet; your advantage (E), using the Basic Omega II System in single- and double-deck games, at about .01, and the number of hands played per hour (T) at about 100. Of course, unusual playing conditions may cause (B), (E), and (T) to vary, somewhat.

FIGURES 5.2 AND 5.3 - PLAYER'S ADVANTAGE VS. BET SPREAD

These charts are a real eye opener. They show how the player's advantage is strikingly influenced by bet spread, number of decks in play, and casino conditions (primarily deck penetration). Notice how, for example, in Figure 5.2 the player's edge varies from a low of about -0.25%, for flat betting against six decks, all the way up to about +1.8%, for a 10:1 bet spread against a single deck.

Figure 5.3 also shows this same dramatic variation. In addition, a comparison of Figure 5.2, which is based on *favorable* casino conditions, with Figure 5.3, which is based on *ideal* casino conditions, shows how important these conditions are to the player's long-term rate of return. A 4:1 bet spread against a double deck in Figure 5.2 (favorable conditions), for example, yields a win rate of only about +1.0%. Yet this same bet spread against a double deck in Figure 5.3 (ideal conditions) yields a win rate of over +1.7%. Quite a difference.

Moral of this story? Pick your games with care.

Figure 5.2

PLAYER'S ADVANTAGE[1]
VS.
BET SPREAD

The Basic Omega II System

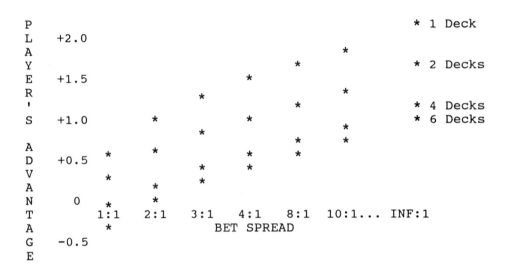

Figure 5.3

PLACER'S ADVANTAGE[1]
VS.
BET SPREAD

The Basic Omega II System

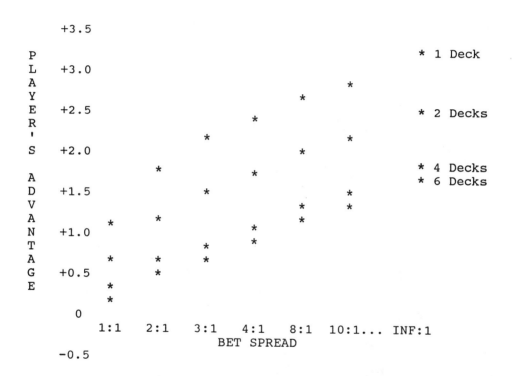

1. THIS CHART ASSUMES <u>IDEAL</u> CASINO CONDITIONS, INCLUDING LAS VEGAS STRIP RULES, ONE PLAYER AT THE TABLE, AND 100% DECK(S) PENETRATION.

HOW LONG TO PLAY

Regardless of where you are playing, it is important to limit your play to 45 minute sessions, or until you win or lose about 15 average bets, whichever comes first.

As a rule, casino bosses are a fairly alert group of people; they have to be for the clubs to stay in business. Usually suspicious to begin with, years of dealing with schemes and scams of every conceivable kind often twist this suspicion into an ugly paranoia. Pit bosses suspect everybody--including each other. They are trained to look for anything unusual so they are constantly scanning their shadowy world, sensing and searching and forever seeking the slightest clue that evil is about.

Unfortunately, one of the things they are scanning for is you! So it's important not to look like a counter; and the cornerstone of effective camouflage is this: use the recommended betting schemes in this chapter, and limit your playing sessions to 45 minutes, as suggested. If you do these two things, you may still be watched, and you may sometimes be suspected, but you will rarely encounter any serious heat.[26]

Of course if you do get some heat, such as two or three bosses, arms folded, heads turned away, whispering furtively and occasionally tossing you an evil little glare, don't wait around for them to descend on you en masse. Just get up, stuff your checks in your pocket, and hit the door. It's also not a bad idea to see if you are being followed. Casino bosses will sometimes do this in order to get your license plate number. This allows them, with a little help from their friends, to find out just about anything they want to know about you.

If you do suspect you are being followed, your best bet is to forget your car and walk immediately to the next hotel/casino. Don't play, and don't hang around the casino area; just get in an elevator and play floor tag for 15 or 20 minutes. By then the Dobermans will have lost the scent, and you can safely return for your car.

----

26. In the next chapter we are going to thoroughly investigate the entire subject of effective camouflage.

BANKROLL, FLUCTUATIONS, AND RISK

Later on, when we get into the theory of Gambler's Ruin, we will investigate more thoroughly this whole fascinating concept of risk versus reward, and just how much of a stake you need to be safe (and just how safe is safe). For now, though, here are some guidelines that will get you into action--and keep you out of trouble.

If you are playing the Basic Omega II System for sport with small change, don't worry about a stake, just have fun. But if you're playing with money that is important to you, I suggest you have a total playing stake of 125 times your maximum bet.

Here's an example. Say you are using a bet spread of $10 to $40. In this situation you need a playing stake of about $5,000 (125 x $40). Assuming a player advantage of 1.67% on your large (above 1-unit) bets (see page 157), this stake would give you about a 96.8% chance of winning indefinitely, with only a small chance of approximately 1 in 31.5 of being wiped out.

If you really want to be safe, bump your stake to 175 maximum bets. This will give you about a 99.2% chance of winning, with only a tiny 1 in 125 chance of ruin. Of course, such a conservative betting strategy will decrease your percentage return on investment (ROI), but you may sleep better at night.

And don't be tempted to press it and play on short money! You would think a stake of, say, 75 maximum bets ought to be safe. But it's not. With an edge of 1.67% on your large bets, a stake of 75 maximum bets will put you at a 1 in 8 risk of being wiped out. These are not the kind of odds I risk serious money on.

Naturally, you do not need to haul all this loot around with you when you play. A trip stake of 40 maximum bets is about right for a weekender, and around 62 is adequate for trips of a week or so.[27] With a 1.67% large-bet advantage, this will give you about a 95% chance of avoiding trip-stake wipeout during any one given trip.

----

27. Here's a tip: Don't carry your entire trip stake around in your wallet--that's way too risky. Instead, keep about 15 average bets to play with and put the rest in a safety-deposit box. All the major hotels offer them to guests free of charge. In addition to the obvious security benefits, this also forces you to take a break and clear your head after a significant loss.

The above probabilities, though not exact, are very close. They are based on ruin calculations that assume a flat bet, invariant advantage, and in some cases reinvestment of all winnings, as well. These assumptions are not strictly valid for Blackjack, so some small errors are inevitably introduced into our results. But for purposes of sizing your playing stake, and laying out the dangers of short money play, they are more than sufficient.

OK, so let's say you've carefully sized your bankroll so as to keep your risk of wipeout to a bare minimum. You're relatively safe from the downside. But what about the upside? What are your chances of winning after an hour's play? After a day's? A week's? This valuable information is contained below in Table 5.8.[28]

These percentages are important because they give you an idea of how long it may reasonably take for your advantage to show. For example, if you're behind after 12, or even 24, hours' play, it's no big deal--just a little bad luck. But if you're still down after, say, 72 hours, it's time to take a hard look at your game. You may be making a lot of mistakes, or playing in second-rate games, or (though unlikely) even being cheated. In any case, if you continue to lose as the hours pile up, a close look to see if the cause goes beyond just bad luck is in order.

Table 5.8

PLAYER'S CHANCE OF WINNING

Hours Played (40 max bets/hr)	Chance of Winning (Basic Omega II)	Chance of Winning (Adv'd Omega II)
1 hr	53.6%	55.0%
6 hrs	59.1%	62.2%
12 hrs	62.7%	67.0%
24 hrs	67.7%	73.3%
48 hrs	74.2%	81.0%
72 hrs	78.8%	85.9%
96 hrs	82.2%	89.3%
192 hrs	90.3%	96.1%
384 hrs	96.7%	99.3%

----

28. This table is for one- and two-deck games; it assumes 40 large bets per hour, and a large-bet advantage of +1.67% with the Basic Omega II System, and +2.25% with the Advanced Omega II System (see pages 157, 161).

SUMMARY

Before we move on, let's take a minute to reflect on what's been accomplished so far.

If you have mastered the material in these first five chapters, you play better than 99.9% of all Blackjack players, worldwide! I mean that literally; there is not one player in a thousand who can outplay you once you have come this far. To get here, you've had to put in some hours, and I want to congratulate you for a job well done.

And not only do you play better than the overwhelming majority of regular players, but you are better grounded in solid Blackjack theory than even some of the world-class players who make their living with the game!

So you have come a long way. You're not world class yet, but you're getting there.

In the next few chapters we're going to explore some of the more subtle and intriguing facets of this interesting game. I hope you enjoy the reading as much as I have enjoyed the writing.

CHAPTER SIX

Camouflage

The young man paused for a moment and looked up through the black evening sky at the huge, dazzling sign above the Dunes hotel in Las Vegas. A smirking impostor of a smile briefly creased his face then, turning away, he walked briskly through the automatic front doors, past the hotel lobby, and headed straight for the casino floor.

In town for less than an hour, he was filled with excitement and anticipation. He could hardly wait to get into action.

Slowly and methodically, he strolled around the Blackjack pits, examining every table, sizing up every game. Warily, he glanced at the casino bosses, searching their faces for any trace of recognition. Finally, satisfied that he was not remembered from some previous encounter, he at last began to relax.

Standing casually behind a table, he counted down the deck as play proceeded. After about 15 minutes, a juicy situation with nearly a 10% player advantage happened to arise. Struggling to contain his excitement, he grabbed an open seat, tossed $1,000 in hundred dollar bills onto the layout and told the dealer, in a practiced voice, to "turn the paper into quarter checks." Carefully stacking the green $25 chips the dealer gave him into neat little piles, he nonchalantly pushed $200 into his betting circle and said something to the dealer like, "OK, let's play some cards." Picking up his hand, he was pleased to see he had hooked a pair of Aces. The dealer had a 10 up but didn't have blackjack. Quickly glimpsing the other players' hole cards, he knew the true count, with only about a quarter deck remaining, was just over +50! That meant that about 60% of the remaining cards were 10s, and even with the dealer showing paint, the player's advantage was over 80% of his original bet! The young man hesitated; 80% was a thundering edge, but dealers had an uncanny way of coming up with miracle hands at the worst possible moments. Pulling himself together, he forced these dark thoughts out of his mind, shoved out another $200, and split the Aces. The dealer tossed two cards face down onto the split Aces, finished with the other players, and flipped over his hole card. Queen of Clubs. The dealer had 20. The kid was nervous now, and it showed on his face. His left eyelid began to twitch, while little beads of sweat formed on his brow, and small white traces of saliva emerged at the corners of his lips. He was not a pretty sight. Fidgeting anxiously, he watched as the dealer worked his way around the table, scooping up chips and cards as he went; finally, the dealer turned over the down card on the first split Ace; Jack of Spades. *Whew.* The young man melted into his seat in relief. No worse than a draw now. Then the dealer flipped over the down card on the second split Ace. Ten of Diamonds. *Yes!! Take that!* he thought, as he rapped the table in triumph. Once more in control, he permitted a knowing little smile to flicker across his face as he raked in the $800--including a fat $400 in profits.

All the while this little drama was unfolding, a fat, stumpy, casino boss, chomping away on his fat, stumpy, cigar, watched the young man from the pit. He sensed something was not quite right. For one thing, the kid seemed a little too practiced, a little too sharp. For another, what was a kid, sporting long hair, faded jeans and a tank top, doing tossing around $100 bills and making megabuck bets? Maybe he was playing with his tuition money, or maybe his dad was rich. Or maybe, just maybe, he had a little something on the game. The boss picked up a red phone in the pit. Simultaneously, a similar red phone upstairs in the "Eye in the Sky" began to softly ring. A thin, sallow-looking man, sitting in front of a bank of glowing monitors, picked up the phone and quietly murmured, "Surveillance, Jensen." "Jensen," came the reply, "this is Cohen in Twenty-One. Take a look at the long-haired kid on 17. See what he's up to, and get back to me." The boss hung up the phone and walked over to the young man's table.

Out of the corner of his eye, the young man saw the casino boss approaching. His stomach muscles tightened, and his eyelid began twitching again. He hated pit bosses. He wasn't too crazy about dealers either. All he wanted was to sit and play. To lose himself in the hypnotic ballet of whirling cards and dancing chips. But pit bosses and dealers were always intruding on this private world. Always hassling him in one way or another. And even when they only wanted to chat and make conversation, it made keeping the count difficult, and maintaining concentration practically impossible. Why couldn't they just leave him alone?

Extending his hand, the boss reached over the Blackjack table and said, "Hello, kid, my name's Cohen. Looks like you're doin' OK tonight." The young man shook hands and, forcing a thin little smile, looked up at the casino boss for a moment, taking care not to lose the count. "Not really," he replied, "you should have seen the bundle I dropped this afternoon at the Stardust." "Yeah?" the boss shot back. "Well, it looks like you're rollin' now." Softening his voice, he continued, "You need anything, kid, you let me know, OK?" "Yeah, I will; thanks for the offer," the young man replied, trying hard to talk and count at the same time.

Not long after the boss walked back into the pit, the red phone began to ring. "Mr. Cohen," the caller began, "this is Jensen. The kid on 17 is a counter. He's in the Griffin[1] book, and there's a note that says he's a professional player. He's good. He's very good. I tracked him through five or six decks, and I don't think he made a mistake. With the money he's betting, he's a threat to make four or five bucks[2] an hour as long as he plays." "OK Tom," Cohen replied, looking up at the young man just as he was turning over a blackjack on another $200 bet. "The kid is '86'; get a picture, then call security. I want that bum outta here now." "Yes sir," came the reply. "I've already got a good face shot, and I'll send over security right away."

The young man never knew what hit him. Deeply involved with a beautiful plus deck, he was just about to make another $200 bet when he felt a heavy hand on his right shoulder. Instinctively turning, he was surprised to see the thick-featured Mr. Cohen, together with three of his uniformed friends, standing directly behind him. "That's it pal, party's over," began the pit boss. As the young man began to protest, the boss cut him off with a hard look and a wave of his hand. "Look, no more Twenty-One. You're way too good. You can play Craps, Roulette, anything else. But no more Blackjack, understand? If I catch you in here playing Twenty-One again, you're going to jail for trespass, got that?" "Yeah, I got it," the young man muttered, as he slid off his seat and headed for the cashier. "Good," shot back Cohen. "Now cash in your checks and get outta here."

As he headed for the cage, the kid was in a daze, really spaced out. The security guards were reading him some Nevada statute about trespass or something, but he was barely listening. The whole thing seemed so unreal, like he was watching it on television. He'd been backed off before, that's for sure. As a matter of fact he'd been backed off at the Dunes before, but no one had ever come

----

1. The Griffin book is a compiled list of undesirables, provided to subscribing Nevada casinos by Griffin Investigations, Inc.

2. In casinospeak a "buck" is $100!

down on him so hard in the past, threatening to toss him in jail and marching him to the cashier with an armed guard of casino Gestapo. *What the hell was this, anyway?* Well, whatever it was, it was serious. As he left the cage and headed for the front exit, he saw Cohen huddled in the pit with the other bosses, staring at him with acid eyes that burned as they glared. The whole experience was more than a little unnerving. Pulling himself together, he reminded himself that Mafia influence and violent solutions were a thing of the past in Las Vegas, and by the time he cleared the exit he was starting to feel a little better. Then he caught the evening headline of the Las Vegas <u>Sun</u>, "Casino Executive Found Murdered in Caesars Palace Parking Lot." Paranoid fears and overactive imagination raging within, he pulled his coat up around his ears and disappeared into the human sea that swelled the banks of the Las Vegas Strip (pun intended).

Unpleasant episodes like this one happen all the time in the casinos of Nevada and elsewhere. Another counter bites the dust. Sometimes these unfortunates really are good, like the young man above, and sometimes they are just amateurs practicing their moves and impressing their friends. Either way the result is the same: they're out on the street, grazing with the sheep, instead of getting in their licks, doing a little fleecing of their own.

A full-blown riot-act barring, like the one above, can put a counter out of business in a casino for years. It can take that long for memory to dim, dossiers to fade, and casino personnel to move up or move on. In the case above, for example, the young man was barred from play at the Dunes hotel for over four years. I know this for a fact--because he was me.

If you have mastered the material presented so far, you can already beat the game. But as you see from my experience at the Dunes, beating the game is one thing; beating the house is quite another. Or, to put it differently, Blackjack excellence is not only about excellent Blackjack, it is also about effective camouflage. So in this chapter we're going to examine the techniques that I, and other successful experts, have developed over the years to avoid being detected as winners.

As you read the material that follows, I want you to think about how you will use it in your play. And when you're finished, go back and read again about my disaster at the Dunes; this time, see how many mistakes you can spot--and what I could have done, and should have done, to stay in business and out of trouble.

HOW TO BET YOUR MONEY

Knowing how to spread your bets in a natural and innocent looking way is the *cornerstone* of effective camouflage. This subject is covered in detail in Chapter Five, and if you have any remaining questions about proper betting, refer back to that section.

Unfortunately, while proper betting technique is *necessary* to effective camouflage, it is not *sufficient* by itself. Just as important is an understanding of how to interact with casino personnel in such a way that an illusion of innocence is created, and the bosses are motivated to overlook any residual suspicions that may still remain.

HOW LONG TO PLAY

As with betting, this topic is covered thoroughly in Chapter Five, and it should be reviewed as necessary. The rule of thumb is to play for 45 minutes, or until you win or lose 15 average bets, whichever comes first. If you limit your play in this way, you will never take a big hit from a cheating dealer, and the bosses won't be able to watch your action long enough to really get a fix on your play.

It is also important to realize that you will be watched very closely when you first sit down to play. This is when the bosses will size you up; if you can get through this initial scrutiny without giving yourself away, the chances are good the entire session will be free of any heat or hassle. So, during these first few critical minutes, it's essential that you keep your bet spread to a minimum, be open and friendly with the bosses, and use every other trick in this chapter to make your play look as innocent as possible.

HOW OFTEN TO PLAY

This is an important topic that is often overlooked when experts give advice on Blackjack, but if you're interested in avoiding the perils of overexposure, then I suggest you pay close attention to the following material.

When I first started playing serious Blackjack, I focused on Las Vegas, in part because it was close to my home, but also because at the time there were a lot of good games to choose from. Now Vegas, then as now, was host to a small underground army of professional Blackjack hustlers, and it wasn't very long before I began to get a close-up look at these mercenaries in action. Some of these players were actually out-and-out card cheats. Others formed teams that worked the clubs by flashing signals back and forth, trading information about dealers' hole cards, "tells," warped decks, incomplete shuffles--you name it. If there was an angle, they played it. But perhaps the most pathetic members of this motley bunch were the counters who had settled down into what they assumed was a strawberry patch, only to find themselves entangled in a wicked bramble of thorns and thistles.

The problem was overexposure. Play long enough, or often enough, and the bosses will bust your act. Just that simple. And these buckaroos would move into low-cost apartments and play day and night, for weeks on end, with scarcely a break. Naturally, before very long they would find themselves bounced from one club after another until they ended up downtown trying to squeeze out a living playing nickel ($5) checks in six-deck junk games in grungy joints like the Las Vegas Club, or the Lady Luck. Many of these people ended up real degenerates; for most of them, the best thing that could happen was a losing streak that would wipe them out--and send them back home for good.

This doesn't mean, of course, that you can't play Blackjack full time. You can. But to do it, you've got to be willing to work the tour: a week in Las Vegas, one in Reno, then off to Atlantic City, the Caribbean, Europe, Asia, and finally back to the good ol' U.S.A. If you enjoy this kind of life style, as I do--then great. But don't get the idea you can just move to Las Vegas or Reno and sign on as a high-paid shill. Believe me, it doesn't work like that. No way.

So keep your face fresh and your identity unknown. Play in a club for one or two 45-minute sessions, on each shift, then back away. Stay out of that casino for at least three months, and when you finally do return, if you think they remember you--take off again. This is not easy to do; it takes a lot of discipline, but you've got to learn to do it, if you want to stay in business.

HOW TO LOOK LIKE A GAMBLER

Casinos want gamblers for customers; they do not want investors. To be successful, therefore, it is very important to look like a gambler; and one of the best ways to learn how to do this, is to watch real gamblers in action.

I have spent literally hundreds of hours, in casinos around the world, carefully observing gamblers at play; and it's amazing how sharply their styles differ from that of the average counter.

Gamblers play for the thrill of the action, and they love to dress the part. If they are playing for serious money in a classy rug joint, like a Caesars Palace, you see them wearing expensive European-cut suits, $200 imported shoes, and enough gold and diamond jewelry to choke a horse.

In the smaller clubs of Reno and downtown Las Vegas, on the other hand, you see the nickel-check gamblers, dressed in their Levis and cowboy shirts, sporting their shit-kicker boots, and puffing away on their stiletto cigars.

Either way the look is right. They are seen, but they are not noticed. They are there to have fun, and they look like they belong.

Counters are not like that; they do not allow themselves to get caught up in the fun and magic of glitzy Gomorrahs like Las Vegas. It's just a business with them, so they dress like they are going to work. Generally they underdress, and if they do dress well, it is usually in a business suit.

Nothing stands out more in a crowded casino than a scruffy young man playing for big money. I learned that one the hard way; I might as well have been wearing a big red "COUNTERS DO IT BY THE NUMBERS" sign on my chest. So observe real gamblers, and do as they do. And remember, while styles change, and fashions come and go, the principle remains the same: dress like a gambler out on the town, hot for some action, and ready for some fun.

HOW TO ACT LIKE A GAMBLER

Many counters have an attitude problem. They see themselves as bandits, thieves that sneak into casinos and make off with as much loot as possible before they are caught. The casino bosses look on counters this way too, so it's not surprising that an adversarial relationship has developed between counters and the casino personnel charged with protecting the house.

This is a game you don't have to play. In fact, if you're going to be successful in beating the house, it's a game you absolutely must not play.

Real gamblers never behave this way. They love to interact with casino personnel, because the more attention they get, the more important they feel. If a gambler is approached by a pit boss, for example, he will smile, shake hands, and chat with the boss for as long as the boss will stay. He will share his triumphs when fortune smiles, and look for sympathy to soothe the sting when lady luck deserts. Counters, on the other hand, both hate and fear the approach of casino bosses. They fear being barred and harassed, but as much as this they hate the intrusion on their private world, an inner space of endless cards and infinite counts, a tranquil place where time is stilled, and mind is bound to an hypnotic obsession profound and aware, yet lost and alone. Hmmm... this ain't bad. Anyway, the average counter suffers a lot of grief before he finally comes to terms with casino management. Actually, most counters never do learn how to handle the casino bosses. They merely play in single-deck games until they are permanently barred there, then they work their way through the double- and four-deck clubs until their action is really not welcome anywhere. Finally, you see them playing in six- and eight-deck garbage games, risking their stake and spinning their wheels, until a really bad fluctuation comes along and wipes them out for good. So sad, and so unnecessary.

Counters are often quite introverted, and they usually have compulsive personalities as well. You almost have to be this way to enjoy sitting at a Blackjack table and counting cards for endless hours. Gamblers, on the other hand, real gamblers, are anything but introverted. They are people oriented, and they love the tension and excitement of the casino. It exhilarates them, and this stimulation spills over into every aspect of their behavior. When they catch a good hand, for example, they may whistle softly in surprise, or if a pit boss is camped at their elbow, they might look up, flash the hand, and give a knowing little wink that seems to say, "Check it out, partner, we've got this sucker in the bag." Instinctively, they understand that the pit boss is not their enemy; on the contrary, he is part of the support system that makes casino gambling so much fun. Pit bosses for their part love real gamblers, not only because they contribute so willingly, and so generously, to the bottom line, but also because nurturing and supporting gamblers is one of the most enjoyable aspects of a pit boss's job.

Before you can expect to manipulate casino personnel to your advantage, you first have to understand a lot more about their world than is obvious to the casual observer. At first glance a pit boss looks to have an enjoyable, if not very challenging, job. He seems to spend a lot of his time trying to make cocktail waitresses, and when he's not doing that, he's either writing out markers and comps for high rollers, counting checks in the table racks, or chatting with the other bosses. Once in a while, just for laughs, he may back off a counter or two, and when things really get slow, he might actually review the performance reports. That's the way it looks from the outside, and in part that's the way that it is. But, believe me, below the surface there's a lot going on that's never seen from above.

To begin with, pit bosses are generally not hired because of *what* they know, but rather because of *who* they know. Even today, when most of the clubs are owned by big hotel chains, rather than mobsters bankrolled by the Teamsters' Central States Pension Fund, being connected to power and influence--having "juice"--is far more important than experience, or a good education, in landing a casino position. This, of course, means that casino bosses are highly insecure in their jobs, for no matter how well they perform, if they do not please the powers that protect them, they will find themselves out on the street. And not only that, but with power struggles and attempted coups going on all the time in the clubs, their protectors, themselves, may fall from grace taking down everyone connected, as well. On top of all this, endless scams are continually attempted against the casinos' banks, and if a boss should have a scheme put over during his shift, he'll find himself under immediate suspicion and probably never be trusted again. So life in the pits can be hard, and a casino boss spends more of his time looking over his shoulder, and looking out for his ass, than doing the things like protecting the house that he was supposedly hired to do.

All this stuff is important, because it points up two essential things: First, if you do anything that makes a boss look bad or incompetent, you are a threat to his job, and you can color yourself gone. Second, and conversely, if you can make a boss look good, or otherwise feed his power needs, he will go to great lengths to keep you around.

If, when you play, for example, you dress and act like an obvious counter, even the most benign pit boss is going to give you some heat, not because he necessarily gives a damn whether you win or lose, but because if he overlooks your behavior his superiors may think he's inept and, with his job on the line, that's a risk he's not likely to take. Also, typical counter behavior, with its aggressive and often grim emphasis on beating the casino into submission, reinforces the territorial imperative and adversarial relationship casino bosses feel toward counters. Seen as an unwanted intruder, they have no choice but to throw you out. Notice that none of this has anything to do with whether you are winning or losing. *Pit bosses do not care whether you win or lose: it's not their money!* All they care about is protecting their careers, and they know allowing smart-aleck counters to run amuck is not the way to do it.

110

This brings us to an important point: while casino managers have strong needs for power, approval, and self-esteem, so do counters. In fact, the greatest satisfaction most counters get from Blackjack is not winning money, but mastering winning. And that's OK, as far as it goes. But remember, the bottom line is winning money, not beating the casino into submission, not showing off for your friends, and not stroking your ego at the expense of the casino bosses. In the end you have to make this choice: you can have the gold, or you can have the glory. You cannot have both--unless you believe as I do, that he who has the gold has the glory.

The key, then, to success is to operate simultaneously on two distinct levels. At the deeper, and fundamental, level you have to maintain a cold, calculating, unemotional approach to the game. You need this objectivity to make the hard decisions required to protect your stake and maximize your winning opportunities. But on the surface you've got to act, and feel, like a gambler. You should walk into a casino knowing you belong. Pick a table seemingly at random. Engage the casino bosses in friendly banter, and when a boss wants to talk cut back to a small bet, slow your play, and chat with him for as long as he wants. And remember, the bosses, not you, are the "experts," so find reasons to seek out their advice--and when they offer it, take it! Most pit bosses play fairly well anyway, and the occasional error will gain you far more in goodwill than it will ever cost you in money. And above all, look like you're having some fun: counters and pit bosses sweat the money, gamblers just play for the thrill.

Warning! This approach has worked for me and kept me on the pro Blackjack tour for over 15 years, but it is not without its dangers. The primary difficulty arises from the exquisite psychological contradiction between the two levels you operate from. At the fundamental level, you are in what psychologists call the "adult" state, characterized by unemotional, goal-oriented behavior. At the gambler level, on the other hand, you are in the "child" state, where behavior is ruled by emotional, self-indulgent, gratification needs. In the day-to-day behavior of normal adults, the cravings of the "child" are mediated by the internalized "parent" before they are realized through the action of the "adult," so there is generally no conflict in the machinery of the mind, and thought is transformed into fact, in an orderly, integrated way. Not so with professional Blackjack. Here the "parent" is put to bed, and the "child" and the "adult" perform simultaneously on parallel levels in opposite directions. It can all get a little confusing. The main danger is that you will get carried away at the gambler level and start compromising your play with careless, and expensive, mistakes. The best way to prevent this from happening is to take a break every 45 minutes or so and review your play. Was your count accurate? How about your betting and the play of the hands? Did you stay too long or allow the game to deteriorate? If you do pick up on any weaknesses in your play, make a mental note, and concentrate on these areas when you return to the game.

Another danger with this technique is that it may actually work <u>too</u> well. One expert I know, for example, became so successful with this approach that he became a favored customer of casino bosses around the world. They courted his action and showered him with attention wherever he went. He developed close and, seemingly, genuine friendships with these people; for a while he was making a mint. Then one day he got careless. A couple of floor managers, who happened to be counters themselves, noticed that my acquaintance, let's call him Hans Christian, was not the foolish gambler he pretended to be. Enraged that he had used and deceived them, his former casino pals quickly spread the word, and before long, not just individual casinos but whole towns were virtually off-limits to his play. As of this writing, he is still out of business, and I doubt he will ever play serious Blackjack again. Not a very happy ending, is it? I think it was Oscar Wilde who wrote something like, "When the gods really want to punish us, what they do is answer our prayers."

Fortunately, this nightmare is easy to avoid. The mistake Hans made was in getting <u>way</u> to close to the casino bosses. Before long, they were exchanging little gifts, showing each other pictures of wives, kids, girlfriends, and pets, and even golfing and playing tennis together. Never, never, develop friendships with casino personnel. Never. It's very important to be *friendly*, but it must stop short of *friendship*. When I walk into a casino, for example, if a boss comes up to me, smiles warmly, and says something like, "Hi, haven't seen you in a while, good to have you with us again." I smile back, return the warm fuzzy feelings, then look for the <u>first</u> opportunity to make for the exit door. *You must maintain anonymity.* In the above example, for instance, I would stay out of that club for three months, and off that shift for at least six months. If, when I finally did return, I saw anything more than the vaguest glimmer of recognition, I would immediately take off again. If you want to stay in business, you've got to have the discipline to do this. Remember, no matter how effective your camouflage is, occasionally somebody's going to bust your act; and when it happens, the less he knows about you, the better off you are.

HOW NOT TO SWEAT THE MONEY

When you play Blackjack at the professional level, it's important to avoid getting emotionally involved with the game. For one thing, it's very hard to keep an accurate count when your heart's pounding and your knees are shaking; for another, when the bosses see you doing this, it looks to them like you care too much whether you're winning or losing--and their attitude toward you may cloud and darken with suspicion and distrust.

The way to maintain this detachment is to consider the cash and chips you play with as just a way of keeping score. If you play for an hour and lose $5,000, for example, you should view this as a temporary deposit of 50 $100 chips into First Caesars Savings Bank, or wherever you happen to be playing. If you can't do this, if you insist on seeing this $5,000 as the loss of a European vacation, or the down payment on a Porsche Turbo Carrera, then you'll always be the victim of your emotions whenever you play for serious dough.

Playing this cool sounds easy to do, but believe me it's not. In fact, unless your father's from Vulcan and you were born with pointy ears, chances are you'll never be able to completely eliminate an emotional response to the game. And that's OK, as long as you're aware of the perils and work constantly to develop the proper approach. Or, as they say in Monte Carlo, "l'attitude comme il faut"--the attitude is the thing.

HOW AND WHEN TO TOKE

Relax, this is not a lecture on smoking. Toking is just casinospeak for tipping the dealer. Most players, and this includes counters, tend to overtip the dealer. They win a $200 hand, for instance, and toss a quarter check ($25) to the dealer. It doesn't seem like much, but do it several times an hour, and I don't care how well you play, you've kissed your edge goodbye. Because of this, many experts never tip the dealer. Their position is, "The dealer doesn't toke me when I lose, so why should I toke him when I win?" This is a hard-nosed attitude, and many dealers will let you know that they don't like it. When you get up to leave the table, for instance, they will mutter something sarcastic like, "Thanks for the bets, sport." Or some other equally hostile little non sequitur.

You can make a case for either side of the toking issue. My own preference is to tip modestly--and to do it when it does the most good.

113

The most important thing is not to overtip. The rule I use is to tip 10% of my average bet, per hour. For example, if I am betting $50 to $200, with an average bet of around $100, I will toke up to $10 per hour (10% of $100). Considering that at this level the swings in your capital are in the thousands of dollars, $10 doesn't seem like much, and you can see why most players tend to overtip. But dealers *do* appreciate tokes in this range. After all, $10 an hour, annualized, is *adding* over $20,000 a year to their salary. Dealers realize this, and believe me, it makes a difference in their attitude.

The best time to toke is when a favorable count occurs near the end of the deck. If the dealer is undecided about whether or not to shuffle, a little toke about here, presented as a bet for the dealer, will often tip the scales and get the dealer to go one more round before shuffling. Of course this is the money round, and if you can usually get it in it will make a big difference in your overall edge.

Notice that you do not just hand the toke to the dealer. You get him involved with your action by placing a small side bet on your hand. Usually I'll kibitz with the dealer and say something tongue-in-cheek like, "OK, if I'm going to sweat out this hand, so are you." Or some other little quip that lets the dealer know I see us as a team. Also, when I sit down to play, I'll normally break the ice with something like, "Have I explained my profit-sharing plan yet?" Dealer smiles. Followed up by, "Well, first off, there have to be some profits." More smiles. Then I'll place a small bet for the dealer and say, "OK, here's a little down payment, let's both get rich." Smiles all around, nods of approval, and a dealer who's now pulling for the right side of the force--me.

HOW AND WHEN TO GIVE IT AWAY

Sometimes, it's good business to make a bad play just for the sake of camouflage. This is a hard thing for many expert players to do. They know it's important to strive for every possible edge, so the thought of giving anything away just goes against the grain. But if you don't occasionally do this, as the late Lawrence Revere noted in his terse and tangled way, "Your disadvantage may be more than your advantage."[3]

----

3. Revere, <u>Playing Blackjack as a Business</u>, p. 118. Actually, Revere was talking about overbetting here, but the principle--that greed is <u>not</u> good--is the same.

The time to make these bad plays is when a pit boss is watching you closely. That's when your "mistake" will have the greatest possible impact.

When you do make a play like this, it should be a genuinely bad play, not one that looks bad but really isn't, like say, doubling on (A,8) vs. 6, which is normally a good play that happens to look bad. One of my favorites is splitting a pair of 10s versus the dealer's 7 or 8. This play looks as ugly as it is, and no one at the table, least of all a pit boss, can watch it without cringing. There is something perversely intriguing about watching other players recoil in horror as I make this play. Sometimes, to really drive 'em crazy, if I happen to pull another 10 to one of the splits--I'll split again, and so on, up to the maximum of four split hands. This move causes delicious chaos--and buys me hours and hours of hassle free play.

It goes without saying, of course, that plays like this are expensive and must be made <u>very</u> sparingly. In effect, you are buying time--playing time--and you don't want to overpay.

Let me give you an example of what I mean by overpaying. A colleague of mine in the fraternity of Blackjack pros, let's call him Hung Long Dong, was one helluva Blackjack player. Originally from Hong Kong, he was a graduate of a top West Coast university and an absolute whiz at anything to do with math or numbers. He played an unbelievably complex point count, complete with fractional card values and a playing strategy that would smoke an IBM mainframe. Yet he played with ease and counted with accuracy, and not only that, but he rarely if ever got any heat. As he once told me, "Blyce, I got magic seeklet, I no get balled[4]--neva" (hey, don't laugh, how's your Chinese?).

Now Dong (his friends called him Long; his girlfriends called him Hung Long) was a joy to watch in action. He had a great act; he would chatter to himself in Chinese while he kibitzed constantly with the dealer and just about everyone else at the table. Pit bosses loved him; he seemed so harmless, and like many Oriental players, he was not afraid to risk big money on the turn of a single card.

Everything seemed to work for Dong, everything except one thing--he was not a big winner. Oh, he had his wins, to be sure, but he had his losses too. Overall, he was ahead of the game, but not by very much. This really puzzled me because I knew the system he played, while very complicated, was also very accurate; and

----

4. Dongspeak for Bryce, secret, and barred, respectively.

I also knew that Dong handled it well. So what could be the problem? As it turned out, the problem lay in Dong's "magic seeklet."

Besides his humorous antics, designed to convince the bosses that he was just another superstitious gambler, Dong relied on bad plays to complete his camouflage. After watching him play for a while, I noticed that he rarely hit soft 18 against a 9 or 10, he never doubled on soft hands, he only doubled on hard hands of 10 or 11, he always insured blackjacks, and he would often stand on 16 against a 10 or an Ace. In addition, every now and then, just for effect, he would toss in a really deviant play. No wonder he was not a big winner. It's a miracle he was a winner at all.

You're probably wondering, as I did, why in the world a player of Dong's ability would do anything as stupid as this? Well, as it turns out, there were two reasons why he made so many "mistakes." First off, he got so caught up in the clown act he put on for the bosses, he really didn't realize just how often he was making these bad plays. And second, he seemed to believe that if he *knew* what the right play was, somehow the Blackjack gods, or something, would protect him even if he made the wrong play anyway. Gambling seems to bring out the irrational in a lot of people--even people, like Dong, who by training and ability ought to know better. Crazy.

Anyway, the lesson is clear. It doesn't matter how well you play in your head; it's what happens on the table that counts. So save your "mistakes" for when it pays, and remember, if you give too much away, you won't get any heat, because all you're doing is beating your... self.

HOW TO PLAY YOUR CARDS

After years of coping with the counter revolution, the great majority of casino bosses have developed at least a working knowledge of what card counting is and how it works. Fortunately, however, very few bosses can spot a counter by the way he plays his cards. This means that you do not have to make many compromises in your play just to prevent detection. There are, however, a few plays you should avoid because they're only made by fools or experts, and it won't take the bosses very long to figure out which category you belong to.

The plays to avoid are as follows: never double down on any soft hand greater than (A,7), never double down on any hard hand less than 9, and only split 10s against a small card if you are sure you are not being watched. That's it. Play the rest of your hands according to the charts.

Let me give you an example of what can happen if you get greedy and go ahead and make one of these plays. Several years ago the Castaways hotel/casino on the Las Vegas Strip[5] was a hot place to play Blackjack. At the time, they had lots of single-deck games, with good penetration, and you could sit and play for hours without getting any heat. Even if they thought you might be counting cards, they would wait until they were sure you could beat the game before taking any action against you.

Anyway, one night at the Castaways I had been playing for several hours when a strange thing happened. Deep into the deck, the count went <u>very</u> plus, a true count so high, it indicated that virtually all the remaining cards were 10s and Aces. Since I had been betting in the range of $100 to $300, to avoid alerting the dealer to this amazing count I placed a "modest" bet of $200. When I picked up my hand I was both pleased and a little surprised to see that I had drawn (A,9). Even more surprisingly, the dealer was showing a 3. As I waited for the dealer to get to me (I was on third base) I kept debating whether or not to double on the (A,9). Mathematically, there was no question; it was the right play. But I knew a move like that, especially with such an obvious plus count, might blow my cover for good. Finally, I just couldn't resist, I shoved out another $200 and doubled down. Peeking at the down card, I wasn't at all surprised to see I had hooked a 10. The dealer flipped over his hole card. Another 10. Still no surprise. Then he took a hit. Eight of Clubs. Surprise! I was in shock. I could not believe it. My 20, and my $400, destroyed by his miracle 21. The whole table let out a howl; a pit boss, hearing all the commotion, drifted over to see what the fuss was all about. Seeing my (A,9) double down, and virtually nothing but 10s and Aces all over the layout, he asked the dealer to spread the remaining cards. The dealer spread eight cards. All eight cards were 10s. The chances of this occurring are exactly one deck in every 58,473. We're talking a rare deck here, folks. The pit boss looked up at me, stared me straight in the eyes and said, "That's it, my friend, no more Blackjack. You just played your last hand." Poorer--a lot poorer--but wiser, I hung my head and shuffled out the door.

----

5. Since leveled to make way for the Mirage.

117

Moral? You want a moral? OK, how's this:

> If your judgment be blinded by greed,
> And good advice you fail to heed,
> Then hold on to your honey,
> Say goodbye to your money,
> 'Cause your wallet is fixin' to bleed![6]

HOW TO CASE A CASINO

Conditions change quickly in the casinos. This is particularly true in the case of Blackjack. One day a club is all single deck, with good penetration; the next day you find nothing but six-deck shoes. The clubs are always experimenting, always trying to put over the worst game they can without losing any business or profits. Sometimes they go too far, and six- or eight-deck shoes, bad rules, and an early cut are surprisingly, and happily, replaced with single- and double-deck games.

So when you walk into a club you never know exactly what to expect, and the only way to know what's going on for sure is to stroll around the Blackjack pits and observe the games for yourself.[7]

Because the clubs are usually crowded with people milling around everywhere, a casual stroll through the casino will not arouse any suspicion. *But standing behind a table and counting down the deck, waiting for a juicy situation to develop before jumping in, definitely will.*

The way I handle this problem is to nonchalantly walk around the pits, noting which dealers are going the deepest into the deck(s) before shuffling, how many decks are in play at each table, what the various table minimums are (usually $5,

----

6. Think you can do better, eh? OK, send me your best Blackjack limerick, and if I like it I'll publish it, with credit, in the next edition of this book.

7. One very useful aid, however, is Stanford Wong's <u>Current Blackjack News</u>. This monthly newsletter updates conditions in all the casinos of Nevada and Atlantic City. It has allowed me to spend less time casing casinos and more time beating them.

$25, or $100), which tables are empty, or nearly so (important in single-deck games), and which tables are getting the most heat from the big guns in the pit (usually the money games).

After digesting all this information, I'll decide which, if any, of the games I want to play in. Having made my choice, I'll step confidently up to the table I have selected, slide onto a seat, turn some paper into plastic, and begin to play. Oh, one more thing, I'm always careful to time my arrival just as the first round of a new shuffle is concluding; this allows me to take immediate advantage of a plus deck, or (since my bet spread is not yet known) to make very small bets on a minus deck until the count is more to my liking.

HOW TO BUY IN

Many players make the mistake of buying in for too much money when they sit down to play. This is a bad move because it draws unnecessary, and unwanted, attention from the pit. If the bosses see that you're loaded for bear, they'll watch you very closely to see whether or not you're shootin' with blanks.

And the bigger you're betting the more careful you have to be. If, for example, you are playing with an average bet of about $10,[8] you can buy in for up to $100. But if your average bet is, say, $50, I suggest you buy in for only $300: six average bets, instead of 10; and, if your action is much bigger than this, I advise you to buy in for no more than four(!) average bets.

Remember, there is nothing that warms up a cold-hearted pit boss faster than the sight of a high roller (seemingly) overbetting his stake.

Here's an example of how this can work in actual play. Say you're betting $50 to $200, with an average bet of about $100. You sit down to play, and buy in for $400. Now $400 is not that big a deal, especially at a quarter ($25 minimum) table, so your buy-in scarcely draws a nod from the pit. As luck would have it, the cards start running against you, and in a period of 10 or 15 minutes you have to make three more $400 buy-ins for a total investment of $1,600. Now, when money starts flying across the table this fast, it's very difficult for the bosses to keep track of just how much you're in for. Let's say at this point the cards begin

----

8. Note, this is an average bet, not a minimum bet; an average bet of $10, for example, represents a bet spread of from $5 to $20.

to turn, and after another half hour of play you have recouped your $1,600 investment plus about another $900. You know it's not smart to push it, so you decide to move on to another club. But, before you go, that initial $1,600 frenzy gives you a perfect opportunity to minimize your win in the eyes of the casino bosses. Continuing to play, you say something to the dealer like, "Well, according to my count, I must be at least even by now." Dealer responds, "You're healthier than that. I think you're up close to a grand." Incredulous, you say, "Really? No way, that can't be right," and, catching the eye of the boss who's been watching your play, you say, "I'm into this game for $2,400, right?" "No," he replies, checking his notes, "I think it's only $1,600." You come back with, "It's got to be at least $2,000; did you see that last $400?" Now, at this point, he's not really sure, because early on money was flying over the table at a furious rate, so, not wanting to admit that he might have missed something, he replies, "Yeah, that's right, but it's only $2,000, not $2,400." "OK," you respond, "thanks for keeping score." Then, rising from the table, you continue with, "Well, I actually made a few bucks for a change. It's only $500, but it's better than I'm used to." And, tossing a nickel ($5) to the dealer, you scoop up your checks and head for the cage.

This tactic is important, because it can make a fairly significant win look like just a little bit of luck. Notice, also, that if you had bought in for, say, $1,000 or $1,200, besides drawing immediate attention from the pit, the bosses would have had a solid handle on your action, and you would never have been able to pull off a snow job like this one.

HOW TO HIDE CHIPS

Another effective way to conceal the extent of a winning session is to discreetly pull checks out of play. You have to be careful how you do this, however, because if the bosses catch you at it they'll assume you're up to mischief, and you'll come under immediate suspicion.

When I play, I usually wear a coat with several large pockets. When the bosses are momentarily distracted, it's not too difficult to palm a few checks and slip them discreetly into one of the pockets.

To make it more difficult for the bosses to detect this move, it's a good idea to keep your chips in casual piles rather than neatly stacked and sorted. This way, the sudden disappearance of a few checks won't be so noticeable. And, as with all such ploys, don't get greedy and overdo it; just wait for the right opportunity, and when it occurs make your move smoothly--and make it fast.

And one last thing, when you go to the cage after a winning session, don't cash in any checks you have pulled out of play; just take them with you and redeem them later on another shift.

HOW TO COUNT YOUR CASH AND CHECKS

Many beginning counters actually move their lips when they count. Because this "tell" is so common, most casino bosses look for this behavior whenever they suspect a player of counting. This situation provides an excellent opportunity to throw the pit bulls off the scent. The trick is to move your lips when you count everything *but* cards. For example, if I decide to count my chips or the cash in my wallet, I will subtly, but pointedly, move my lips as I count. The bosses can't help but notice this. Later on, when they observe my behavior as the cards come out, the absence of any lip movement then will lead them to believe that I'm not counting cards. And don't ham it up, let the bosses think they're really sharp to have picked up on such a subtle "tell."

PLAYING WITH A PARTNER

One of the very best ways to keep the bosses distracted and uninterested in your action is to play with an attractive female partner. The power of sexual excitement should never be underestimated, and if your partner has the talent to turn on the bosses to the point where the little head is telling the big head what to do--you are absolutely home free.

One beautiful young woman I often play with[9] is an absolute master of the dry seduction. Not only is she dynamite to look at, with long black hair, large exotic brown eyes, and a pair of truly bodacious ta-tas, but her seductive movements and flirtatious mannerisms are calculated to have maximum effect on the stallion ganglia. She seems to love this little game, and it's not unusual to have three or four casino bosses clustered around her, gushing and blushing like awkward

----

9. Come on, we're talking Blackjack here.

schoolboys, while I sit next to her, the invisible man, playing for hours on end without hassle or heat.

Be careful, however, when you pick your partners. If possible, don't let them know you're a counter. If you do level with them, be sure that they can be trusted. Remember, if they do their job right, they'll get hit on continually, and you never know; one of the bosses just might get lucky. If that happens, your cover is in danger of being blown for good.

HOW TO CHOOSE A PIT BOSS

Pit bosses have a number of responsibilities, and busting counters is just one of them. Equally important are the public relations and promotional aspects of the job. Because personalities differ, some bosses take these latter duties more seriously than others; and your job is to find those bosses who are more interested in stroking you than poking you.

My own preference is for female and minority bosses. Because they often attain their positions through affirmative-action quota programs rather than through the usual good ol' boy network, they generally are not very well connected, and consequently feel especially insecure in their jobs. Lacking a power base to operate from, the last thing they want to do is make waves. Mostly, they tend to keep their noses clean and make as many friends as possible. They are often very responsive, even grateful, for some friendly attention and positive reinforcement.

All this means that if you cultivate these people properly you can buy yourself not only many hours of hassle-free play, but thousands of dollars worth of RFB[10] comps, as well.

Remember, gamblers are the lifeblood of any casino, so they all compete aggressively for "good" players. One of their most effective marketing tools is player comps, and based on your action you can--and should--expect to receive up to 40% of the casino bosses' estimates of your expected losses in RFB comps and other premium goodies. This, of course, is one of the great perks of casino gambling, and carefully choosing and manipulating the casino bosses to your advantage will allow you to employ and enjoy this comp-counting tactic to the max.

----

10. Casino shorthand for *room, food,* and *beverage,* respectively.

HOW TO HANDLE GETTING BARRED

No matter how well you play or how clever you are, once in a while you are likely to get barred. The way you handle these traumatic little episodes will have a great bearing on your future success when you play in these clubs again.

The best way to deal with these situations is to avoid all confrontations and get out as fast as possible. Don't make a fuss, and don't waste time protesting your innocence. Just pick up your checks and crash the doors. If you have a car, even a rental, just leave it there and walk away. This is important, because a lot of clubs will have a security "floater" follow you out to the parking lot to get your license number. This allows them, with a little help from their friends, to find out who you are, where you live, and sometimes even where you work.

After a few hours you can come back for your car, but stay out of that casino for at least three months, and off of that shift for at least six months. When you finally do return, be alert for any hint of recognition. If you find it, get out immediately! If you are patient, eventually they will forget you, but it is amazing how long some pit bosses can remember a face.

HOW TO REMAIN ANONYMOUS

The clubs like to know what they are up against, so they will go to great lengths to find out as much as possible about anyone who plays big enough, often enough, or well enough to potentially pose a threat. Naturally, it is in your interest to avoid this intelligence net as much as possible, and the less you tell them, the better off you'll be.

When I play, for example, I never use my real name. If they run one of my AKAs through the central computer, they're not going to come up with a thing--and that's the way I like it. I never use casino credit either; credit applications ask a lot of questions that are none of the casinos' business. I play strictly cash. Once in a while a boss will press this point and suggest I apply for a line of credit. I just say I have this little problem with compulsive gambling and find it safer to play only cash. They love the sound of that, and they generally never bring up the subject again.

Remember, casinos often pool credit and security information. So, if you're "86" in one casino, any other club that can identify you from the shared intelligence may bar you from play as well.

DISGUISES

Up until a few years ago, if you were barred, or otherwise tagged as an undesirable by the bosses, this unfortunate situation lasted about as long as the pit bosses' memories. Even if they had a small, grainy photo of you it was buried in a book along with pictures of hundreds of other undesirables, and your chances of being identified from it were pretty slim. Today, unfortunately, this is no longer generally the case.

In many of today's modern casinos, sophisticated, 21st-century technology allows surveillance personnel to take high-quality, head-shot photos of you, automatically scan them into a computer, together with any other information they may have, and "key" the whole thing by name, AKAs, sex, race, age, identifying characteristics, etc., all without your slightest knowledge. Next time you come in, they press a few keys and, bam! You're busted.

This is scary stuff, and it demands a response. The best response I know of is wearing disguises.

Disguises don't have to be elaborate. They just have to be effective. The most important thing is to change (or obscure) your facial appearance. Wigs, fake mustaches, eyeglasses, and hats are good. Depending on where you're playing, cowboy hats, sports caps, and specialty hats all work well. I usually go for a "theme" look. On one trip I might wear a sports cap with matching jacket and tennis shoes; next time it's jeans, cowboy hat and shit-kicker boots. The important thing is to make it very hard for the bosses to finger you from surveillance photos or identifying characteristics. Also, be very careful <u>not</u> to wear unique or unusual jewelry--this is a dead giveaway, and the bosses look for it.

Some pros don't have the patience for disguises, but their use can definitely prolong your playing life, and, for me, wearing disguises is all part of the spy vs. spy gamesmanship that makes professional Blackjack so much fun.

SUMMARY

Well, there you have it. Just about everything I know about camouflage is here. Of course, it is true that some things simply defy description, but in time you will gain a "feel" and judgment through play that no one can really teach you. In the meantime, if you will learn and use the concepts described in this chapter, you will have already taken a giant step down the road to professional Blackjack.

CHAPTER SEVEN

The Advanced Omega II System

If the chapter on camouflage is the soul of this book, then this is surely the heart. In fact, if the copy in your hands were missing every chapter except this one, this book would still be worth many times the price you paid for it.

The Advanced Omega II System is the most powerful and accurate level 2 Blackjack system ever devised. And even though less powerful systems continue to sell for a hundred or more dollars every day, I have included this powerhouse at no additional charge. Why have I done this? Good question. My accountant asked me the same thing. I guess the answer has to do with values and viewpoints. Unlike most other Blackjack authors, I do not make my living selling books and systems on Blackjack. I make my living *playing* Blackjack and selling Apple and IBM computers through my chain of computer specialty stores. My purpose in writing this book really has been to offer the knowledge I have gained through years of play on the pro Blackjack tour to anyone interested enough to read it and to study it. And I guess I have to admit to some ego tripping, as well. For unlike other trained professionals, pro Blackjack players have to maintain a very low profile to be successful. This book finally gives me an opportunity to showcase my thoughts and reach for a little recognition, as well.

Anyway, enough of that, let's get down to cases. In this chapter we're going to perfect the Basic Omega II System of Chapter Five. We'll be using the same count, the same betting strategy,[1] the same stake, the same camouflage techniques, the same everything--except for one thing. We will <u>not</u> be using the same playing strategy. Instead of the rather crude strategy of the Basic Omega II System, we will use a sophisticated and accurate playing strategy developed through extensive computer research and modeling. And, fortunately, because nearly everything you have learned so far works with the Advanced Omega II System, it shouldn't take you very long to master this system and put it into play.

----

1. For convenient reference, the Bet Spread and Betting Indices tables of Chapter Five are included near the end of this chapter as Tables 7.8, 7.9, 7.10, and 7.11.

One refinement, in particular, bears mentioning. Every other modern Blackjack system I have analyzed has suffered from the same rather subtle defect in the calculation of the playing indices for certain doubling-down and pair-splitting situations. Essentially, the authors of these systems have assumed that whenever doubling the original bet (through doubling down or splitting) won more money (or lost less money) than not doubling the bet, then the bet should be doubled. This analysis works for Basic Strategy, or any other strategy yielding a non-positive expectation for the player, but it has a flaw when applied to positive expectation strategies such as the Advanced Omega II System. In effect, the player is winning more money because he is betting more money, but he is doing so with a slimmer edge. The disagreeable consequence of this is that he raises his risk of ruin. The doubling-down and pair-splitting indices for the Advanced Omega II Strategy have been corrected for this anomaly and are, therefore, the most accurate yet developed.[2]

In Chapter Five, we estimated the player's advantage, using the Basic Omega II System in high quality single- and double-deck games, at about 1.0%, and in four-deck games at about .75%. Using the Advanced Omega II System, under the same conditions the player's advantage rises to approximately 1.5%[3] in one- and two-deck games, and to about 1.1% in four-deck games. This is a 50% increase

----

2. The proper way to calculate these bet-doubling indices is to provide for doubling down and pair splitting when such strategies will not only win more money (or lose less money), but when they will not dilute the player's overall advantage, either. This point occurs when the added gain from the bet doubling, expressed as a percentage of the original bet, is equal to the player's overall percentage edge. That is exactly what we have done with the Advanced Omega II Strategy. Another valid approach, that of calculating these indices so as to maximize the log of the expected win, is not really feasible due mainly to real-world betting constraints necessitated by camouflage considerations.

3. Actually, under ideal conditions (head-to-head play; single deck, dealt to last card; 10:1 bet spread; Las Vegas Strip rules) the player's advantage is 3.8%. You will sometimes see claims of 3.0%, or more, made by Blackjack authors for their systems. As you can see from the above conditions, however, these are theoretical yields only, and they bear little resemblance to what is attainable in the rough and tumble of real casino play.

in power, and it makes the Advanced Omega II Strategy well worth learning and using.

There are over 150 variable playing decisions in the Advanced Omega II Strategy and, not surprisingly, they are not all equally important.

In fact, Blackjack pundit Donald Schlesinger has determined that just the following 18 plays will give you over 75% of the total possible gain from strategy variation based on the true count.

I suggest, therefore, that you start by mastering these *"Fabulous 18,"* playing the other hands with the Basic Omega II Strategy, and only adding other playing decisions as you become comfortable and proficient.

When you do add other plays, begin with those decisions between +10 and -10; these, together with the *Fab 18,* will give you over 95% of the total possible gain from strategy variation.

Fabulous 18

Insurance	12 vs. 5
16 vs. 9	12 vs. 6
16 vs. 10	11 vs. A
15 vs. 10	10 vs. 10
13 vs. 2	10 vs. A
13 vs. 3	9 vs. 2
12 vs. 2	9 vs. 7
12 vs. 3	10,10 vs. 5
12 vs. 4	10,10 vs. 6

In multiple-deck games, because most of our advantage comes from spreading our bets rather than from varying our strategy, learning the remaining double-digit decisions (especially the minus ones) is of very little value.

In single- and double-deck games, however, strategy variation is significantly more important, so if you plan to play primarily in these games I suggest you eventually learn all the playing decisions in the Advanced Omega II Strategy.

LEARNING THE ADVANCED OMEGA II STRATEGY

The tables that follow present the Advanced Omega II Strategy in all its numeric splendor. This strategy, as with any Blackjack strategy, is best learned by making up flash cards, shuffling them in random order,[4] and practicing until your responses are quick, effortless and absolutely accurate.

Practice Charts 4.1 and 4.2 of Chapter Four are also a good way to perfect your knowledge of the Advanced Omega II Strategy, as well as an excellent way to stay sharp once you've got the strategy wired.

Occasionally, apparent contradictions can occur with the Advanced Omega II Strategy (or any Blackjack strategy, for that matter) in which different decision tables appear to give conflicting advice. For example, Table 7.3 indicates that hard 8 should be doubled against a 6 any time the true count is +5 or greater. Yet Table 7.5b indicates that (4,4), also hard 8, should be split against a 6 if the true count is 0 or greater. So what do you do with (4,4) vs. 6 and a true count of, say, +7: double, split, or punt? In this case, splitting takes precedence.

The general order of decision priority for the Advanced Omega II Strategy is as follows:

1. Surrender
2. Splitting
3. Doubling
4. Stand/Draw

After you have mastered this strategy using flash cards and Practice Charts 4.1 and 4.2, you are ready to put the Advanced Omega II System into play. Start small; just build from your playing experience with the Basic Omega II System, and when you are completely comfortable with your new strategy, you can begin to play for more serious money.

---

4. Actually, in practice, I separate the strategy by subgroup (stand/draw, doubling, splitting, etc.). Within a strategy subgroup, I practice the playing decisions in randomly shuffled (dis)order.

STANDING VS. DRAWING (Hard Hands)

In Chapter Four, when we studied the Basic Strategy, we learned that within Basic Strategy there is a correct play for every player hand against each dealer up card. In the Basic Omega II System of Chapter Five, we modified this to a correct play for every player hand against each dealer up card *within a true count range*. In the Advanced Omega II System of this chapter, this idea of a correct play *contingent* upon the true count is carried to its logical conclusion. In the Advanced Omega II Strategy, instead of a fixed play assigned to each situation, many of the strategy decisions are assigned *playing indices*. These are numbers, plus or minus, that indicate at what true count a particular playing option is invoked.

In Table 7.1, for instance, the decision is simply whether to stand or draw. And, as you can see, although some of the more extreme plays continue to be fixed, most of the playing decisions are now conditional upon the true count. For example, we would stand holding hard 12 versus the dealer's 6 if, and only if, the true count were -2 or greater. If the true count were less than -2, we would hit.

The same is true with all the other conditional playing decisions of Table 7.1: stand if the true count is equal to or greater than the playing index, hit if the true count is less than the playing index.[5]

In general, the greater the true count, the more likely we are to stand. This is reasonable because as the true count rises, so do our chances of busting if we decide to draw to our hand. This goes for the dealer too. So with big plus counts, even against a strong up card, it often pays to stand and hope the dealer is stiff and busts when he draws to complete his hand.

It is also interesting to note that, when we are stiff ourselves, we stand with lower true counts against a 9, 10, or A than we do against a 7 or 8. This seems strange when you consider that the dealer figures to have a stronger hand with, say, a 10 up than he does showing a 7. The reasoning behind this little puzzler is that with a 7 or 8 up, if we don't break on the draw, we will probably win, but when the dealer is showing paint, even if we catch a card, we will probably lose

----

5. And remember, a larger negative number, such as, say, -18 is less than a smaller negative number, like -17.

anyway. So in these situations, with even a modest plus count, it generally pays to stand--and pray (hard).

Table 7.1

STANDING VS. DRAWING
Hard Hands

The Advanced Omega II Strategy

PLAYER	DEALER'S UP CARD									
HAND	2	3	4	5	6	7	8	9	10	A
17	S	S	S	S	S	S	S	S	S	-10
16	-14	-17	-19	-22	-20	15	14	7	0	14
15	-10	-10	-14	-17	-17	22	21	15	6	18
14	-6	-7	-10	-12	-12	H	H	H	15[1]	22
13	-1	-3	-5	-8	-8	H	H	H	H	H
12	5	2	0	-2	-2	H	H	H	H	H

LEGEND: S=STAND
H=HIT

----
1. IF YOUR 14 CONSISTS OF (7,7), STAND AT +1 OR GREATER IN
SINGLE-DECK GAMES; +6 OR GREATER IN DOUBLE-DECK GAMES; +11 OR
GREATER IN FOUR- OR MORE DECK GAMES.

STANDING VS. DRAWING (Soft Hands)

As with the Basic Strategy of Chapter Four, standing versus drawing with soft hands using the Advanced Omega II Strategy is simple, intuitive, and completely straightforward.

Most of the decisions in Table 7.2 continue to be fixed, and learning the few variable ones won't put much of a strain on your brain. Just stand if the true count is greater than or equal to the playing index; otherwise hit.

Remember, however, that <u>doubling down</u> takes precedence over standing versus drawing; so (A,6) vs. 6, for instance, would normally only be hit if doubling down on soft hands were not allowed.

Table 7.2

STANDING VS. DRAWING
Soft Hands

The Advanced Omega II Strategy

PLAYER	DEALER'S UP CARD									
HAND	2	3	4	5	6	7	8	9	10	A
A,8	S	S	S	S	S	S	S	S	S	S
A,7	S	S	S	S	S	S -22		H	H	0[1]
A,6	H	H	H	H	H	H	H	H	H	H

NOTE: DOUBLING DOWN NOT CONSIDERED.

LEGEND: S=STAND
         H=HIT

----
1. STAND +2 OR GREATER IN FOUR- OR MORE DECK GAMES.

DOUBLING DOWN (Hard Hands)

There is nothing exceptional about Table 7.3. I could have included some rare situations where it mathematically pays to double on 5, 6, and 7, but these moves should never be made in casino play, so I have left them out.

Double down if the true count is greater than or equal to the playing index; otherwise hit.

Obviously, the greater the true count, the more likely we are to double. It doesn't take a rocket scientist to figure out that when the deck is loaded with 10s, hard doubles are likely to result in gonzo hands. And, as an added bonus, if the dealer turns out to be stiff, he will find himself drawing from a deck that is bursting with bust cards.

Also, while you're reviewing these strategy tables, if some of the plays don't seem to make good sense, go back and review Chapter Four on Basic Strategy, especially the material relating to Tables 4.1 through 4.10. There is a wealth of information and insight in those pages that should help you over any rough spots now.

Table 7.3

DOUBLING DOWN
Hard Hands

The Advanced Omega II Strategy

PLAYER	DEALER'S UP CARD								
HAND	2	3	4	5	6	7	8	9	10	A
11	-17	-18	-19	-21	-23	-12	-9	-6	-6	2
10	-13	-15	-17	-19	-21	-10	-6	-2	9	8
9	4	0	-3	-7	-9	7	17	H	H	H
8	H	17	12	7	5	H	H	H	H	H

LEGEND: H=HIT

DOUBLING DOWN (Soft Hands)

Because soft doubling is not as intuitive as most other aspects of the game, Table 7.4 will probably take you longer to learn than any of the other strategy charts. You can speed up this process somewhat by looking for patterns in the playing indices, and by increasing your feel for the game by reviewing the material on Table 4.4 (Basic Strategy).

With (A,2) through (A,6), the question is whether to double down or hit. Double if the true count is greater than or equal to the playing index; otherwise hit.

With (A,7), (A,8), and (A,9), we either double down or stand (except with (A,7) vs. 8, 9, 10, A, see Table 7.2). And remember, as we pointed out in Chapter Six (Camouflage), doubling with (A,8) or (A,9) can be hazardous to your playing life (in fact, in the good ol' days of mob rule, it might have been hazardous to your life--period); so you do have to be careful when you make these aggressive plays.

Table 7.4

DOUBLING DOWN
Soft Hands

The Advanced Omega II Strategy

PLAYER				DEALER'S UP CARD						
HAND	2	3	4	5	6	7	8	9	10	A
A,9	S	16	13	10	9	S	S	S	S	S
A,8	S	9	6	3	2	S	S	S	S	S
A,7	2	-2	-8	-12	-12	S	*	H	H	*
A,6	2	-5	-9	-16	-19	23	H	H	H	H
A,5	H	6	-3	-10	-16	H	H	H	H	H
A,4	H	8	0	-7	-11	H	H	H	H	H
A,3	H	10	2	-4	-8	H	H	H	H	H
A,2	H	11	5	0	-3	H	H	H	H	H

LEGEND: S=STAND
        H=HIT
        *=SEE TABLE 7.2

SPLITTING PAIRS

There aren't any real surprises in Table 7.5a. Aces and 8s continue to be split more often than any other pairs. Fours, 5s, and 10s are still rarely, if ever, split; and the other pairs are or are not split depending on the count and how likely the dealer is to break when he draws to complete his hand.

Generally, just split a pair if the true count is greater than or equal to the appropriate index in Table 7.5a. If the true count is less than the index, hit or stand, depending on the situation.

A couple of special cases, however, need some special attention. Both (3,3) vs. 7 and (8,8) vs. 10 are handled differently. In both of these situations, you split the pair if the true count is *less* than the playing index. If the count is greater than or equal to the index, you hit with (3,3) vs. 7, and stand holding (8,8) vs. 10.

Table 7.5b gives the playing indices if doubling down after splits is permitted. This option shifts the balance in favor of splitting in some marginal situations, and it is worth learning if you often play in clubs where doubling on any two cards is allowed.[6]

----

6. As opposed to doubling on any *first* two cards.

Table 7.5a

PAIR SPLITTING

The Advanced Omega II Strategy

PLAYER HAND	DEALER'S UP CARD 2	3	4	5	6	7	8	9	10	A
A,A	-18	-19	-20	-21	-22	-15	-14	-13	-13	-7
10,10	S	15	12	9	8	S	S	S	S	S
9,9	-1	-5	-6	-10	-8	15	P	P	S	12
8,8	P	P	P	P	P	P	P	P	8[1]	P
7,7	-14	-18	-21	P	P	P	*	*	*	*
6,6	4	-1	-4	-9	-12	H	H	H	H	H
5,5	*	*	*	*	*	*	*	*	*	*
4,4	H	*	*	*	*	H	H	H	H	H
3,3	14	6	0	-7	P	14[2]	H	H	H	H
2,2	13	4	-5	-12	P	P	H	H	H	H

LEGEND: S=STAND
         H=HIT
         P=SPLIT
         *=SEE TABLES 7.1, 7.3, OR 7.6; (4,4) IS 8,
          (5,5) IS 10, AND (7,7) IS 14.

----

1. SPLIT <u>LESS</u> THAN +8; ELSE STAND.

2. SPLIT <u>LESS</u> THAN +14; ELSE HIT.

Table 7.5b

PAIR SPLITTING

The Advanced Omega II Strategy

PLAYER	DEALER'S UP CARD									
HAND	2	3	4	5	6	7	8	9	10	A
A,A	-18	-19	-20	-21	-22	-15	-14	-13	-13	-7
10,10	S	15	12	9	8	S	S	S	S	S
9,9	-3	-7	-10	-11	-13	8	P	P	S	9
8,8	P	P	P	P	P	P	P	P	12[1]	P
7,7	-15	-18	-21	P	P	P	-1	*	*	*
6,6	-2	-6	-8	-12	-22	H	H	H	H	H
5,5	*	*	*	*	*	*	*	*	*	*
4,4	H	14	7	3	0	H	H	H	H	H
3,3	-3	-11	-15	-18	P	15[2]	H	H	H	H
2,2	-7	-9	-13	-18	P	P	15	H	H	H

```
LEGEND: S=STAND
        H=HIT
        P=SPLIT
        *=SEE TABLES 7.1, 7.3, OR 7.6; (5,5) IS 10,
          AND (7,7) IS 14.
```

----

1. SPLIT <u>LESS</u> THAN +12; ELSE STAND.

2. SPLIT <u>LESS</u> THAN +15; ELSE HIT.

SURRENDER

Table 7.6 presents late surrender only. Early surrender is rarely encountered these days, so it's not worth wasting brain power on. If you do encounter early surrender somewhere, use the strategy found in Table 4.6 of Chapter Four (Basic Strategy); this will give you about 90% of the possible gain from early surrender.

As with the Basic Strategy version, we generally only late surrender when we are holding a nearly hopeless stiff, like 15 or 16, against the dealer's strong up card--like a 10 or an Ace. However, as you can see from Table 7.6, sometimes with big plus counts the player's disadvantage can exceed 50% even with more makable hands against weaker up cards. When this occurs we just "toss 'em in for half," and hope the Blackjack gods cut us a little slack on the next hand.

Late surrender if the true count is greater than or equal to the appropriate index in Table 7.6; otherwise stand, draw, or (rarely) split, depending on the situation.

Late surrender, unfortunately, is not a big money maker. The gain varies from .02% (flat betting with Basic Strategy) to about .20% (variable betting with the Advanced Omega II System). The main virtue of late surrender is that it moderates negative swings in your playing stake.[7] This is an important consideration that should not be underestimated. Even with your edge, the casinos will always enjoy one important advantage: they have more money than you do, which means they can ride out bigger losing streaks than you can. So, an option like surrender that flattens out downward fluctuations in your capital is a powerful weapon that should be used whenever possible.

----

7. Of course, it also moderates positive swings in your playing stake as well, but these won't help you as much as bad runs will hurt you.

Table 7.6

LATE SURRENDER

The Advanced Omega II Strategy

PLAYER	DEALER'S UP CARD			
HAND	8	9	10	A
17	S	S	23	S
16[1]	10	2	-4[2]	-1
15	14	6	0	5
14[3]	22	12	6[4]	10
13	H	H	13	*

LEGEND: S=STAND
H=HIT
*=SEE TABLES 7.1, 7.7

----

1. EXCLUDING (8,8), EXCEPT AS NOTED.

2. SURRENDER AT +3, IF 16 CONSISTS OF (8,8).

3. INCLUDING (7,7), EXCEPT AS NOTED.

4. SURRENDER AT +2, IF 14 CONSISTS OF (7,7).

INSURANCE

There is no change from the Basic Omega II System with respect to insurance; continue to take insurance <u>only</u> when the true count is +6 or greater.

OVER/UNDER

Over/under is a betting option introduced at Caesars Tahoe in 1988 that is beginning to show signs of longevity. It consists of two even-money side bets: the player may either bet that his first two cards will total over 13, or that they will total under 13. Aces count 1; 13 always loses; the maximum bet is usually $100, and over/under bets may not exceed the amount of your original wager.

The player's average disadvantage with the over bet ranges from a low of -6.5% in an infinite-deck game, up to about -6.8% in a single-deck game. The player's average disadvantage with the under bet remains constant at about -10.1% regardless of the number of decks in play.

That's the bad news. The good news is that over/under is a highly volatile, beatable option (especially in single- and double-deck games), with the advantage swinging back and forth between the player and dealer as the cards are dealt out.

And fortunately, though not optimal, the Omega II Count is a strong count to use for over/under. In fact, using the Omega II Count to make appropriate over/under bets up to the amount of your original wager will *increase* your overall advantage by about .8% in single-deck games, by about .5% in double-deck games, and by nearly .3% in six-deck games. That's a *lot*, and it makes the over/under option a major source of potential winnings.

Although over/under is generally only offered in selected six- and eight-deck games, it has occasionally shown up in single- and double-deck games, as well. So be alert and keep your eyes open; over/under in a single-deck game is a solid-gold key to the casino's vault.

One note of caution is in order. Because over/under involves making an additional wager, it does moderately increase your risk and potential loss. Therefore, if you frequently play over/under, I suggest you increase your bankroll by about 10%. This will limit your risk of ruin to an acceptable level.

With the Omega II Count, make the over bet at a true count of +8 or greater, and make the under bet at a true count of less than -11.

NO-HOLE-CARD CASINOS

In many foreign casinos, including a lot of cruise ships, the dealer does not take a hole card. In some of these clubs you lose any additional money wagered on double downs or splits if the dealer gets a blackjack. In others, you lose only your original bet. Play as usual if you lose only your original bet, but if additional money wagered on doubles and splits is lost to the dealer's natural, then make the following changes to the playing strategy for the Advanced Omega II System: (1) Never split or double down against an Ace, (2) Never double down against a 10, and (3) Never split 8s against a 10 (however, continue to split Aces against a 10 as usual).

If you lose only your original bet, your edge is not affected by this rule; however, in those clubs where you lose the extra money bet, your advantage is reduced by about .13%.

IF THE DEALER HITS SOFT 17

As you know from our earlier discussions, in about half of the casinos in the world, the dealer hits soft 17. This rule has a modest effect on the standing versus drawing playing strategies of the Advanced Omega II System. Therefore, when you are playing where this rule is in effect, make the following changes to Tables 7.1 and 7.2: (1) Stand 12 vs. 6 at -5 or greater, (2) Stand 13 vs. 6 at -10 or greater, (3) Stand 14 vs. 6 at -14 or greater, (4) Stand 13 vs. A at +21 or greater, (5) Stand 14 vs. A at +14 or greater, (6) Stand 15 vs. A at +10 or greater, (7) Stand 16 vs. A at +5 or greater, (8) Stand 17 vs. A at -7 or greater, and (9) Always hit soft 18 against an Ace.

Table 7.7 presents these changes in regular matrix fashion.

This rule will cost you about .16% when you are playing the Advanced Omega II System. This is actually a little less than the .20% it costs you with Basic Strategy. The difference has to do with the increased accuracy of the Advanced Omega II Strategy and the fact that this rule has less effect against plus counts--when we will be making our bigger bets--than it does when the count is minus.

Table 7.7

CHANGES IF THE DEALER
HITS SOFT 17

The Advanced Omega II Strategy

PLAYER	DEALER'S UP CARD	
HAND	6	A
A,7	*	**H**
17	*	**-7**
16	*	**5**
15	*	**10**
14	**-14**	**14**
13	**-10**	**21**
12	**-5**	*

LEGEND: H=HIT
        *=SEE TABLES 7.1, 7.2

Table 7.8

BET SPREAD TECHNIQUE

Single-Deck Games
Las Vegas Rules[1]

Bet	W/L	Count[2]	Bet < 1/2[3]	Bet > 1/2[4]
1	W	(+)	2	2
1	L	(+)	2	1
1	W	(−)	1	1
1	L	(−)	1	1
2	W	(+)	2	2
2	L	(+)	2	2
2	W	(−)	1	1
2	L	(−)	1	1

----

1. This is a reprint of Table 5.4 of Chapter Five. See that section for a more complete explanation of this table.

2. In this context, (+) does not mean any plus count; it means a count sufficiently plus to mathematically justify the indicated bet. (-) also is relative; it means a count that is either actually minus, or one that is insufficiently plus to mathematically justify a larger bet. The Betting Indices tables list these critical betting counts.

3. This means the next hand will be dealt from the *first* half of the pack.

4. This means the next hand will be dealt from the *second* half of the pack.

Table 7.9

BET SPREAD TECHNIQUE

Double-Deck Games[1]
Las Vegas Rules[2]

Bet	W/L	Count	Bet < 1/2	Bet > 1/2
1	W	(+)	2	2
1	L	(+)	2	2
1	W	(−)	1	1
1	L	(−)	1	1
2	W	(+)	4	4
2	L	(+)	4	2
2	W	(−)	1	1
2	L	(−)	1	1
4	W	(+)	4	4
4	L	(+)	4	4
4	W	(−)	2	2[3]
4	L	(−)	2	2

----

1. This is a reprint of Table 5.5 of Chapter Five. See that section for a more complete explanation of this table.

2. Or single-deck games with Reno rules.

3. Resist the temptation to cut back to a 1-unit bet in these situations. Such a big drop just looks too suspicious; wait for the next hand to back off to 1 unit.

Table 7.10

BET SPREAD TECHNIQUE

Multiple-Deck Games
Las Vegas Rules[1]

Bet	W/L	Count	Bet < 1/2	Bet > 1/2
1	W	(+)	2	2
1	L	(+)	2	2
1	W	(−)	1	1
1	L	(−)	1	1
2	W	(+)	4	4
2	L	(+)	4	4
2	W	(−)	1	1
2	L	(−)	1	1
4	W	(+)	8	8
4	L	(+)	8	4
4	W	(−)	1	1
4	L	(−)	1	1
8	W	(+)	8	8
8	L	(+)	8	8
8	W	(−)	1	1[2]
8	L	(−)	1	1

----

1. This is a reprint of Table 5.6 of Chapter Five. See that section for a more complete explanation of this table.

2. This is aggressive play, and it does not look especially innocent; however, if you expect to beat multiple decks, you've got to back off fast against minus counts.

Table 7.11

THE BETTING INDICES[1]

Las Vegas Rules[2]

REMAINING DECKS

BET SIZES	6	5	4	3	2	1.5	1	.75	.5
Bet = 2 units	+20	+15	+10	+7	+4	+3	+2	+1	0
Bet > 2 units	+27	+21	+15	+11	+7	+5	+3	+2	+1

Reno Rules[3]

REMAINING DECKS

BET SIZES	6	5	4	3	2	1.5	1	.75	.5
Bet = 2 units	+27	+21	+15	+11	+7	+5	+3	+2	+1
Bet > 2 units	+34	+27	+20	+15	+10	+7	+4	+3	+2

All index numbers indicate the *running* count.

----

1. This is a reprint of Table 5.7 of Chapter Five. See that section for a more complete explanation of this table.

2. Las Vegas Rules are as follows: double down on any *first* two cards, resplit all pairs except Aces, and the dealer may (downtown), or may not (Strip), hit soft 17.

3. Reno Rules are as follows: double down on *first* two cards totaling 10 or 11 only, resplit all pairs except Aces, and the dealer hits soft 17.

FIGURES 7.1 AND 7.2 - PLAYER'S ADVANTAGE VS. BET SPREAD

These two charts give you an accurate idea of the power and results you can expect from the Advanced Omega II System over a wide range of casino conditions.

Some of the yields in Figure 7.2 (ideal conditions) are nothing short of spectacular. While it's true you don't often see games dealt to the bottom anymore, it still pays to keep your eyes open. Occasionally a small club will deal an old-fashioned game for a few weeks until the pros swoop down and kill it. If you're alert, you can sometimes get in on the fun before the bones are picked clean. Good hunting.

Figure 7.1

PLAYER'S ADVANTAGE[1]
VS.
BET SPREAD

The Advanced Omega II System

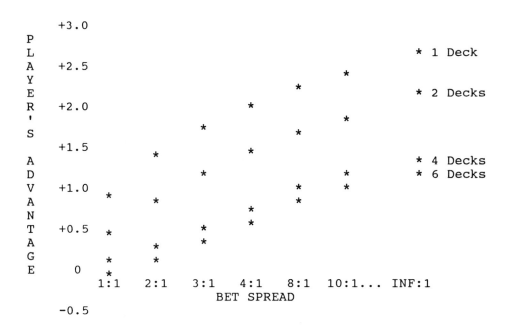

----
1. THIS CHART ASSUMES <u>FAVORABLE</u> CASINO CONDITIONS, INCLUDING LAS
VEGAS STRIP RULES, THREE PLAYERS AT THE TABLE, AND 70% DECK(S)
PENETRATION (75% WITH FOUR AND SIX DECKS).

Figure 7.2

PLAYER'S ADVANTAGE[1]
VS.
BET SPREAD

The Advanced Omega II System

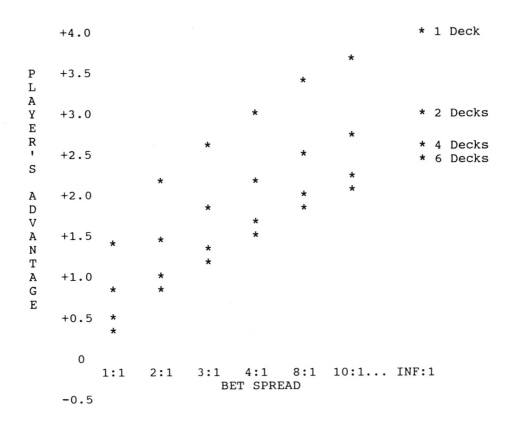

----
1. THIS CHART ASSUMES <u>IDEAL</u> CASINO CONDITIONS, INCLUDING LAS VEGAS STRIP RULES, ONE PLAYER AT THE TABLE, AND 100% DECK(S) PENETRATION.

SUMMARY

The Advanced Omega II System is not only one of the top performing Blackjack systems in terms of raw power, it is also very enjoyable to use in actual play. It is slick. It reminds me of a high-powered car roaring through a canyon in all-out pursuit, every part performing perfectly, the entire machine a high-performance extension of body and being. The Advanced Omega II System feels like this in actual play, a smooth, powerful extension of your own mind.

And consider this: by the time you have mastered the Advanced Omega II System and the earlier material on camouflage and money management, you will be, as far as the casinos are concerned, an international terrorist, armed and dangerous: armed with knowledge, and a danger to the bottom line. Kind of an exciting prospect, don't you think? Lock and load. Let's rock 'n' roll!

CHAPTER EIGHT

The Theory of Gambler's Ruin

You do not need the information in this chapter to win with the Blackjack strategies presented in this book. But as you know by now, I'm a believer in mastering the fundamentals. So if you have any head for math at all and can follow simple equations through basic algebra, I suggest you give this chapter a long, hard look. Someday when you've been losing and you're tempted to overbet your stake to get even (and you will be), there is a good chance the material presented here will save you from a financially fatal mistake.

Winning Blackjack follows what mathematicians call a random walk with an upward drift. What this means is that the game will rock back and forth, with winning streaks mixed with losing streaks, but overall the trend will be steadily upward. Steadily upward, and relentlessly upward, but, unfortunately, not necessary immediately upward. You can think of the swings in the game as analogous to a drunk staggering up the street. With any luck he will eventually get to where he is headed, but the path is going to be twisted and tortuous to say the least.

This is why even with an advantage you need a substantial playing stake to be a winning Blackjack player. Bad runs of luck can, and will, sometimes dominate your results for hours and hours on end. I have personally experienced losing streaks that lasted for over 7,500 hands, and during computer simulations I have occasionally seen relentless poundings that went on for tens of thousands of hands before finally turning around. Fortunately, because a computer plays more Blackjack in a few hours than you could play in several lifetimes, you are very unlikely to experience anything as bloodcurdling as all that. But it is sobering just to know that it could happen.

I think you get the idea. Gambling, even gambling with an edge, involves risk. This is why countless people have spent countless hours trying to devise schemes and scams to protect themselves from bad runs of luck. As a matter of fact, the entire discipline of probability theory was developed not as you might suppose by high-minded intellectuals hoping to fathom the mysteries of the universe or something, but rather by inveterate gamblers, like the 17th century mathematicians Blaise Pascal, Pierre de Fermat, and Christiaan Huygens to name three, who were just looking to get an edge on their gambling opponents and protect themselves from downward swings in their playing stake.

SIZING YOUR PLAYING STAKE

These pioneers in probability theory were obsessed with the problem of gambler's ruin: namely, how big a stake do you need to be safe, and just how safe is safe?

They realized that the operative factors in calculating the chance of ruin were the player's expectation (E), his total number of units (bets) of playing capital (C), and the amount he wants to win before quitting (W). Eventually the following formula[1] for calculating the player's probability of ruin (R) for even-money games was developed and proved:

$$R = \frac{((1 + E)/(1 - E))^W - 1}{((1 + E)/(1 - E))^{W+C} - 1}$$

Now for us W, the amount we want to win, is essentially infinite. This simplifies things, and reduces the above equation to:

$$R = ((1 - E)/(1 + E))^C$$

In addition, for a game like Blackjack, where some trials are neither won nor lost at even money, this equation can be shown to take the more general form:

$$R = ((1 - E_d)/(1 + E_d))^{C_d}$$

Where $E_d = E/d_{(1)}$, $C_d = C/d_{(1)}$, and $d_{(1)} \sim 1.1$ (see page 161).

Let's plug some numbers into this formula and see what we can expect. Because both our expectation and our bets vary with the count in actual play, and because studies have shown that the fluctuations in our playing stake are heavily

----

1. Feller, <u>An Introduction to Probability Theory and Its Applications</u>, p. 314.

influenced by maximum bets, we will use our average expectation for large (above 1-unit) bets as (E), and our maximum bet as the basic unit in sizing our stake (C).

Research has shown that in one- and two-deck games the average expectation for large bets (E) is about +1.67% for the Basic Omega II System, and about +2.25% for the Advanced Omega II System.[2]

So, based on these values for (E), let's calculate the chance of ruin (R) for playing stakes (C) of from 25 to, let's say, 275 maximum bets. The results are shown in Table 8.1.

Now you can see why in Chapter Five I recommended a playing stake of at least 125 maximum bets. Even with a stake this large and a 2.25% large-bet advantage, your chance of ruin is a small, but not insignificant, 1 in 105; with a slimmer 1.67% edge, your risk rises to a larger, though still reasonable, 1 chance in 31.5.

Considering that the upside is that you will go on winning unlimited amounts of money forever, I think most people would consider this small chance of ruin an acceptable risk.[3]

Actually, things aren't even quite this good, because the formula we used assumes total reinvestment of all winnings. In this way your stake just keeps getting bigger and bigger, and unless a big loss occurs early in your career, before long your stake is large enough to withstand virtually anything the Blackjack gods can throw at you.

Some big-time pro players actually do this. They put most of their winnings into short-term CDs, or other liquid accounts, and only spend the earned interest, saving the growing principal for when they retire from serious Blackjack--or in case they need it. If you have the financial resources, and the discipline, to do this, great; if not, know that your chances of being wiped out are a little higher than the numbers here would suggest. Personally, I invest some of my winnings, spend some of my winnings, and trust the Blackjack gods to save their worst for someone else.

----

2. Assuming the playing conditions and betting schemes considered here.

3. Of course, the formula we used assumes flat betting and a constant expectation (E). Obviously, these things are not strictly true for Blackjack, so we have, necessarily, substituted average large-bet expectation and maximum bet, instead. Consequently, the results here, though close, are approximate.

Table 8.1

PLAYER'S CHANCE OF RUIN[1]

CAPITAL (C) (Units)	CHANCE OF RUIN (R) (E = +1.67%)		CHANCE OF RUIN (R) (E = +2.25%)	
25 Max Bets	50.1508%	(1 in 2.0)	39.4601%	(1 in 2.5)
50 Max Bets	25.1511%	(1 in 4.0)	15.5710%	(1 in 6.4)
75 Max Bets	12.6135%	(1 in 7.9)	6.1443%	(1 in 16.3)
100 Max Bets	6.3258%	(1 in 15.8)	2.4246%	(1 in 41.2)
125 Max Bets	3.1724%	(1 in 31.5)	0.9567%	(1 in 105)
150 Max Bets	1.5910%	(1 in 62.9)	0.3775%	(1 in 265)
175 Max Bets	0.7979%	(1 in 125)	0.1490%	(1 in 671)
200 Max Bets	0.4002%	(1 in 250)	0.0588%	(1 in 1,701)
225 Max Bets	0.2007%	(1 in 498)	0.0232%	(1 in 4,310)
250 Max Bets	0.1006%	(1 in 994)	0.0092%	(1 in 10,870)
275 Max Bets	0.0505%	(1 in 1,980)	0.0036%	(1 in 27,778)

----

1. NOTE, THAT HALVING THE NUMBER OF MAXIMUM BETS INCREASES THE CHANCE OF RUIN TO THE SQUARE ROOT OF THE ORIGINAL RISK. THIS MEANS IF YOU CUT YOUR BETS IN HALF AFTER LOSING HALF YOUR STAKE, THE OVERALL CHANCE OF RUIN IS REDUCED TO THE ORIGINAL RISK TIMES THE SQUARE ROOT OF THE ORIGINAL RISK. CAUTION: THIS IS A RISK MANAGEMENT TECHNIQUE, NOT AN EXCUSE TO OVERBET YOUR PLAYING STAKE.

The sizing of your playing stake is also heavily influenced by your overall financial strength, as well as several important psychological considerations.

Let's say, for example, you earn a high five-figure salary as a stockbroker. You enjoy Blackjack but have no ambition to be anything more than just a strong recreational player, betting, say, $10 to $40. How much of a playing stake do you need? Not much. Around 50 maximum bets, or about $2,000, will do nicely. This will give you about a 84.4% chance of winning indefinitely with the Advanced Omega II System. Even if you do get wiped out, it's no big deal; just save up another $2,000 from your regular job, and before long you're back in business. In a sense, your total stake is really the sum of all the discretionary income from your regular job.

On the other hand, suppose you're earning the same high five figures, hustling the same stocks and bonds, but now you have dreams of being enshrined in the Blackjack Hall of Fame as one of the all-time, big-time winners. What now? If you're betting $100 to $400 you'd better have a stake of at least 125 maximum bets, $50,000, because otherwise, if you run into a really bad run of cards and get wiped out, you're out of business forever, at least at that level. In other words, if you cannot readily replenish your stake from other sources of income, you have to be very, very conservative in sizing your playing stake.

As a matter of fact, I would not play at that level with a stake of only $50,000, even though my chances of winning unlimited amounts of money, indefinitely, are better than 99%. Why? Consider this: Let's say I eventually hit a really bad run of cards and drop, say, $32,500. This can happen. Now I've only got a stake of 43.75 maximum bets left, and my chance of total wipeout has risen from 1 in 105 to nearly 1 in 5. I've just seen 65% of my stake disappear; can the other 35% be far behind? In a situation like this, you need steely eyes bluer than mine to maintain the composure, concentration, and professional detachment you need to play winning Blackjack for serious dough.

But I would never let myself get into a hole like that. When I play Blackjack at a level that cannot be readily replenished from other sources of income, I maintain a playing stake at least twice as large as any loss I am even remotely likely to encounter. This generally means a minimum of 175 maximum bets. In the above example, for instance, I consider a bankroll of at least $70,000 absolutely essential. If you never lose more than half your stake, you can keep your fears and your demons under control. Lose much more than that, however, and you can kiss your composure goodbye, and probably before long the last of your stake, as well.

Additionally, it is absolutely imperative that you never play with money you cannot afford to lose. Winning Blackjack requires a cool, calculating, unemotional head; but if you play with the mortgage money, or even with the car payment, you will find every lost hand a dagger to the heart, every losing streak a brutal, mind-numbing hammering. This is not fun. Beyond that, it is both stupid and unnecessary. Play with money you can afford to lose; and know this: you do not have to start big to win big. Later on, I'm going to show you how one world-class Blackjack duo parlayed $500 into $250,000 in less than five years. It can be done.

SIZING YOUR TRIP STAKE

Of course, hauling huge amounts of money around a gambling town is not such a good idea. As a matter of fact, it's a downright dangerous idea. This revelation has given rise to the concept of trip stake, whereby instead of toting all your loot along on each visit to casinoland, you merely stuff your pockets with enough cash to back your action and reduce your risk of trip-stake wipeout to an absolute bare minimum.

Now, the equations we used to calculate playing stake won't really do the trick for us here, because their main variable is target win (W). But, in calculating trip stake, we don't care about target win; what we care about is riding out the losing streaks that can occur during the course of a typical trip. In other words, the problem is how to size our trip stake so we don't get wiped out by unfavorable deviations from the expected win that can happen any time we go out to play. Fortunately, probability theory has an answer for us.

Two measures of risk--variance and deviation from an expected norm--have been thoroughly investigated by mathematicians, and a set of equations useful to us here have been developed.

Variance is defined as the sum of the squares of the differences between the theoretical expected result and all possible deviant outcomes multiplied by their respective chances of occurrence. The standard deviation is simply the square root of the variance.

Fortunately, in a game like Blackjack the relative standard deviation[4] reduces

----

4. Expressed as a decimal fraction.

to the simple expression $d_{(r)} = d_{(1)}/\sqrt{N}$, where $d_{(1)}$ is the standard deviation for one hand in units (about 1.1), and N is the number of trials considered. One standard deviation includes about 68% of all results, and two standard deviations takes this out to over 95% of all possible outcomes. For our purposes, two standard deviations is enough.

Let's take a look at a couple of examples to see how this works in practice. First, let's see what kind of money we need to take along on a weekender.

You can generally figure to play about six hours a day. If you play much more than this you'll end up overstressing yourself both mentally and physically, which not only isn't much fun but can also be expensive due to errors caused by tension and fatigue.

So, figuring six hours a day, you can get in about 12 hours play in a two-day weekend. Generally, about 40% of your bets will be large bets; all of which we will consider to be maximum bets in our ruin calculations. So, at around 40 maximum bets per hour, you'll wager about 480 maximum bets (trials) per trip.

Plugging N = 480 into our formula for relative standard deviation yields $d_{(r)} = .050$ or, expressed as a percent, $d_{(r)} = 5.0\%$. This is one standard deviation; $2d_{(r)}$ is double this, or 10.0%. Since our normal large-bet expectation is +2.25%, this means we have to be ready to absorb a loss of up to -7.75% (2.25% - 10.0%) of our total maximum-bet action for the trip.

If we bet, say, $25 to $100, our total maximum-bet action in 12 hours play would be $100 x 480 = $48,000; -7.75% of $48,000 is $3,720. With a maximum bet of $100, $3,720 represents 37.2 maximum bets (units).

Or consider a longer trip. Say you're going to go to Las Vegas for seven days and want to know how much money you need to bring along. In this case N = 1,680, $2d_{(r)} = 5.37\%$, and our potential loss is -3.12% (2.25% - 5.37%) of our total maximum-bet action, which works out, assuming a maximum bet of $100, to $5,242 or 52.4 maximum bets (units).

Notice an interesting thing; two standard deviations, $2d_{(r)}$, is smaller (5.37% vs. 10.0%) for the longer trip than it is for the shorter one, but you need more units of capital (52.4 vs. 37.2) for the longer trip than you do for the shorter one. The reason, of course, is that as the relative standard deviation is falling with trials, the amount of money bet is increasing. Eventually, however, as N increases and $2d_{(r)}$ ultimately falls to less than 2.25%, our potential for loss will virtually disappear. Play long enough and our edge must assert itself, losing streaks or not.

As it turns out, with an average large-bet advantage of 2.25%, a trip of about 10 days (2,400 maximum-bet trials) exposes you to the greatest $2d_{(r)}$ dollar risk. Shorter trips have a larger $d_{(r)}$, but with less action they result in a smaller dollar risk, and though longer trips have more action the $d_{(r)}$ is small enough to reduce or even virtually eliminate the risk of loss. This means that with a 2.25% edge on your large bets, even for extended trips, you never need to take along more than about 53.8 maximum-bet units to be 95%[5] safe from trip-stake wipeout. With a 1.67% large-bet edge, your $2d_{(r)}$ dollar risk is greatest at about 18 days (4,320 maximum-bet trials), and it takes about 72.5 maximum-bet units to be 95% safe.

SIZING YOUR BETS

While a playing stake large enough to ride out bad runs of luck is obviously essential to winning play, knowing how to size your bets is just as important to your ultimate success.

In the Betting Indices table of Chapter Five (which applies to both the Basic and the Advanced Omega II Systems) our bets increase as the count rises. Intuitively, this makes sense: since our advantage rises as the count rises, it seems reasonable to save our bigger bets for the bigger plus counts.

And, in fact, mathematical analysis bears out this intuitive approach: the greatest gain, consistent with acceptable risk, is achieved by betting a percentage of our stake in fixed proportion to our percentage edge. Exactly what percentage of our stake we bet in any given situation is dependent upon our advantage in that situation and what overall chance of ruin we are willing to accept.

Along these lines of fixed proportional betting, the ultimate scheme is one developed a number of years ago called "congruent fixed fraction betting," also known as the Kelly System. With the Kelly System, we bet a percentage of our *current* stake just equal (congruent) to our percentage edge in any given situation.[6]

----

5. This value is 95%, rather than the 97.7% you might suppose, because some trip-stake wipeouts that occur before the scheduled end of a trip would recover if funds were available to continue playing. Since no such funds are available here, our overall risk of trip-stake wipeout rises to just over twice the end-of-trip value.

6. Assuming for simplicity, an even payoff game and noncoupled probabilities.

If, for example, we have a current stake of, say, \$5,245.23, and an advantage in a particular situation of 1.55%, we would bet exactly \$81.30 on that hand (1.55% of \$5,245.23).

Because the betting strategy in the Kelly System is a function of both the player's advantage and the size of his current stake, it not only max's out the player's rate of win, it does so with a theoretical chance of ruin of exactly zero.

Furthermore, as you would expect, if fixed-fraction betting is used, but bets are sized at less than the Kelly criterion, the risk of ruin remains zero, but we will win at a slower rate. Conversely, as we increase our bets above about twice the Kelly criterion, negative fluctuations will eventually drive our playing capital toward zero, and our chance of ruin will be, for practical purposes, one hundred percent!

Interestingly enough, however, if we use fixed-fraction betting but size our bets at greater than one but less than about twice the Kelly criterion, we will again win more slowly than with Kelly but with a zero chance of ruin. This seems strange. It's certainly not hard to understand how overbetting can lead to disaster, but how can betting more than the Kelly criterion yield a reduced win rate and a zero risk of ruin? You would think that if bigger bets in favorable situations don't wipe you out first, they would be bound to win you more money.

Suspense killing you? Well, without getting too deep into the mathematical gymnastics of the thing, the basic answer is that the bigger bets result in bigger downward fluctuations that, although not large enough to overwhelm your stake, will eventually depress it so that on average your bets, in dollars, will be smaller than Kelly bets, even though they are bigger as a percentage of your current stake. What? Say that again. No.

Well, all right. To understand how the Kelly System increases your capital, consider that in N trials there will be W wins and L losses, such that $N = W + L$.[7] Now the Kelly System is a special case of fixed-fraction betting where the fraction bet (f) is congruent to the percentage advantage for each particular trial. Furthermore, it can be shown that for the general case the player's initial capital C_0 will change with successive trials such that the player's total capital C_N at the

----

7. Pushes, for our purposes, will be considered null hands and will not be counted.

end of any series of trials is defined by the expression:[8]

$$C_N = C_0(1 + f)^W(1 - f)^L$$

Now the average ratio R, as N increases without bound, that C_0 would have to be multiplied by N times to yield C_N, is defined (rather intuitively) by the expression:

$$R = \lim_{N > Inf} \sqrt[N]{\frac{C_N}{C_0}}$$

Substitute the equivalent $C_0(1 + f)^W(1 - f)^L$ for C_N, and the above expression can be shown to yield the following form:

$$R = (1 + f)^{W/N}(1 - f)^{L/N}$$

Now W/N is the fraction of trials that are won. Let's call this fraction (p). L/N is the fraction lost; call it (q). Of course (p + q) = 1. Substituting the notation (p) and (q), let's rewrite the above expression this way:

$$R = (1 + f)^p(1 - f)^q$$

Now obviously if your initial capital C_0 is going to get bigger, R must be larger than 1. Otherwise successive multiplications by R would yield a progressively smaller C_N.[9] In the above equation defining R, it can be shown (and you can easily verify it for yourself) that this occurs for a range of values of (f) greater than 0 but less than about 2(p - q).[10]

----

8. Wilson, <u>The Casino Gambler's Guide</u>, Appendix G. This book contains a description of the Kelly System, as well as numerous other interesting betting schemes.

9. In the trivial case where R = 1, C_0 does not change.

10. This is true for the range of values for (p - q) found in casino Blackjack.

As a matter of fact, if we take the derivative of R with respect to (f), dR/df, in the above equation, and set the result to zero to max out R with respect to (f), we end up with the expression f = (p - q), which is of course the Kelly criterion, as (p - q) is the player's expectation.

So here we are, back to where we started: the Kelly criterion f = (p - q) will maximize our win rate consistent with a zero chance of ruin. Smaller (f)s will win but more slowly; (f)s greater than about twice the player's edge, 2(p - q), will give you a severe case of wipeout, and values of (f) greater than (p - q) but less than about 2(p - q) will win but, again, more slowly.

In addition, in Blackjack, because some hands are neither won nor lost at even money with respect to the original bet (naturals, doubles, splits, insurance, and surrender), it is necessary to divide the Kelly criterion as derived above, f = (p - q), by the variance for one hand of Blackjack in units $v_{(1)}$ (about 1.3) to arrive at the optimum Kelly bet.

There now, wasn't that fun? There's just nothing like a little clarification to get over the rough spots, is there?

Anyway, the reason we are spending so much time exploring the Kelly System, and proportional betting in general, is because they form the theoretical basis for the betting strategies presented in this book. Beyond that, if you can understand how and why these systems work, your intuitive grasp of the game will increase significantly, and you will be much less likely to try tempting, but fallacious, alternatives.

Now, having said all these great things about the Kelly System, it's time to address a few hard, real-world facts. First off, no form of rigorous proportional betting can be used in actual casino play, and that definitely goes for the Kelly System. It's easy enough to do it on a computer, but, for any and all of the following reasons, there's no way do it for real:

1. Money is not infinitely divisible.

2. The casino always has a minimum and a maximum bet.

3. The player must bet, even when his expectation, (p - q), is zero or negative.

4. Bets generally cannot be made in odd-change amounts.

165

And beyond all that, can you imagine the effect on a dealer if you jacked your bet from $1 to, say, $125 from one hand to the next. Poof! Instant shuffle. Do it again. Poof! Instant 86.

So, because of these limitations, the Betting Indices table of Chapter Five was created with both the ideal of proportional betting and the reality of casino play in mind. It is a thoughtful compromise between theoretical probabilities and real-world possibilities.

Mathematicians interested enough in Blackjack to write about it often become fascinated with proportional betting. They like its elegance and its power. So, naturally, when they create a betting strategy of their own, they keep it as close to the ideal as they can and still make any kind of claim to practical use.

The problem with this approach is that it complicates play, which leads to errors, and ends up costing a lot more in mistakes than it ever earns by squeezing out a little extra theoretical profit. In addition to this, finely graduated betting points make the camouflage betting techniques of Chapter Five more rigid, and therefore less natural looking and effective.

Nevertheless, compared to the ideal of true proportional betting, the Betting Indices tables presented in this book differ enough to increase your chance of ruin slightly. This is the price of functionality with practicality, and the obvious fix is to size your stake in a conservative enough way to compensate for any increased volatility.

DR. J. AND THE PERFECT PARLAY

Before we leave this subject, I want to share an experience I had in Reno several years ago that I think you may find interesting.

One afternoon at Harrah's I had been playing, and losing steadily, for about an hour. The club was busy and small-time players kept plopping down, making a few bets, then getting up and leaving. Maybe it was just because I'd been losing, but it seemed like about every time the count got really good, some wanna-be cowpoke from Resume Speed, Nevada, or somewhere, would wander up, plunk down a few bucks on a couple of holes, and proceed to eat up the good cards until the dealer shuffled, then get up and drift off, leaving me muttering to myself, and sinking deeper and deeper into a dark and moody funk.

I needed a break, bad, and I was about to get up when a couple, decked out like Roy and Dale and well into their fifties, sat down and proceeded to engage in a needling banter that apparently had been going on for some time. It went something like this: Man pulls $800 in bills out of his wallet and tells the dealer to "Color it half 'n' half, black and white."[11] Before the paper even hits the felt, the wife starts in with, "Frank, haven't you lost <u>enough</u>?! This was supposed to be a vacation, but your gambling is turning it into a nightmare!" Frank, sounding slightly juiced, comes back with, "Gladys, shut up! I know what I'm doin'!" Then turning to the dealer, "Jus' ignore her I think she's havin' another hot flash or somethin'." Dealer smiles kind of wryly, then, naturally, colors the cash and slides the checks across the table to our beleaguered Blackjack buckaroo.

Now, at first, this bickering sort of annoyed me, and I started to get even more pissed than I already was. But then, as I was getting up to leave, for some perverse reason it suddenly struck me that this domestic skirmishing might prove kind of amusing, so, cutting back to a quarter waiting bet, I decided to stick around for a while and watch proceedings, well, proceed.

First thing, even before making a bet, cowboy Frank looks up, and making a little drinking motion with his right hand, says something to the dealer like, "How 'bout some whiskey, pardner." Dealer, allowing a condescending smile to tug at his lips, turns to the pit boss behind him, and calls out, "Cocktail."

Now Frank's ready for some action, and he shoves out a $200 bet. Immediately the dealer calls out, "Checks in play," but before the boss can react, Gladys jumps in with, "What are you doing? Start slow, for Chris' sake, Frank. See how he's running before you go hog wild!" Grumblin' and mumblin', Frank pulls back $150, leaving a $50 bet. As it turns out, Gladys saved our boy Frank some loot here, because the count just happened to be minus in a very big way, and both Frank and I saw our four-card 20s lose to the dealer's five-card 21.

About this time the cocktail waitress shows up. Frank orders a gin and tonic. Gladys says alcohol gives her hives and orders tonic only, with a twist, no ice. I order a Coke and settle into my seat. There's something about these two that's beginning to intrigue me.

Nothing much happened over the next several decks. Oh, on a couple of occasions, Frank jacked up his bet only to have Gladys knock it down; but again, as before, this didn't hurt him because he happened to pick very minus counts to get inspired.

----
11. At Harrah's, black checks are $25 and whites are $100.

Then something unusual occurred. About midway through a deck, the count went very plus, really ballistic. For once Frank's timing was right, and he placed a $200 bet. Naturally, I expected Gladys to slap him around and make him back off. But she didn't. She seemed kind of distracted. Maybe she just didn't notice. Anyway, the cards came out. Bang, blackjack Frank. Very nice.

Now the cocktail girl shows up. Gin and tonic, Frank; tonic only, with a twist, no ice, Gladys; and a Coke for me. Only Gladys makes a mistake and picks up the gin and tonic. Frank, already half in the bag, doesn't notice and takes a healthy pull on the tonic. I sip my Coke, and I start to get this strange feeling that somehow, someway, things are just a little bit out of sync.

Gladys takes a couple of small hits on the gin and tonic, doesn't seem to notice it's not straight tonic, and promptly excuses herself to go to the ladies room--gin and tonic in hand. Frank continues to pound the tonic only, with a twist, no ice, and I'm still sippin' my Coke--trying hard to shake this very weird feeling that somehow something is not quite right.

The funny thing is, the more Frank hammers down the tonic, the more wasted he seems to get. Psychological intoxication, I guess. Anyway, Gladys comes back. No gin. No tonic. Just a very empty glass. I thought she was allergic. Hmmm...

By now, wasted or not, Frank is really into the game. And he plays pretty well, too. In fact, in 20 minutes of play, as far as I can tell, he hasn't made a mistake. Easy hands and luck, I guess, or maybe there's something to that old saw about God taking care of drunks and little children, after all.

Of course, about every fifth or sixth hand he tries to bet the farm, but Gladys usually cuffs him around and makes him take it back. And it's a good thing too, because Frank seems to have a unique talent for making big bets on minus counts.

Then lightning strikes. The count goes really plus, with no Aces out. Big, big, plus deck. Now, as it happens, Gladys had let Frank get away with a $100 bet on the last hand, which he won. So Frank decides to let the $200 ride. And bet another hole for $200 more. $400 in total. *Jeez, luckout move,* I think to myself. But, of course, Gladys is going to screw it up and make him pull it back. But luck is really ridin' with him this time: Gladys is preoccupied chatting with a pit boss and doesn't pick up on Frank's huge and incredibly well-timed bet.

Cards come out. I get a pair of Queens. Frank has (10,King) on the first hand, and a pair of 9s on the second. Dealer has an Ace up. Uh oh. I take insurance. Frank looks over at me with a pained expression on his face; he takes insurance on both hands. *Good move, Frankie boy,* I think to myself. The dealer takes a peek. No blackjack. I smile. Frank smiles. Gladys looks over and sees what's going on. I expect her to either kill Frank or stroke out on the spot. Probably both. But this is not what happens.

Instead, Gladys gazes coolly at the layout. She just takes it all in, no emotion at all.

Frank sheepishly shows her his pair of 9s. He knows, and I know, he's had it. The right play, the advanced play, with this kind of monster count, is actually to split the 9s against the dealer's Ace. With this move Frank would have a fighting chance. Of course, Frank doesn't know this. This is why Frank is going to get his butt kicked. Eighteen against an Ace, especially with a big plus count, is your basic dead-meat hand.

Gladys contemplates the pair of 9s for a long moment, very intense, then pats Frank on the shoulder, twice. One, two. Frank gives her a fleeting kind of "really?" look, and proceeds to split the 9s. My jaw drops. The dealer shakes his head. Card to first 9: Ace. Card to second 9: Ace. Dealer flips over his hole card: 8 of Clubs.

No sooner has the dealer paid the hands than Frank scoops up the $1,200 in checks off the layout and, turning to Gladys, says something like, "Well, dear, maybe my luck's finally gunna change, after all." "Maybe so," she replies, "but let's quit for awhile before you give it all back, OK?"

And off they go, arm in arm, pockets bulging with $100 checks. Frank and Gladys, looking for all the world like a couple of extras from the Lawrence Welk polka parade.

Now somewhere during that last hand the scales finally began to fall from my eyes, and at last I saw Frank and Gladys for what they were: a team, an act. About the smoothest pair of professional card hustlers I have ever seen. Frank shoves out the money. *Gladys* counts the cards and controls the action. Very, very, slick. And very, very, effective.

There's more...

So, I'm sitting there, dazed and amazed, watching Frank and Gladys disappear up the escalator toward the second floor coffee shop. Finally, I looked up. The dealer had this impatient, "Well, pal, we gunna play cards, or what?" expression on his face. I hesitated. Then I figured, what the hell, this might be worth pursuing. So I got up, tossed a nickel[12] to the dealer, and headed up the escalator in hot pursuit of the polka prince and his dynamic dolly.

As I entered the coffee shop, I looked around and immediately spotted Frank and Gladys seated at the counter--with a spot open next to Gladys. *Hmmm, I thought, this might not be so tough, after all.*

I walked over and sat down. I figured if I was going to get anywhere, I had to open up first. So, catching Gladys' eye I said, "Hi, my name's Lance Pearson.[13] Looked like you two were doin' pretty good down there." Frank reached over to shake hands, "Good to meet ya, Lance, this is my wife, Gladys, and I'm Frank Ja...." "Dr. J. Everybody just calls him Dr. J.," Gladys cut in, before Frank could finish giving me what was probably, and foolishly, his real last name.

Well, this is it, I thought to myself, *make your move.* "Listen," I began softly, leaning over, so no one else could hear me, "I take my Blackjack seriously. I, uh, count cards, if you know what I mean, and I do pretty well at it, too. But from what I saw downstairs, you two are in a league of your own." I figured maybe flattery and a little humility might work. I figured right.

Frank smiled this big ear-to-ear grin. He was just too proud of himself not to bask in the warm glow of a little recognition. Gladys, on the other hand, was not about to give it up so easy. "What do you mean, exactly, Lance?" she came back, very noncommittal like.   "What I mean, Gladys," I continued, in hushed conspiratorial tones, "is that you and Frank have a hell of an act. None of the bosses in the pit, or the dealer, not even me until that last hand, picked up on what you two were doin' down there. It was beautiful. Really nice. On top of that you're one heck of a counter, Gladys. What do you play, Revere APC, HI-OPT II, what, exactly?" Gladys didn't answer. She just sat there for a minute looking at me. Wheels turning. Sizing me up. Finally, she spoke, "Revere APC, Lance, what do you play?" *Bingo!* "Same thing," I said, smiling. "Maybe you can give me a pointer or two."

And now, of course, they both opened up. It turns out, Frank was an engineer with a Silicon Valley electronics firm, and Gladys was a high school math teacher. Somehow, Frank had picked up the Blackjack bug about six or seven years ago

----

12. Casinospeak for $5.

13. I said open up. I didn't say open up with the truth.

and had become a small, but steady, loser in the clubs around Reno, Lake Tahoe, and Carson City. Gladys, always practical, figured if he was going to do it, he ought to do it right. So she bought him a copy of Revere's <u>Blackjack as a Business</u>, and popped $200 more for the <u>Revere Advanced Point Count</u>. Now, as you may remember from our discussion in Chapter Five, this strategy is strong, but it's also tough to learn and tough to use. Way too tough, as it turned out, for Frank. So, Gladys figured it was up to her. She told me she mastered the system in about six months and then set about teaching Frank how to bet with the count and play the hands with Basic Strategy. After that, it was just a matter of developing a set of signals and polishing their act to get to where they were when I found them.

Naturally, I couldn't resist asking them how they were doing, overall. Frank, not one to pass up a chance to do a little bragging, reached into Gladys' purse and pulled out a little black notebook. "We're doin' great, Lance. See this; it's a win/loss record of every trip we've ever made. Countin' this one, that's 129 trips in just under five years." "Really," I said, "that's a lot." "Oh yeah," Frank continued, "every other weekend we're out playing. All over the place too, not just Reno and Tahoe. We go to Las Vegas, Laughlin, lots of little towns you probably never heard of. Last year we even spent two weeks in the Caribbean. It was great. We made a small fortune."

"Mind if I take a look?" I said, as innocently as possible, reaching toward the little notebook. "I could definitely use the inspiration." "Yeah, I guess so," Frank replied, "sure why not?" But Gladys didn't necessarily buy into that idea. "Frank, he's a nice young man, but that's private, you know?" "Ah, come on, honey, it can't hurt. Like he says, give him a little inspiration, OK?" Not waiting for an answer from the hesitating Gladys, I reached for the notebook in Frank's outstretched hand.

"Jesus! you two ever lose?" I said, as I scanned through the notebook, looking at one win after another. "Oh yeah, we lose sometimes," volunteered Gladys. "Yeah, but not very often," countered Frank, with a wink and a smile.

"What's your gross win, Frank? Looks like it must be way over a hundred and fifty grand," I said, matter-of-factly. "Make that way over two hundred grand, Lance, my boy. In fact, counting this trip, it's just over two hundred and fifty thousand!" replied a very self-satisfied Frank.

"No shit!?" I exclaimed. "Excuse my language, Gladys, but that's incredible. How the hell did you get a big enough stake?" "What stake?" replied Frank. "We started out with just over $500."

And it was true. They started out betting $5 to $25, logged a couple of wins, and never looked back.

I <u>had</u> to have a copy of this notebook. A parlay of this kind is really tough to do, and I wanted to study it a lot more closely than I could in a few minutes over coffee.

I knew there was a copy machine at the front desk, which also happened to be on the second floor just around the corner from the coffee shop. So, I took my best shot.

"Frank, what you two have done is amazing. It just blows me away," I began. "It would mean a lot to me if you'd let me photocopy your win/loss record so I could study it and learn from it." Frank's hot button was flattery, and I was pushing it real hard. "I don' know, Lance. What do you think, honey?" *Damn!* I thought. *She'll never go for it.* "Lance," Gladys began, looking me hard in the eyes, "you know a lot more about us than you should know. But that's Frank. Sometimes he's a little bit, well, a little bit too trusting. If you want to photocopy the notebook, go ahead. With what you already know, it won't make that much difference. But one thing, if you ever see us again, you don't know us and we don't know you. Agreed?" "Yes, OK, absolutely, Gladys," I stammered, surprised as hell she was really going to let me do it.

So we walked over to the front desk, together, and I copied the six pages of Dr. and Mrs. J.'s win/loss trip record. On the way over, Gladys told me that their big-time Blackjack playing days were about over. Frank's health wasn't that good, and the strain of big-money play was beginning to take its toll. They'd decided to use their winnings to buy a nice farmhouse in a small town in Vermont near where Frank was born, move there in a year or so, and retire on their pensions. They'd had a great adventure, but now the adventure was just about over.

I thanked and shook hands with both of them, gave Gladys a little buss on the cheek, and as we wished each other luck, and turned to go our separate ways, Frank looked back at me and said, "Show it to your Blackjack buddies, Lance. Show 'em how it's done." And then they were gone.

Well, Blackjack buddies, take a look at Table 8.2. Take a long look, 'cause *that* is how it's done.

Table 8.2

DR. J.'S PERFECT PARLAY

Trip #	Bet Spread	Result	Trip #	Bet Spread	Result
1	$ 5 - $ 25	+$ 300	43	$25 - $100	+$2225
2	$ 5 - $ 25	+$ 395	44	$50 - $200	+$5235
3	$ 5 - $ 25	**-$ 40**	45	$50 - $200	+$4650
4	$ 5 - $ 25	+$ 170	46	$50 - $200	+$ 935
5	$ 5 - $ 25	**-$ 210**	47	$50 - $200	+$3095
6	$ 5 - $ 25	+$ 985	48	$50 - $200	+$3985
7	$ 5 - $ 25	+$ 105	49	$50 - $200	+$4930
8	$ 5 - $ 25	+$ 30	50	$50 - $200	+$5200
9	$ 5 - $ 25	+$ 380	51	$50 - $200	+$2910
10	$ 5 - $ 25	+$ 285	52	$50 - $200	+$5850
11	$10 - $ 50	+$ 450	53	$50 - $200	+$1425
12	$10 - $ 50	+$ 600	54	$50 - $200	**-$4950**
13	$10 - $ 50	+$ 790	55	$50 - $200	**-$3550**
14	$10 - $ 50	**-$ 300**	56	$50 - $200	+$7120
15	$10 - $ 50	**-$1105**	57	$50 - $200	**-$9455**
16	$10 - $ 50	+$ 900	58	$50 - $200	**-$3360**
17	$10 - $ 50	+$ 520	59	$50 - $200	+$3650
18	$10 - $ 50	+$1010	60	$50 - $200	+$3300
19	$10 - $ 50	+$ 330	61	$50 - $200	**-$2250**
20	$10 - $ 50	**-$ 330**	62	$50 - $200	**-$ 210**
21	$10 - $ 50	**-$ 285**	63	$50 - $200	+$3000
22	$10 - $ 50	+$1300	64	$50 - $200	+$4545
23	$10 - $ 50	+$ 500	65	$50 - $200	+$5895
24	$10 - $ 50	+$ 450	66	$50 - $200	+$4270
25	$10 - $ 50	**-$1190**	67	$50 - $200	+$5925
26	$10 - $ 50	**-$ 800**	68	$50 - $200	+$1200
27	$10 - $ 50	**-$1230**	69	$50 - $200	+$6765
28	$10 - $ 50	+$1830	70	$50 - $200	+$5625
29	$10 - $ 50	+$1020	71	$50 - $200	+$4635
30	$10 - $ 50	+$1080	72	$50 - $200	+$3555
31	$10 - $ 50	+$1610	73	$50 - $200	+$7770
32	$10 - $ 50	+$1400	74	$50 - $200	+$6125
33	$10 - $ 50	+$1010	75	$50 - $200	**-$9120**
34	$10 - $ 50	+$ 515	76	$50 - $200	**-$4860**
35	$25 - $100	+$3085	77	$50 - $200	+$5430
36	$25 - $100	+$1640	78	$50 - $200	+$2785
37	$25 - $100	+$3030	79	$50 - $200	**-$8940**
38	$25 - $100	+$3500	80	$50 - $200	+$1600
39	$25 - $100	+$3595	81	$50 - $200	+$1770
40	$25 - $100	+$1240	82	$50 - $200	+$5560
41	$25 - $100	+$2225	83	$100 - $400	+$10520
42	$25 - $100	+$2550	84	$100 - $400	+$ 6380

173

Table 8.2
(continued)

DR. J.'S PERFECT PARLAY

Trip #	Bet Spread	Result	Trip #	Bet Spread	Result
85	$100 - $400	+$ 8060	127	$100 - $400	+$ 8965
86	$100 - $400	+$ 7620	128	$100 - $400	**-$ 3580**
87	$100 - $400	**-$15760**	129	$100 - $400	+$ 4740
88	$100 - $400	+$14575			
89	$100 - $400	**-$ 7690**	Total Win ($):		$253910
90	$100 - $400	+$ 7585	Total # of Wins:		97
91	$100 - $400	+$11040	Total # of Losses:		32
92	$100 - $400	**-$ 4585**			
93	$100 - $400	+$20130			
94	$100 - $400	**-$ 3760**			
95	$100 - $400	+$ 4330			
96	$100 - $400	+$ 6525			
97	$100 - $400	**-$ 3610**			
98	$100 - $400	+$ 2805			
99	$100 - $400	+$ 1440			
100	$100 - $400	+$14725			
101	$100 - $400	+$13185			
102	$100 - $400	**-$ 7735**			
103	$100 - $400	+$ 2535			
104	$100 - $400	+$13890			
105	$100 - $400	+$ 2015			
106	$100 - $400	+$ 3255			
107	$100 - $400	+$ 6095			
108	$100 - $400	**-$ 6450**			
109	$100 - $400	**-$12275**			
110	$100 - $400	+$ 2970			
111	$100 - $400	**-$ 7260**			
112	$100 - $400	+$ 3940			
113	$100 - $400	+$ 3335			
114	$100 - $400	+$16580			
115	$100 - $400	+$ 5845			
116	$100 - $400	**-$ 4025**			
117	$100 - $400	**-$ 385**			
118	$100 - $400	+$ 6055			
119	$100 - $400	+$ 7035			
120	$100 - $400	**-$13245**			
121	$100 - $400	+$ 1185			
122	$100 - $400	+$ 1625			
123	$100 - $400	+$ 6165			
124	$100 - $400	**-$ 6955**			
125	$100 - $400	+$ 3395			
126	$100 - $400	+$ 5070			

And it is a truly amazing record. Because they didn't keep track of how many hours they played on each trip, it's hard to calculate their exact win percentage. But figuring about 12 hours per trip, and about 100 hands per hour, they played a little over 150,000 hands of serious Blackjack in a little less than five years. Based on this, and adjusting for bet size, I estimate their win rate at about +1.6%. Which, of course, is outstanding.

And take a look at some of those runs. From trip 28 to trip 53, they never lost! That's 26 wins in a row! God, that *is* incredible! Notice also, that they never lost more than three times in a row, and that only happened once. Jeez, I'm getting jazzed, all over again.

Understand, a parlay like this requires a tremendous amount of skill and discipline. Anywhere along the line it is easy to overbet your capital and blow the whole thing. But Frank and Gladys definitely had the right stuff. Notice, too, how they steadily increased their bets as their stake got larger.[14] This is about as close to the Kelly criterion as you can get in the real world with a system based on proportional betting.

Well, there's your inspiration, comrades, sort of a little reward for struggling through the first part of this chapter. And one more thing. Remember, the Advanced Omega II System is a little stronger than the Revere APC and a lot easier to play.

SUMMARY

I know some of this chapter was fairly heavy going; and, as I mentioned before, you don't really need this material to win with the systems in this book. But, I also know that two of the areas where even strong, seasoned players often get into trouble are in sizing their stake and sizing their bets. There are just a lot of temptations along the way to overbet and hope for the best.

But if you understand the principles here, really understand what sound betting strategy is all about, you are much more likely to resist these fatal seductions. And with some guts, some heart, and a bit of luck, there is no reason why you can't match, or even exceed, the impressive success of the wily Dr. and Mrs. J.

----

14. And, of course, if at any time a losing streak had significantly cut into their current stake, they would have *reduced* their bets, proportionately.

CHAPTER NINE

Special Weapons and Tactics

Welcome to advanced commando training. This is where you'll get the really wicked weapons and terrible tactics that take you beyond card counting into the world of the hustler, a dark domain where mercy and quarter are neither offered nor given.

This is war. A war that is forever changing and evolving. Casinos develop countermeasures. Counters and card hustlers develop measures to counter the countermeasures. And so on, and so on, with no end in sight.

Here are some of my favorite plays. They've made me a lot of money over the years, and I think you'll find them an interesting and powerful addition to your Blackjack war machine.

THE FREE HIT

With a fairly big minus count, the Advanced Omega II Strategy actually says to hit hard 17 against an Ace. This play looks very bizarre, so bizarre, in fact, that if you play your cards right you can get away with a free hit. This is how to do it: if the count is sufficiently minus, and you are dealt hard 17 against the dealer's Ace, act distracted and hold your cards in a casual, sort of uninterested way. When the dealer gets around to you, scratch for a hit. Just as the card hits the table glance at your hand and act startled. If the hit card is a 4 or less, whistle softly, mumble something about blind luck, and slide your hard 17 under your bet. If you bust, however, show the dealer your hard 17, tell him you weren't really paying attention and, of course, would never hit hard 17, intentionally. Most of the time the dealer will buy this story and toss the hit card into the return tray; sometimes he will ask for an OK from a pit boss first, but it's rare that your request for mercy will be denied.

Keep this play in mind if you are holding a stiff (12 through 16) against an Ace as well. When you hit the stiff, if you draw hard 17, and the count remains sufficiently minus, you can still make the above play for a free hit.

176

One word of caution. Don't make this play more than once per session. Greed is _not_ good. Greed can get you barred.

THE BOTTOM CARD

Sometimes, against some dealers, you will get a glimpse of the bottom card before the cut. If you cut the cards yourself you can put this card anywhere you want. If the bottom card is small, cut very thinly; this will put the bottom card near the bottom of the deck, and the dealer will shuffle before he gets to it. In effect, the deck starts off with a plus count equal to the value of the bottom card. If the card is large (Ace or 10) I generally cut it to about the middle of the deck, where I know it will be dealt before the shuffle. If you can vary the number of hands you are playing, you can also cut a large card to near the top of the deck and get it as your first card for a big advantage on that hand.

Another nice move is to cut the deck so that the bottom card ends up as the dealer's hole card. This takes practice, but if you can do it, it's worth it. For example, say it's your cut, you're playing with two other players, and you happen to see the bottom card. If you cut the bottom card to nine cards from the top of the deck, the dealer will get it as his hole card. Naturally, knowing the dealer's hole card adds a certain accuracy to your play.

If another player cuts, make note of where the bottom card goes and adjust the count and your play accordingly.

THE CUT CARD

Just as with the bottom card, sometimes you will get a peek at the cut card. Occasionally, this will happen when another player cuts the cards; when you do the cutting yourself, however, you can often arrange it so you see the cut card nearly every time.

This technique only works in single- and double-deck games, and only in those clubs that offer the deck to the player to cut, rather than giving him a plastic cut card to place in the deck.

The idea is to slightly tilt the top part of the deck toward you as you cut it away from the bottom part. For this move to work, you have to make it fast and angle the deck just barely enough to get a quick glimpse of the card as you cut it away from the deck.

No matter how fast or how smooth you are, however, some dealers will pick up on what you're doing, and they may not like it. So, if you get some flak, back off. A lot of dealers, though, will let it go if you're not too obvious about it.

Naturally, when you see the cut card, adjust your count immediately. The cut card goes to the bottom of the deck and is never dealt.

THE BURN CARD

Another card you will sometimes see is the burn card.

After the cut, most casinos burn, or discard, the top card before they begin to deal.

A lot of clubs, nowadays, simply toss this card into the return tray; some, however, especially in single-deck games, still follow the traditional practice of placing the burn card face up on the bottom of the deck.

Experienced dealers do this by rolling the top card to the bottom of the deck with a very quick wrist snap. When this is done properly, the burn card is just about impossible to see. Some dealers, however, aren't as fast or as smooth; with these guys you can generally see the burn card every time.

If you do see this card count it immediately, for as with the cut card it is never dealt.

One of the sweetest things in a single-deck game is to see the bottom card, cut it where you want it, glimpsing the cut card as you do, then catch the burn card as the dealer rolls it over.

Seeing these three cards can often give you better than a 1% edge right off the top of the deck!

WARPS AND TELLS

Tells

Some dealers give away their hole card when they check an Ace or 10 up for blackjack, but you generally have to be alert and watch a dealer very closely to pick up on these "tells." For example, many dealers will take a double peek at a 4 in the hole with a 10 up because a 4 looks similar to an Ace; others will "stroke the dukes" as they neatly align their hand with a 10 up and a 10 in the hole. Still others give themselves away by body language or facial expressions as players scratch for hit cards.

The bottom line is that once the dealer checks his hole card, he knows whether he has a strong or a weak hand, and he may give this information away with subtle tells.

It pays to watch for this. I recently played against a dealer who developed a small but uncontrollable eye tic every time he had a small card in the hole with a 10 up. This information allowed me to play him for a stiff in these situations, and during the 40 minutes he was "on" I won at an incredible rate.

And how's this for the ultimate giveaway: A couple of years ago I was playing at the Nugget in Carson City when a middle-aged, rather hard-looking, woman dealer came on. She'd obviously been a dealer for a long time--maybe too long, as it turned out.

Anyway, she started dealing; immediately I noticed that when she slid her hole card under the up card she lifted the front of the hole card just a little. Just a little bit, but sometimes just a little bit's a lot. I ordered a drink; I took a few sips, and I began to get very "drunk" very fast. With each sip, I sunk lower and lower into my seat. My eyes got glassy; my speech got slower; my coordination began to suffer. What a shame, another sheep about to get sheared. Except this sheep, now at eye level with the table, could see the dealer's hole card every time she slid it under. This sheep was about to do some shearing of his very own.

I stopped counting. No need. Knowing the dealer's hole card gives the player an advantage, with proper play, of nearly 10%![1] Even with the compromises I had to make to avoid giving myself away (such as not hitting hard 17 or more, or doubling down on soft 20), my advantage was still in the 7% range.

I placed my maximum bet of $200 and just kept it there. No bet spread at all. She was on for 40 minutes, and during that time I made a small fortune. After a while she started shuffling every two or three hands. Fine. She could shuffle every hand for all I cared. When she moved to another table, I wobbled off after her. Same result. Finally, after more than an hour, and in the glare of intense pit-boss scrutiny, I decided that I'd had enough fun and asked for a chip tray to carry my stacks of green and black checks to the cashier's cage. As I left the table I tossed a quarter ($25) check to the dealer. She was worth it.

----

1. See Table 9.1 for the proper Basic Strategy when the dealer's hole card is known.

Table 9.1

BASIC STRATEGY

When Dealer's Hole Card is Known

DEALER HAND	MH[1]	MS	PLAYER'S ACTION DOUBLE DOWN Hard	Soft	SPLIT
2,2	14	18	10,11		A,7,8
2,3	13	18	10,11		A-3,6-9
2,4	12	18	9-11	17,18	A-3,6-9
3,3	12	18	8-11	13-19	A-4,6-9
2,5	17	18	10,11		A-3,7,8
3,4	17	18	9-11		A-3,7,8
2,6	17	18	10,11		A,7-9
3,5	17	18	10,11		A-3,7-9
4,4	17	18	10,11		A-3,7-9
2,7	17	19	10,11		A,8,9
3,6	17	19	10,11		A,8,9
4,5	16	19	10,11		A,8,9
2,8	16	19	11		A,8
3,7	16	19	11		A
5,5	16	19	11		A
4,6	17	19	11		A
2,9	16	18			A
3,8	15	18			A
4,7	14	18			A
5,6	14	19			A
2,10	12	18	8-11	13-19	A-4,6-9
3,9	12	18	8-11	13-19	A-4,6-9
4,8	12	18	8-11	13-19	A-4,6-9
5,7	12	18	8-11	13-20	A-4,6-10
6,6	12	18	8-11	13-20	A-4,6-10
Hard 13	12	18	7-11	13-20	A-4,6-10
Hard 14	12	18	5-11	13-20	A-4,6-10
Hard 15	12	18	5-11	13-20	A-4,6-10
Hard 16	12	18	5-11	13-20	A-4,6-10
Hard 17	17	18			2,3,6-8
8,10	18	19			2,3,7-9
9,9	18	19			3,6-9
9,10	19	19			9
10,10	20	20			
A,A	16	18	11		A,8
A,2	15	18	10,11		A,7,8
A,3	14	18	10,11		A,7,8
A,4	13	18	10,11		A,2,6-9
A,5	13	18	9-11	17,18	A-3,6-9
A,6	17	18			A-3,6-8
A,7	18	19			2,3,7-9
A,8	19	19			9
A,9	20	20			

----
1. MH IS THE PLAYER'S MINIMUM HARD STANDING TOTAL.
   MS IS THE PLAYER'S MINIMUM SOFT STANDING TOTAL.

Although I've been back to the Nugget several times since then, I've never seen her again. I bet she's still dealing somewhere though, and sooner or later our paths will cross again. Anyway, I sure hope so.[2]

When you find a consistent tell, stick with the dealer. Follow him around from table to table. This is not unusual; people follow "lucky" dealers around this way all the time.

Also, make note of his name, the casino, what shift he deals on, what he looks like, and just what his tell is. This is very valuable information, and you'll want it for the next time.

Be careful, however, of dealers with inconsistent tells, or dealers who know they have a tell and compensate for it with offsetting behavior. These guys can really mess you up. One dealer, for example, had the common tell of taking a double peek with a 4 in the hole, but he knew he did this and compensated by sometimes randomly double peeking other hole cards. So you have to be careful. Just be sure of the tell before you risk any money on it.

Because tells are so powerful for the player, many casinos no longer have the dealer check his hole card with a 10 up. This costs the casino money by wasting time when the dealer has blackjack, but these casinos believe (probably correctly) that this loss is less than the loss due to tells. A lot of casinos still do check for blackjacks with a 10 up, however, so this technique is not likely to become obsolete any time soon.

Warps

Warps are really another kind of tell. But here the cards, rather than the dealer, tell the tale.

Warps can happen any time the dealer or the players handle the cards. Intentionally warping or bending the cards is a form of card marking--and that's cheating. I do not cheat. I advise you not to cheat, as well. Not only is it illegal, but to me there isn't much satisfaction in winning by cheating, either. With a little practice anyone can do that. But beatin' 'em at their own game, that's where the real fun is.

----

2. This, of course, went beyond just a tell; this was what I call a "show-and-tell," also sometimes known as "front-loading."

And, fortunately, honest warps occur too. One common way this happens is when the dealer checks for a blackjack. The right way for the dealer to do this is to carefully lift up both the up and hole card without bending them. New dealers are careful to do this. Old hands, however, especially ham-fisted male dealers, will sometimes bend the top card (the Ace or 10) as they check the hole card. The result is that after a while most of the 10s and Aces will have a small but noticeable concave bend to them. This means that in subsequent hands when you see a *convex* bend to the dealer's face-down hole card, it must be either an Ace or 10. This is valuable information. Very valuable information.

Because single and double decks are changed frequently, it is unusual to find them badly warped in this way. Multiple decks, however, are usually only changed once each shift, so there is plenty of time and opportunity for them to get good and warped.

The best way to find a warped deck is to look around for a shoe game and a dealer that really gives his hand a good bend when he checks for blackjacks. Then observe the dealer's hole card; see if you can consistently tell when he has an Ace or 10 in the hole by the convex warp of the hole card. When you find a deck you can read like this stay with it. Count and play as you normally would until you pick up on a hole card, then vary your play based on this new information.[3]

Sometimes when a pack of cards have been in play for a while, a few of them will pick up a random warp here and there through rough handling. Be on the lookout for this. If you can identify several cards this way it's money in the bank. Not only can you use the information to read the dealer's hole card, but occasionally you can even read the warp on the top card in the shoe.

As with tells, fewer cards are being warped these days because most casinos no longer check for blackjacks with a 10 up. But some casinos still do check and, in any case, random warps can and do occur.

Reading warps and tells is a real art. And although we've touched on some of the more common ways you can exploit them to your advantage, there are advanced techniques used by virtuoso hustlers in Las Vegas, and elsewhere, that go considerably beyond our discussion here.

----

3. Generally, because the pack contains four times as many 10s as Aces, play the dealer for a 10 in the hole. However, if the dealer has an Ace up and you lose your insurance bet, the warped hole card must obviously be an Ace.

END PLAY

End play as we knew it in the good ol' days B.T. (before Thorp) is just about gone today, but there is a variation on this theme that does occasionally show up. It works like this: A few casinos deal double-deck and multiple-deck games down to a plastic cut card, then shuffle right in the middle of the hand. This is not the usual way; most clubs finish the round and then shuffle, but a few do shuffle when they reach the cut card.

If you play in a club like this, position yourself at or near first base (holes one or two), preferably with two or three other players to your left, toward third base. When the count goes plus down deep near the cut card, vary the number of hands you play to ensure that each of your hands gets a card, but the dealer reaches the cut card before he deals his up card. Alternately, you can play so that each of your hands gets two cards, and the dealer only gets his up card and has to shuffle before he deals his hole card.

The other players to your left give you some margin of error in determining how many hands to play; this is because the further downstream a player is, the less likely he is to get a card before the shuffle. Of course, the dealer is the last player downstream, so it's not hard to arrange things so that the shuffle comes before he deals to his own hand.

Done right, you will get one card more from the plus deck than the dealer will. With one or both of the dealer's cards coming from a freshly shuffled, probably somewhat minus deck, you figure to have a big overall advantage on all your hands.

In clubs like this, you can also end play the dealer when the count goes really minus late in the pack. In this situation, the idea is to force the dealer to shuffle with as many small cards as possible still on the table. You can do this by playing several holes, usually three or four, all with minimum bets; then hit and split wherever possible to eat up as many cards as you can without busting,[4] until you force a shuffle.

----

4. Actually, you just don't want to bust hands comprised of several small cards. Hands with 10s and Aces in two or three cards should be busted, so they're included in the shuffle.

As soon as the dealer shuffles, count the cards on the table to pick up the new count; then stand on all your hands, regardless of their totals,[5] and wait for the next round.

The beauty of this move, of course, is that it removes a number of small cards from the newly shuffled pack. You can make maximum bets right off the top, and keep them there as long as the count remains plus.

This is a nice move, but it looks fairly bizarre in practice, so don't overdo it; just save it for those few really minus counts way down deep near the end of the pack.

THE QUADRUPLE DOWN

I almost didn't include this one. It's just a little too raw for my taste. Although I don't consider it actually cheating, there is no doubt that it's right on the ragged edge.

There is, however, also no doubt that a lot of card hustlers have made a lot of money with this one.

It goes like this:[6] Normally, when a player is going to double down, he waits until the dealer gets around to him, then places his cards face up on the layout and slides an additional wager equal to his original bet next to that original bet. That's the way it's usually done, but that's not the only way it can be done.

Here's another way: Position yourself near third base at a full table. When you have a double-down situation, turn up your cards and double your bet immediately; don't wait for the dealer to work his way around to you. One more little thing. When you double your bet, place the additional wager *on top* of the original bet, not next to it, side-by-side.

When the dealer gets around to you, one of two things is going to happen: (1) He will notice that you have doubled your bet, so he will size it side-by-side, himself, deal the double-down card and move on. In this scenario, he may or may not ask you to place your double-down wagers next to your original bet in the future. (2) He doesn't realize you have doubled your bet, so he will pause, give

----

5. So as not to waste cards from the freshly shuffled plus deck on minimum bets.

6. Compare Stanford Wong, Winning Without Counting, p. 211.

you an expectant look, and wait for you to double your wager. So, give him what he wants, double your bet. Of course, when you do, you are actually *quadrupling* your original bet, for a big-time boost to your overall advantage.

But don't get greedy. One time per playing session is about the limit, and pick your dealers carefully. Also, when you make this play, act as if you're distracted and aren't really paying much attention, that way when the dealer prompts you to double your bet, it's believable that you might not remember you have already doubled down.

OK, OK, I know, this is a chiseling play more suited to card hustlers than card counters, but if the dealer *invites* you to quadruple your bet is it really polite to just say no?

TEAM PLAY

Ah, team play. Or should I say dream play? This is definitely one of my favorites.

The basic idea of team play is to have several counters making minimum bets and playing Basic Strategy, situated at tables around a casino, while the money player, the Big Player,[7] sort of hangs out waiting for subtle signals from the counters that a shoe has gone plus. When that happens the Big Player saunters over and begins making large bets, one after another, until the dealer shuffles or the count goes minus. At this point if the BP gets the high sign from another counter, he wanders over to that table. Otherwise he drifts over to the bar, or to some other convenient place where he can watch the counters, and waits for the next plus shoe. Really, a very simple concept.

Team play was originally developed as a way to counter the use by casinos of multiple decks. Of course, multiple decks were originally put in by casinos to stop, or at least slow down, counters. So, team play can be seen as a classic historical example of the ongoing battle of measure and countermeasure that continues in the casinos to this day.

In earlier chapters, I made the point that although multiple decks are not particularly difficult to count, such games do yield a slower win rate than one- and

----

7. To my knowledge this term was coined by Ken Uston in his fascinating book on team play, <u>The Big Player</u>.

two-deck games, primarily because during play the density deviations of the various cards are smaller. In other words, multiple decks are less volatile than single and double decks, so there are fewer, and smaller, winning opportunities to exploit.

But it is this very flatness, this stability of multiple-deck games, that makes them perfect for team play. This is because when a shoe finally does go plus, it is likely to stay plus right down to the shuffle, thus affording camouflage to the Big Player's action. This contrasts sharply with single-deck games, where the true count jumps all over the place from one hand to the next.

Also, the fact that four-, six-, and eight-deck shoes, unlike one and two decks, yield many, many hands between shuffles makes them ideal for team play. In fact, the greater the number of decks in play, the better off we are! My personal favorite is eight-deck shoes. Before I got involved in team play, I avoided Atlantic City, with its mostly eight-deck games, like the plague. Now I'm there with my team so often I think I'm starting to pick up a Jersey accent.

Although there are a lot of ways to run a team, this is how I do it. First off, you have to assemble a team. My teams consist of the Big Player (me) and four or five counters.

Four or five counters is about right, because with this many different games being monitored, there is almost always at least one plus shoe. This makes it possible for the Big Player to just naturally stroll from table to table, seemingly on whim. With fewer counters, the win rate is less, and the BP has the problem of what do when none of his counters is signaling plus shoe.

Generally, I have found it both difficult and expensive to coordinate gambling trips to faraway places with a lot of team members, so I recruit my counters locally.

In Las Vegas, Atlantic City, and all the major gambling towns, there is a large underground of pro and semi-pro counters and hustlers. These guys are always looking for an easy way to make a buck or two at the tables, and they are usually pretty easy to spot as they prowl the casinos, as well. When you meet one, you meet his friends; pretty soon you know them all. It's not hard to tie in with the local hustler network.

Once you've made the right contacts, it's easy to recruit local counters for team play.

When I'm going to Las Vegas or Atlantic City for a team hit, I usually call a few days ahead and set up a meeting with my intended four or five counters. That way, when I arrive it's easy to get together, work out the details, and get down to business with a minimum of lost time.

Now, you have to be careful with local talent. These guys are usually hustlers. Many of them cannot be trusted--certainly not with money that is not their own.

You also want to be careful to select counters who can actually count. Test them on this. Don't take their word for it. It's also better if they use the same, or at least the same level, count you do. This way when they pass you the count, you know what it means.

And no drinking of alcoholic beverages during the playing day. Not just at the table; I mean not at all. Period.

When they play on my team, they play my way, or no way.

If I run into an attitude problem, he's history. No excuses; no second chances. I'm nice about it. I don't make enemies, but I don't make exceptions either. You have to be this way if you're going to risk your serious money on someone else's count.

Most BPs give their counters small stakes to play with. I do not. On my team they play with their own money. If they win, they keep it. If they lose, it's their problem.

I usually schedule team trips for three days, five or six hours per day, for a total of 15 to 18 actual hours of total play.

At the end of each day we have an accounting, and I show the counters just how I'm doing. Right down to the last penny. You may not trust them, but it's important that they trust you. I am square with my counters. I never cheat them. They get every cent they're due. Get them to trust you, depend on you; never give them a reason to finger you to the casino bosses.

At the end of the third, and last, day, we meet for a final settlement. I split my winnings 65/35. Sixty-five percent for me. Thirty-five percent split equally among the counters. Once in a while (about one time in four) the trip is unsuccessful, and I lose. In that case, I eat the entire loss.

In solo play, against one and two decks, I average a win rate of about 1.5%. In team play my win rate against six- and eight-deck shoes is about 2.0%. However, I am spending 35% of each win on counters. You might think this would leave me with 65% of the 2.0% for a net win rate of 1.3%. Not so. Remember, when I lose I eat the entire loss, so my net win rate is reduced to about 1.0%. However, because every bet in team play is a maximum bet, my actual dollar win is significantly larger in team play than in solo play with the same maximum bet. In addition, even though the average bet in team play is larger than in solo play, so is the average player advantage. This results in a probability of ruin for team play that is about the same as in solo play.

In other words, team play not only makes multiple decks more playable, it makes them ideal. Bring on the shoes!

Oh, one more thing. Keep your signals simple, subtle, and very natural looking. Nothing too tricky. And nothing that might look artificial or contrived to the casino bosses. It's also desirable to have several levels of signals to indicate various plus counts. This way, you can distinguish a really hot shoe from one that is only slightly plus (in Las Vegas or Atlantic City, use an Ace-adjusted Omega II true count of +5, or equivalent, as the minimum count to "call in" the BP).

Team play takes work, but if it's done right you can make a fortune with it.

THE RENO SHUFFLE

This one's a beauty. The first time I stumbled onto it I couldn't believe my eyes.

It happened like this: I was playing at Harolds Club one bright spring morning several years ago. I had been losing steadily for about half an hour, and decided to get more aggressive with my bet spread to make up for Harolds rather tough Reno rules.

After a few minutes of this, spreading my bets $50 to $250, the dealer began to shuffle whenever I jacked up my bet over $100. She was so consistent in doing this that, on a lark, I decided to test her. The count went moderately *minus*; I jumped my bet from $50 to $150. Instant shuffle. I cut back, waited for another minus deck, and tried again. Same result: immediate shuffle. I couldn't believe my eyes! I couldn't believe a dealer would let me control the action this way, but she was. So now, I began to play as follows: I bet $200 off the top and kept betting $200 until the deck went significantly minus. At that point, I jacked my bet up to $300; presto, the dealer shuffled away the bad cards. I cut back to $200, and started the process all over again! Is this beautiful or what?

This continued for about another 40 minutes or so, until I finally decided I'd had enough fun for one session.

Since then, I have found several casinos, all in the Reno area, that can be controlled this way. One dealer, apparently out of frustration, actually asked me, as she was shuffling away a minus deck, "Do you know it's illegal to make a dealer shuffle the cards?" I just smiled innocently and asked her how a player could make the dealer shuffle the deck.

I have never been able to work this gambit anywhere but Reno; I'm amazed that it works at all. Maybe the altitude and thin air have something to do with it; I don't know. What's especially surprising is that this caper only comes into play *after* the casino suspects you of being a counter. Yet I have occasionally worked this play for hours on end with no additional heat. Unbelievable. Unbelievable, but true.[8]

SAND BAGGING

Generally speaking, you have to limit your bet spread to fairly modest limits to avoid being detected as a card counter. There are, however, a couple of techniques that will enable you to greatly increase your overall effective bet spread. One of these I call Sand Bagging.

Sand Bagging works like this: Say, you're playing in a single- or double-deck game and the count goes really bad. Few or no Aces and a big, big minus count. Most of the time, in situations like this, you just have to cut back your bet, play your cards and hope for the best. Occasionally, however, when you see this coming you can work it another way. *You can create an excuse to stay out of the hand*, as well as the next hand or two, until the dealer shuffles. There are several ways you can do this. One of my favorites is to pull my wallet out, start counting my cash and checks, slowly, and just motion the dealer to pass me by when he pauses for me to place my bet.

Another good diversion is to spill a small amount of your drink, just enough to require a little mop-up job. With a little practice, you can learn to milk this simple task for, say, two, three hands, no problem.

Or how about this one: The count goes bad; you place a small bet and lose. In seeming disgust, you make a big deal about it and refuse to play the next hand, saying something to the dealer like, "Jeez pardner, cut me some slack! I'm afraid I'm goin' to have to sacrifice my friends here 'til the cards turn around." Then

----

8. Compare Edward O. Thorp, Beat the Dealer, rev. ed. p. 127.

you just sit there and watch the other players get slaughtered for a hand or two until the dealer shuffles. Yeah, that one works great.

Against multiple decks, because you get so many hands between shuffles, it's even easier. Just get up, head for the john, and time your re-entry to coincide with the shuffle. What could be easier than that?

So, as you can see, there are a lot of ways to make this play. The basic idea, however, remains the same: Find a convenient, and believable, excuse not to get involved with really bad decks. And the payoff is big. In effect, your bet spread rises by as much as 50% (e.g. from 4:1 to 6:1), which is important for really good results in today's tougher games. Not bad. Not bad at all.

SHORT CHANGING

Short Changing is a variation on the Sand Bagging theme. It goes like this: Say, you're playing quarter ($25) checks at a nickel ($5) game. After a while you're bound to pick up some small change from minimum bet blackjacks. You could just stack this stuff onto some quarters the next time the count is right, but don't. Just hang onto it. Wait for a really bad count, then bet this blackjack "junk," saying something to the dealer like, "Mind if I get rid of this stuff? I never know what to do with it."

This looks natural. A lot of regular players do this. And, like Sand Bagging, it allows you to get out of bad decks real cheap.

TRACKING SLUGS

How would you like to sometimes play in double-deck games where the dealer not only deals down to the last card, but is nice enough to slip in several extra 10s and Aces, as well--all with full approval of the casino bosses?

Think I've been in the sun too long? Read on.

In multiple-deck games (especially four- and six-deck games) it is often possible to follow a block (slug) of cards through the shuffle, and use this information to your decided advantage.

It works like this: Say, you're playing in a four-deck game where they deal three decks and cut off one (this is typical). When it comes time to shuffle, it is common for the dealer to take the undealt slug from the shoe and place it on top of the cards from the discard tray. Then, typically, the dealer will divide the four decks into two blocks of two decks, each. Obviously, one of these two-deck blocks will contain the undealt slug sitting right on top. Next, the dealer will take about a half deck from each of these two blocks, shuffle them together, and place this shuffled "pick" off to the side. This process will be repeated, with each new shuffled pick placed on top of the previous one, until both of the two-deck blocks have been thoroughly shuffled together to form a new four-deck pack.

"Thoroughly," however, like beauty, is often in the eye of the beholder.

In the above scenario, for instance, the undealt slug from the shoe would end up shuffled into the *bottom* two decks of the newly shuffled four-deck pack. After the cut, this two-deck slug could end up anywhere, but if you watch closely you'll see where it goes. Of course, if *you* cut, you can put it right at the top of the shoe.

And, not only do you know where this two-deck slug is, *you also know its count*. Why? Consider this. Let's say the running count at the end of the last round before the shuffle is, say, +15, with three "extra" Aces. This means that the undealt (10-rich) slug must have a running count of -15, because a "balanced" count has an equal number of positive and negative points. Now, during the shuffle, this -15 slug will be mixed up with another deck to form a two-deck block. Since the undealt slug has a count of -15, the remaining three decks must, necessarily, have a combined count of +15. On average, this +15 count will be evenly spread among the three decks, so each of the three decks can be assumed to have a count of +5. This means that the two-deck slug we are tracking would on average have a running count of -10 (-15+5). By similar logic, it can be shown that this two-deck slug would also, on average, contain two "extra" Aces (+3-1).

Now, as play resumes with the reshuffled pack, "sand bag" or "short change" until you get to the Ace/10-rich two-deck slug then revert to a running count of +10, with two "extra" Aces, and bet and play accordingly (estimating the true count for the *entire* slug as +10/2 = +5, with one "extra" Ace per deck).

There are many variations on slug-tracking through the green-felt jungle, and it does take some practice, but it can be an important way to increase your advantage in multiple-deck games.

COMPUTERS

Computers are my business. Outside Blackjack, computers are what I do. I sell them through my computer specialty stores; I work with them; I play with them, and I program them, for fun, favor, and profit.

One thing I don't do with computers is use them to count cards at Blackjack. I consider that little more than a crutch for players too lazy or too slow to learn how to count on their own.

Besides, if the casino bosses spot you using a concealed Blackjack computer, they'll most likely have you arrested and confiscate the computer. That could be unpleasant, not to mention expensive.

Overall, it's just not worth the hassle.

Not worth it--except for this:

About a year ago a friend of mine, Mr. P., a noted computer engineer and general mathematical wizard, called me at the office and asked me if I would be interested in seeing a demonstration of a small concealable Blackjack computer that he had developed in collaboration with a Mr. F.

This computer had a very special talent: It could read the dealer's hole card!

Now, to say the least, I was interested. I was also very, very skeptical. Especially so, because Mr. F. is a well-known Las Vegas card hustler and slight-of-hand master, deluxe. There is virtually nothing Mr. F. cannot do with a deck of cards.

But my friend Mr. P. assured me he had programmed the thing himself, and believe it or not--it actually worked!

So, with skepticism intact, and a fresh, unopened pack of Bee No. 92 cards in hand, I headed off to Mr. P.'s.

Arriving at Mr. P.'s, I was shortly joined by the infamous Mr. F., and Mr. F.'s Las Vegas showgirl companion, the lovely and leggy Ms. Beverly K.

Now, down to cases. Sitting on the dining room table was a shuffled deck of cards and a small black box about the size and shape of a pack of cigarettes. Two small switches, which looked like tiny accelerator pedals, rose side-by-side from the top of the box.

They called their little creation, Black Magic.

I assumed nothing. Rather, I should say, I assumed the worst. As far as I was concerned their deck was marked, the table was rigged, and there was absolutely no way Mr. F. was going to touch the cards.

No problem. "Pick a spot on the floor; you deal, and use your own cards," Mr. F. generously offered.

OK, but I was still suspicious. Anyway, we all plopped down in the middle of Mr. P.'s living room, and I opened up and thoroughly shuffled the deck I had brought along with me. I mean thoroughly.

Finally, satisfied, I cut the cards myself, and began to deal seven holes, face up. As I did, Mr. P. manipulated the tiny switches on Black Magic, entering in the cards as they fell. No one touched the cards but me. All the hands were played by Basic Strategy. I dealt two rounds of seven holes each, carefully dealing, picking, and paying in standard casino fashion. "Time to shuffle," I said. "Fine," replied Mr. F. "We've already got a 'working deck.'"

So, I shuffled again, and began to deal another round. I played out the first three hands and then gave a hit card to hand number four. It was the 5 of Clubs. Just as I was about to hit it again, Black Magic gave off with a series of beeps. "Ask it again; make sure," Mr. F. said to Mr. P. "I'm sure," replied Mr. P. "The hole card's a 7; 7 of Hearts to be exact." I flipped over the hole card. Seven of Hearts. Amazing.

And this was no fluke. Black Magic could finger the dealer's hole card about 75% of the time. The reason it sometimes missed is because the "working deck" it creates as the cards fall is incomplete because the shuffle comes before the end of the deck. It just doesn't "see" all the cards. But because it knows the composition of a full pack it also knows which cards it has not seen. So, although it sometimes can't determine the dealer's hole card (if it happens to be one of these undealt cards) it never makes a mistake and indicates the wrong hole card. It either knows what the hole card is and says so, or it says nothing. Most of the time it knows.

Can this really be true? Yes, as it turns out, it can.

I am not going to give away the exact algorithm (computer program) Black Magic uses, but I will say that the basic principle is that the dealer's hole card is the only card that is dealt but not immediately seen. Think about it.

You want a little more? OK. Consider this: suppose you know the order of the pack (the working deck); suppose further that you link each card, so that card 1 is paired with card 2; 2 with 3; 3 with 4, and so on. Suppose, also, that as the cards are shuffled the order of the pairings does not change, but merely spreads out as other cards are inserted between them. In other words, after the shuffle, card 1 still precedes card 2, but now there are several additional cards inserted between cards 1 and 2. This, of course, is an oversimplification; sometimes the pairings do reverse order, but when that happens Black Magic is programmed to compensate for it.

Assume, for the moment, however, that no such reversals occur. Black Magic starts with a working deck, and the order of the pairings is maintained right through the shuffle: card 1 precedes 2, 2 comes before 3, and so on, right to the end of the deck.

Now comes the deal. As soon as Black Magic "sees" the second card of a pairing, but has not yet seen the first, it knows the first card of the pairing has been dealt but not yet seen. Hmmm, what card do you suppose that could be? Black Magic knows: the dealer's hole card. Yeah, it's that simple--and that slick.[9]

The actual algorithm Black Magic uses is, of course, a lot more complicated than the simplification above.[10] This is especially true for the multiple-deck version of Black Magic (called Multiple Magic), which has to distinguish between different cards of the same rank and suit, but the basic idea remains the same.

Black Magic is a stunning tribute to the innovative brilliance of Mr. F. and the engineering genius of Mr. P.

It's also a terrifying nightmare to casino bosses everywhere.

If you're interested in these intriguing little toys, get to know the Las Vegas and A.C. undergrounds, and check the classified ads in the major newspapers in L.A., Las Vegas, New York, and New Jersey. You may find what you're looking for. But they don't come cheap. The going price for Black Magic is $10,000.[11]

CASINO PROMOTIONS

Casinos are always running promotions of one kind or another. They have to if they want to keep the players coming and the action humming.

----

9. You may wonder whether more thorough shuffling could defeat Black Magic. A recent study by mathematicians Persi Diaconis of Harvard University and Dave Bayer of Columbia shows that it would take at least seven shuffles to overwhelm Black Magic. Casinos do not shuffle seven times. Not yet.

10. For instance, Black Magic actually links the cards in triplets of three rather than in pairings of two. This is what allows it to compensate for reversals. The simpler "pairings" technique has been presented here for demonstration purposes only.

11. And be forewarned: their legal status is in doubt, and many casinos consider the use of Blackjack computers to be outright cheating.

These come-ons often take the form of bonus coupons redeemable for slot play or table-game action.

Once in a while a really good one comes along. In the spring of 1991, for example, the Edgewater hotel/casino in Laughlin ran a promotion for hotel guests checking into their new 26-story tower. It worked like this: in addition to other goodies, they gave you a coupon that allowed you to select any blackjack of your choice and be paid at 2:1, instead of the usual 3:2. A nice fat 50% bonus. Unfortunately for them, they forgot to include all the little strings that usually go along with such freebies. For instance, they had no rule about only one coupon per person, and no restrictions on transfer of the coupons from one person to another. They really should have been more careful.

So, never one to pass on free money, I cruised the $2 tables and promptly bought up a couple dozen of these little beauties at the bargain price of $5 each.

Next, after a discreet wait, I showed up at the $25 tables and proceeded to cash in my coupons on $100 blackjacks. Every time I did this I profited to the tune of $50 (less the $5 I paid for the coupon).

Needless to say, over the next few days, I made a lot of money with this one.

Of course, not every promotion is as good as this, but a surprising number of worthwhile giveaways are available. It definitely pays to keep your eyes wide open.

JUNKETS

If you like the idea of flying the world first class, staying in top-notch hotel/casino resorts, and eating in five-star gourmet restaurants, all absolutely free, you may want to consider casino junkets.

Gambling resorts offer junkets to lure high-rolling premium players into their casinos.

Generally, they expect you to deposit from $5,000 to $15,000 into the casino cage, and play one or more of the major table games (Blackjack, Baccarat, Roulette, or Craps) at a level of at least $50 per bet, four or more hours a day.

That's it. Give them the action they want, and they're more than happy to shower you with first-class, VIP treatment.

You have to be careful with junkets, though. The main problem is that you usually have to give them your real name, and when you play, they monitor your action closely.

For these reasons I do not do junkets to casinos I depend on for regular, serious play. This means I generally stay clear of Nevada and Atlantic City. For me, these are working towns, not party towns.

But the resorts in Monaco on the French Riviera, Aruba, Nassau, Paradise Island, and elsewhere in the Caribbean, all over the Orient, and cruise ships from California to the Caribbean to the Mediterranean all offer gambling junkets that include everything you could ever want in red-carpet, all-expense-paid, free vacations.

When I go on one of these little adventures, I check into the Blackjack rules, customs, and reputation of the resort in question, very carefully, before I put up any money.

Depending on what I find, I either play serious money to win or just the minimum to keep the casino bosses happy and the comps coming. Either way, I end up way, way ahead of the game.

You can arrange junkets directly with the resort or cruise ship line, or through travel agents and brokers who specialize in gambling promotions.

Either way, after you've been on one or two, your name will start showing up on sucker lists, and you'll begin to get solicitations from all over the world. Trust me on that one.

Handled right, junkets are worth a minimum of $25,000 a year in free first-class vacations. Not counting your winnings. I love junkets.

THE FIVE-CARD TRICK

This one's my favorite, so I've saved it for last.

When you bust you only *lose* if the dealer takes your bet. Sometimes, if you bust with 22 in five or more cards a careless dealer may think you have 21--especially if you smile, whistle softly and slide your hole cards under your bet.

This slippery play generally earns 200% every time the dealer "buys" it.

SUMMARY

Well, there they are. Just about every crafty, scheming, devious tactic I have picked up in over 15 years of serious money play on the pro Blackjack tour.

Combined with the Advanced Omega II System, they constitute a method of play that is virtually invincible. Good hunting!

CHAPTER TEN

Casino Cheating

No book on Blackjack would be complete without a discussion of the highly charged and controversial subject of cheating.

The casinos, as we discussed earlier, are continually being assaulted by cheating players and insider scams.

But that's their problem and not our concern here. What we care about is the possibility of being cheated by casinos doing a little scamming of their own.

Does this happen? Do casinos sometimes cheat players at Blackjack and other games?

Yes, without question, they sometimes do.

The mere fact that the Nevada State Gaming Control Board, though not noted for aggressive enforcement, has nevertheless closed down several large clubs for cheating is proof positive that some violations do occur.

The range of "expert" opinions of just how commonly this happens runs from those who believe the problem is rampant to those who believe it's exceedingly rare.

I believe the truth lies somewhere in between.

If cheating were common, however, neither I nor any other pro player could win, certainly not at the rate some of us do win at.

Consider Dr. J., for example. He played about 155,000 hands of serious Blackjack. Assuming high-quality games, high-quality play, and *no* cheating, his theoretical win rate should have been +1.5% plus or minus .4% (+1.1% to +1.9%). In fact, he won at the rate of about +1.6%, which is right up in there. Obviously, Dr. J. encountered little, if any, cheating.

I am not an expert at detecting cheating. In general, I know what to look for, but a sleight-of-hand master like, say, Mr. F. of Chapter Nine, would have no trouble picking my bones clean before I ever knew what happened.

Yet I continue to win at a rate well within the theoretical range, so it is clear that I, like Dr. J., have not encountered much, if any, cheating.

I feel confident in saying that in the large, legal casinos of Nevada and Atlantic City you are very unlikely to encounter any casino-sanctioned cheating. Smaller clubs, especially in out of the way places, might be a little riskier.

Now, having said that, I have to tell you that I have personal knowledge that a small amount of cheating does, in fact, occur.

Consider this: A few years ago I was in Las Vegas for a weekender and walked into a large downtown club. As I strolled around the pits looking for a good game, I was startled to see a dealer I recognized as a colleague from my days as a systems analyst with the Data Systems Division of Litton Industries. Let's call him Gary.

He recognized me, too, so I sat down and began playing for small stakes while we chatted about old times and what we'd been doing for the last couple of years. After a few minutes the table began to fill up, so Gary and I agreed to meet for coffee on his break, and I wandered off to another game.

Anyway, later on, as we sat over coffee getting caught up, it became clear that Gary was going through some rough times. It turns out his marriage of 10 years had broken up, so he had left Southern California for a new start in Las Vegas.

Unfortunately, things really weren't getting that much better. He had hoped to get a lucrative job on the Strip dealing Craps or Blackjack at a major hotel, but he soon realized that without the right connections the best he could hope for was a job downtown in some grind joint dealing for scale plus small-change tokes. Barely enough to cover his rent and child-support payments.

So after a while, hurting badly for money, he fell in with a local Fagin-like hustler whose specialty was recruiting Blackjack dealers down on their luck, training them to deal seconds,[1] and then showing them how to cheat regular players and dump the excess profits back to him. All "winnings," of course, to be split down the middle, 50/50.

He told me this sordid stuff in part to get it off his chest, but also in part to see if he could recruit me for the team. They needed a fresh face to dump the money to.

Thanks. But no thanks. I absolutely do not cheat.

----

1. The single most common technique used by cheating dealers is to surreptitiously identify the top card of the deck by "peeking," and then hold it back for later use by dealing the second and subsequent cards immediately below.

But I might be amenable to a little, shall we say, demonstration. It's rare to observe these boys at play, so I thought it'd be worth a few bucks to take a look at the real thing in action.

This idea seemed to amuse Gary, so we agreed to the following little scenario: I'd show up at the club at about 2:30 a.m., when things were generally really slow. I'd hang around until Gary's table was empty, then plop down, buy in for $40 in silver, and, according to Gary, be treated to the most incredible run of bad "luck" I had ever experienced.

Curious as to just how he planned to separate me from my $40, I asked him what moves he was going to use. He just smiled and said, "You'll see, Bryce. Just watch the deck in my left hand when I reach down to check for a snapper."[2]

So promptly at 2:30 a.m. I strolled into the club. There was Gary at an empty table, the deck fanned out face-up on the layout.

I sat down, bought in for $40, and placed a $1 bet on the table.

Gary smiled pleasantly, shuffled the cards, and after the cut began to deal.

Out came the cards. Ace up for Gary. (Ace,8) for me. "Insurance?" he asked. "Not this time," I answered. He checked under the Ace. No blackjack. I slid my soft 19 under my bet, and gave Gary this skeptical little "well, let's see your stuff" kind of look. Gary flipped over his hole card: 4 of Spades. He took a hit: 6 of Diamonds. Uh oh, twenty one. As he scooped my buck into the rack and tossed my cards into the return tray, he gave me a knowing little wink.

Hmmm... how'd he do that?

Then I remembered what he'd said about his left hand and checking for blackjacks. A couple of hands later he dealt himself a 10 up; this time I watched real close as he looked under the 10. Everything seemed normal, except as he rolled his left hand over to act as a shield against anyone else seeing his hole card, he lifted the edge of the top card away from the rest of the deck with his left thumb. Not by much, maybe an eighth of an inch or so. But it was enough. Now as he checked his hole card, he also got a peek at the top card in the deck. I had (10,7) so I stood. Gary flipped over his down card: 2 of Clubs. He promptly hit it with the 8 of Spades for 20. Another loser for me. And this is how it went. Anytime Gary needed the top card to complete his hand, he saved it by dealing seconds to me until it was his turn to draw. If he couldn't use the top card himself

----

2. A "snapper" is casinospeak for a blackjack.

but thought it would help my hand, he would deal me seconds and then, if necessary, rip a second to his own hand, as well. And, if he thought the top card would hurt my hand, he would deal it to me honestly and then complete his hand in the usual way.

Because the dealer will have an Ace or 10 up almost 40% of the time, this simple tactic will wipe out any player it is used against in very short order.

And so it did. Within 20 minutes my $40, at $1 per hand, was history.

And this was just what he called the "weak bust-out"; the "strong bust-out" supercharged this scam by having the dealer peek at the top card as he was picking and paying at the end of the round. Then, if the top card were an Ace or 10, he would deal seconds to the players and save the Ace or 10 for his up card; otherwise, he would deal it honestly. With this added feature assuring the dealer an Ace or 10 up over 60% of the time, the player loses at an incredible rate.

Scary stuff.

I was able to see what Gary was doing because I was expecting the move; he told me where to look, and he was just obvious enough about it so I was sure to catch on. But cheating dealers don't usually conduct clinics. If this had been for real I doubt I'd have seen a thing.

Rogue dealers like this *do* exist. They are rare, and you will probably never come up against one, but it pays to be on the lookout, nevertheless.

In addition to camouflage, this is the reason you never want to lose more than 15 average bets against any one dealer. Losing 15 bets to a cheating dealer hurts, but it's not fatal. Grimly hanging on no matter what happens can not only blow your cover, it can also blow your entire trip stake, as well.

There are lots of other ways a cheating dealer can fleece a player. They run the gamut from stacked decks, to marked cards, to bogus pick-ups, to, well, you name it. Thorp gave a fairly thorough rundown in Beat the Dealer, and other good books on the subject are available as well.[3]

Don't be overly concerned about cheating. Certainly, do not assume that just because you have a sustained run of bad luck you are being cheated. It's probably just that: bad luck. Hang in there; it'll turn around. If it doesn't, it's far more likely you are making a lot of mistakes than being cheated.

But keep your eyes open. You never know. Gary might still be out there.

----

3. One in particular, Dealing with Cheats by A. D. Livingston, is worth a look.

CHAPTER ELEVEN

The Omega II Blackjack Machine

This is the final piece, the last but essential element in your comprehensive system for beating the game of casino Blackjack.

Up to now we have concentrated on strategy, camouflage, tactics, and technique, but in this chapter we're going to learn how to evaluate the many different, and constantly changing, Blackjack games offered in order to select those games that give us the best return on our action.

To do this we're going to study, and learn to use, a system of integrated computer programs I have developed called the Omega II Blackjack Machine.

I originally developed the prototype of the Blackjack Machine for my own purposes: to sort out the hype and the hoopla from the real and the rational, so I could determine for myself exactly what advantage I had in the games in which I played.

Casinos are continually making wild and exaggerated claims that are loaded with distortions, deceptions, and outright deceit; and, believe it or not, sometimes even pros get sucked in by these come-ons.

As an example, the Las Vegas Club in downtown Las Vegas has advertised for years that it has the most liberal Blackjack rules in the world. Strictly speaking, this may well be true, for, in addition to the already liberal rules common to most casinos in the area, the Las Vegas Club allows late surrender, resplitting of Aces, double on any two, three, or four cards, including after splits, and, as if that weren't enough, any six-card unbusted hand is an automatic winner! No doubt about it, these are some mighty fine rules. What they somehow forget to mention, however, is that they deal a six-deck game, shuffle just past the middle of the pack, and break even earlier than that if they think someone might be watching the cards. The bottom line is that a Basic Strategy player is down about .1% off the top, and even an aggressive bet spread, coupled with a very strong system, will yield an advantage of less than 1.0%. In other words (except for exploiting the occasional warped card), this game is not worth playing, good rules or not.

And yet one respected authority on Blackjack stated for the record that the Las Vegas Club was such a pushover that, "If you can't beat this game, you might as well take up poker."

Another renowned expert was recently quoted as saying that Caesars Palace is one of the most profitable places to play Blackjack in all Las Vegas. Whereas, in reality, Caesars Palace offers a six-deck game that is no better than the one at the Las Vegas Club, which makes Caesars Palace probably one of the least, not most, profitable places in Las Vegas to play Blackjack.[1]

How can experts make mistakes like this? Well, sometimes they just flat-out blow it; they're human like the rest of us. Other times they seem seduced by the mood and tone of the casino. The above expert,[2] for instance, told me that what he really meant was that Caesars Palace was one of his *favorite* places to play because it welcomed his action and was tolerant of marathon playing sessions by obviously skilled players. That is nice. But it does not make Caesars Palace an especially profitable place to play Blackjack. Pity the poor readers who took this expert at his word and risked serious money on the Caesars Palace game. I hope Lady Luck had mercy on 'em--but I wouldn't bet on it.

So, if even the experts sometimes go astray, what chance does the average counter have of picking games he figures to really clean up on?

The answer, unfortunately, is not much. Of course, it is true that if you limit yourself to single- and double-deck games with good rules and customs, and follow the recommendations set forth in this book, you'll do fine. The problem is that sometimes you're going to want to play in games that deviate from this norm. Say you're going on a junket to a casino where they only deal four-deck games with less than ideal rules, but the sky's the limit as far as bet spreads are concerned. What then? Do you play serious money, or not? Or suppose a casino deals a double-deck game with tough Reno rules, but deals down to almost the last card. Is this a good game, or not? Or say you choose to occasionally play in

----

1. Even team play suffers significantly when the pack is only dealt out, as it is here, about half way before reshuffling.

2. It is not my intention to disparage other experts but rather to show that even pros can sometimes be taken in by the confusing array of rules, customs, and claims that casinos use to promote their games.

somewhat second-rate games so you don't burn out your welcome at the really good clubs. That's a sensible idea, but where do you draw the line? Which games are marginally good, and which are just plain marginal?

And even in good single- and double-deck games it's important to know what your theoretical advantage is so you have something to compare your results against; for, even though you'll never be spot-on with that edge, if you don't get close in time you may be doing something wrong (like making a lot of counting errors).

So the variations are infinite, and so are the possibilities. The casinos give, and the casinos take away, and without some way to evaluate the effect of all the many rules and customs commonly found, there's just no reliable way to consistently pick acceptable games and know what your advantage is.

Enter the Omega II Blackjack Machine.

OVERVIEW

Essentially, the Omega II Blackjack Machine is designed to allow you to simulate the play of a virtually unlimited set of strategies and bet spreads against practically any traditional Blackjack game you are likely to encounter in the legal casinos of the United States and abroad.

The Blackjack Machine comes complete with a selection of strategies to choose from; these include the Basic Strategy (for both one and multiple decks), the Basic Omega II Strategy, and the Advanced Omega II Strategy. In addition, it is easy to create, modify, and analyze any other strategies of your choice.

All during a simulation test run, as well as at the conclusion, the Omega II Blackjack Machine continuously displays the player's win (or loss) rate, as well as a wide array of other interesting and valuable information.

In addition, you can use the Blackjack Machine to focus on specific aspects of play; you'll find this an invaluable tool in gaining real insight and understanding of the game.

INSTALLATION

The Omega II Blackjack Machine is a system of four integrated computer programs written for the Macintosh LC series with IIe option and Apple II series of computers.

The system will run on any Macintosh LC, LC II, or LC III with IIe option, Apple IIe, or IIgs computer with a 5.25" drive and a minimum of 64K of RAM. It is supplied on one 5.25" diskette,[3] and, although not required, a CPU accelerator card is recommended for the eight-bit Apple IIe.

All standard Macintosh LC series and Apple II series compatible monitors, both monochrome and color, are supported.

It is completely autoloading; merely place the program diskette in DRIVE 1 and boot the system (or enter RUN HELLO <RETURN> at the screen prompt).

THE OPENING MENU

After the system boots and the title screen is briefly displayed, the opening menu will appear. It should look like Figure 11.1.

If this screen is not displayed, you have a problem. Check your computer, disk drive, and monitor to make sure they are operating properly. If they are, the problem is with the Omega II Blackjack Machine program diskette.

In this case, return the defective diskette to the address on the order coupon, and it will be replaced free of charge.

Now, let's take a look at the six opening menu selections one by one, in order.

1. REVIEW AND CHANGE STRATEGY CHARTS.

When the Blackjack Machine boots, it automatically loads the single-deck Basic Strategy into its RAM resident strategy tables.

Press **1 <RETURN>** to get to these strategy tables.

The first screen you'll see is the Pair Splitting Strategy (PA), laid out in a grid with the player's pairs (from (A,A) to (10,10)) descending on the left, and the dealer's up cards (from A to 10) across the top.

As stated at the top of the screen, X indicates don't split, and P indicates split.

To find out how the computer will handle any given pair against any up card, simply find the intersection of that pair and the dealer's up card.

----

3. To receive the Omega II Blackjack Machine program diskette, please mail in the order coupon at the back of the book. IBM / MS-DOS users, please note the ad for the Omega II Blackjack Casino on the above-referenced order coupon.

Figure 11.1

OPENING MENU

The Omega II Blackjack Machine

*** OMEGA II ***

1.   REVIEW AND CHANGE STRATEGY CHARTS.

2.   LIST ALL CHANGES SINCE LAST RESET.
     OPTION - SAVE REVISIONS ON DISK.

3.   HIGH SPEED SIMULATION TEST RUN.
     OPTION - MODE 1 OR MODE 2.

4.   RESET FIXED OR VARIABLE STRATEGY.
     OPTION - LOAD REVISIONS FROM DISK.

5.   CATALOG OR DELETE REVISION FILES.

6.   EXIT OMEGA II.

PLEASE ENTER SELECTION:

Example: You want to know how the computer will play (6,6) against the dealer's 7. Just find (6,6) on the left, and follow across to the right until you intersect with the dealer's up card of 7. In this case, you'll find an X, indicating the computer (playing Basic Strategy) would not split (6,6) against a 7.[4]

Now, at the bottom of the screen you'll see a line of text that asks, "DO YOU WANT TO CHANGE THIS STRATEGY?". Answer Y OR N <RETURN>; any other response will be ignored.[5]

If you answer N <RETURN>, you will proceed immediately to the next screen (the Soft Doubling Strategy (SO)); however, if you enter Y <RETURN>, you will be given the opportunity to change any, or all, of the Pair Splitting Strategy (PA).

----

4. With a fixed strategy, like the Basic Strategy here, the decision to split or not is independent of the count, so as you scan the (PA) table, you'll see only Xs and Ps, indicating there are no decisions conditional on the count. All that matters is the player's hand and the dealer's up card. However, you can also load *variable* strategies, such as the Advanced Omega II Strategy, into the Blackjack Machine (option 4 at the opening menu). When a variable strategy is resident, in addition to Xs and Ps, you may also see positive and/or negative numbers indicating that the decision to split or not is conditional on the true count.

The Omega II Blackjack Machine uses a true count based on 100 cards. This means that the true count is calculated using the following formula: TC = (Running Count)x100/(Remaining Pack).

Example: The running count is -12, and there are 57 cards remaining in a double-deck game; the true count, therefore, is: (-12)x100/(57) = -21.

Note, this is different from the way we calculate the true count in actual play. There the TC is based on 52 cards, not 100. The reason for this change is that using 100 cards yields larger (absolute-value) true-count playing indices than 52 cards would. This makes rounding errors in the playing indices less significant than they would otherwise be (however, if desired, an *effective* true count based on 52 cards can be created by multiplying the card values by .52).

5. Actually you can also respond to any (Y/N) prompt with a simple <RETURN>; this will be accepted as N <RETURN> by the Blackjack Machine.

In this case, the following line of text appears, "ENTER CHANGE: **PAIR,** UPCARD, CODE?"

This option allows you to make modifications to existing strategies, as well as to create whole new strategies of your own, for later analysis. For instance, the Basic 6 strategy, which is included on the Omega II Blackjack Machine program diskette, consists of seven changes which optimize Basic Strategy for multiple decks; this strategy was created using the change option we're discussing here.

Notice the word "PAIR" is highlighted in inverse video; this indicates that the first information required is the selection of the player's pair. Enter A through 10 <RETURN>.[6] Any other response will be ignored.[7]

After the pair is entered, the highlight will shift to the word "**UPCARD,**" indicating the dealer's up card must now be specified. Enter A through 10 <RETURN>. Any other response will be ignored.

After both the player's pair and the dealer's up card have been entered, the highlight will move to the word "**CODE,**" indicating the final required entry is the desired strategy change code. Enter X for don't split, or P for split. Any other response will be ignored.[8]

As the strategy change is performed by the Blackjack Machine, the new index code will flash in inverse video in the strategy grid, and the message "CHANGE REGISTERED" will appear.[9]

After a strategy change is completed by the Blackjack Machine, the prompt will return to the "DO YOU WANT TO CHANGE THIS STRATEGY?"

----

6. One character only! For instance, enter 7 <RETURN> for (7,7).

7. Except you may also respond here with a simple <RETURN>; this will return you to the previous prompt.

8. Except, of course, if this were a variable strategy, such as either the Basic or the Advanced Omega II Strategy, in addition to X and P, index numbers from -99 to 99 would also be accepted.

9. However, if you specify an existing index code, the message "CHANGE ALREADY EXISTS" will appear, and you will be given the chance to specify another change.

message; at this time either additional changes can be made, or you can proceed to the next screen.

The next screen is the Soft Doubling Strategy (SO).

This screen is laid out in similar fashion to the (PA) strategy, except that player soft hands from 12 (A,A) to 19 (A,8) are listed on the left, and, as with (PA), the dealer's up cards appear across the top.

Soft 20 (A,9) and soft 21 (blackjack!) are not listed because the Blackjack Machine always stands on these hands and no changes are, therefore, permitted.

As the legend at the top of the (SO) screen indicates, the possible strategy codes are S for stand, H for hit, D for double down (or hit if doubling not permitted), and B for double down (or stand if doubling not permitted).[10]

Changes to the (SO) strategy are made in the same manner as with the (PA) strategy. In response to the message, "ENTER CHANGE: HAND, UPCARD, CODE?" first enter the player's hand (12 through 19) <RETURN>, then the dealer's up card <RETURN>, and finally the change code <RETURN>.

As with the (PA) strategy, as many additional changes as desired can be made to the (SO) strategy.

After all desired changes have been made, proceed to the next screen (the Hard Hand Strategy (HA)) by responding to "DO YOU WANT TO CHANGE THIS STRATEGY?" with N <RETURN>.

The Hard Hand Strategy (HA) lists player hard hands from 9 through 17 at the left and, as with the (PA) and (SO) strategies, the dealer's up cards appear across the top of the grid.

Hard hands of less than 9 or more than 17 are not shown because the Blackjack Machine always plays these hands the same way (hitting hard hands of 8 or less and standing on hard hands of 18 or more).[11]

----

10. With variable strategies, the B code is not permitted because the (SO) variable strategy algorithm is programmed to know when to hit and when to stand if the rules do not permit doubling down. And, of course, variable strategies permit index numbers of from -99 to 99.

11. Actually, some hard hands of 8 or less, say (3,3), and some hard hands of 18 or more, say (9,9), may at times be handled by splitting. The Omega II Blackjack Machine avoids potential strategy conflicts by prioritizing the order in which strategy decisions are performed. The order of priority is: surrender, splitting,

As the legend indicates, the possible strategy change codes are S for stand, H for hit, and D for double down.[12]

Changes to the (HA) strategy are made in the same way as with the (PA) and (SO) strategies. In response to the message, "ENTER CHANGE: HAND, UPCARD, CODE?" first enter the player's hand (9 through 17) <RETURN>, then the dealer's up card <RETURN>, and finally the desired change code <RETURN>.

After all desired changes have been made to the (HA) strategy, return to the opening menu by responding to "DO YOU WANT TO CHANGE THIS STRATEGY?" with N <RETURN>.

2. LIST ALL CHANGES SINCE LAST RESET.
   OPTION - SAVE REVISIONS ON DISK.

This selection from the opening menu allows you to list, and save to disk, any strategy changes you may have made from option 1 (review and change) above. In addition, any changes previously saved to disk, and currently loaded into the Blackjack Machine's strategy tables, will also be displayed.

To get to this selection, press **2** <RETURN>.

If you have made no strategy changes, and the only strategy resident is the auto-loading single-deck Basic Strategy, then when you select this option, the CHANGE LIST screen will display, "NO CHANGES WERE MADE TO STRATEGY. PRESS 'RETURN' FOR MENU:". However, if changes to the current strategy have been made, or a previously created change file has been loaded into memory (option 4 from the opening menu), then the CHANGE LIST screen will indicate the number of changes made and ask if you want to "SAVE THE CHANGES ON DISK (Y/N)?". If you respond Y <RETURN>, you will be prompted to give an appropriate name[13] to the change file, and upon so

----

doubling down, standing and drawing.

12. And in addition, as always, variable strategies also permit index numbers of from -99 to 99.

13. Filenames may be up to 10 alphanumeric characters long.

doing, this file will be saved to the Blackjack Machine's program diskette (or any other formatted diskette in the boot drive) for later use.

At this time, the changes made will be listed for your review. The changes are presented in the following format:

Strategy Table, Player's Hand, Dealer's Up Card, Strategy Change.

For example, let's say in the Pair Splitting Strategy (PA), you changed the Basic Strategy playing code for (3,3) against a 7 from split (P) to don't split (X). In this case, the change would be listed as follows: PA 3 7 X.

Or say in the Soft Hand Strategy (SO), you changed the playing code for soft 18 against the dealer's Ace from hit (H) to stand (S). This would be listed as: SO 18 A S.

Or, as a final example, say in the Hard Hand Strategy (HA), you were to change the strategy code for hard 9 against the dealer's 2 from double (D) to hit (H). In this instance the change would appear as: HA 9 2 H.

At any time during the listing of changes, you can freeze the screen by pressing <CONTROL> S; when you are ready to resume scrolling the changes, merely press <RETURN>.

When all the changes have been listed, the message "THE CHANGE LISTING IS COMPLETED. PRESS 'RETURN' FOR MENU:" will appear. At this time press <RETURN> to go back to the opening menu.

3. HIGH SPEED SIMULATION TEST RUN.
   OPTION - MODE 1 OR MODE 2.

This selection is the guts of the Omega II Blackjack Machine; everything else is basically just support for this option.

To enter the simulation option, press **3 <RETURN>**.

At the first screen, you will be asked to enter a four-digit "randomizer" code. This code can be any random four-digit number of your choice. The purpose of this number is to "seed" the computer's pseudo random-number generator to ensure that the simulation is free of any residual bias. Blackjack simulations are very sensitive to bias in the playing algorithm, and this "seeding" adds an additional level of randomness to the process.[14]

After the Blackjack Machine seeds the pseudo random-number generator, you will be given a choice of two different simulation modes to select from. As the screen explains, in mode 1, every hand is dealt from the same subset of cards; this allows you to analyze specific situations in the game.[15] As an example, with mode 1, you could run a simulation to find out just what the player's advantage is holding (10,9), in a Las Vegas Strip double-deck game, against the dealer's 10,[16] using the Advanced Omega II System, and a true count of, say, +9.

You'll find that being able to focus in this way on virtually any aspect of play is an invaluable tool of both discovery and insight, as you journey along toward real mastery of the game.

Mode 2, on the other hand, is not designed to explore specific situations in the game but rather to test complete Blackjack systems against almost any set of rules and customs desired. In mode 2, the game is dealt as it would be in a casino, with each hand coming from an increasingly depleted deck until the "dealer" shuffles.

Let's begin with mode 1. Press **1 <RETURN>** from the "PLEASE SPECIFY MODE DESIRED (1 OR 2):" prompt.[17]

After the Blackjack Machine loads the high-speed mode 1 simulation program from diskette, you will be asked to respond to the message, "FIXED OR VARIABLE STRATEGY (F/V)?".

----

14. As a matter of fact, they are so sensitive that the Blackjack Machine does not rely on the pseudo random-number generator provided in Applesoft Basic; it's just not good enough. In its place, a *very* well-tested and reliable algorithm used in mainframe airfoil simulations has been used, instead. This binary file can be found on the Blackjack Machine's program diskette; it is called USRND.

15. And even to create whole new strategies, as I did, for instance, with the Advanced Omega II Strategy.

16. And, if you chose, you could further limit this simulation to only those situations when the dealer does not have blackjack.

17. There are three acceptable entries at this prompt: 1 <RETURN>, 2 <RETURN>, and just <RETURN>. <RETURN> will take you back to the opening menu.

You must respond either F <RETURN> or V <RETURN> at this prompt. No other entries will be accepted.

As we discussed in an earlier chapter, there are two fundamental types of Blackjack strategies: *fixed* strategies, such as Basic Strategy, where the play of the hands is independent of the count, and *variable* strategies, such as the Advanced Omega II Strategy, where the playing decisions are very much dependent on the count.

If you respond F <RETURN>, the single-deck Basic Strategy will be loaded into the Blackjack Machine's strategy tables.

If you respond V <RETURN>, no default strategy will be loaded into memory, but the Blackjack Machine's strategy tables will prepare to accept a variable strategy, such as the Advanced Omega II Strategy.

You will then be asked, "DO YOU WANT TO LOAD A REVISION (Y/N)?". This option allows you to load a change file from diskette into the Blackjack Machine's strategy tables.

The program diskette comes with one fixed change file, called BASIC 6. This file optimizes the single-deck Basic Strategy for multiple-deck games. There are also two variable change files: A OMEGA II (the Advanced Omega II Strategy) and B OMEGA II (the Basic Omega II Strategy).

Of course, you can also create any number of additional fixed or variable change files with selection 1 from the opening menu and save them to diskette with selection 2.

If you have specified a fixed strategy (F <RETURN>), you aren't required to load a revision file, because the single-deck Basic Strategy is automatically loaded into memory. Of course, you may, if you choose, overlay the single-deck Basic Strategy with any fixed change file available on diskette (such as BASIC 6).

If you select a variable strategy (V <RETURN>), however, since no strategy is autoloaded into memory, you must select a variable revision file (such as A OMEGA II or B OMEGA II).

In any case, if you respond Y <RETURN> at this prompt, you will be asked to "ENTER THE NAME OF REVISION FILE:". This prompt will accept the name of any appropriate change file on the diskette in the boot drive. If you have selected a fixed strategy (F <RETURN>), you must select a fixed change file; if you have chosen a variable strategy (V <RETURN>), you must select a variable change file. If you choose an improper filename, you will be returned to the previous prompt.

After the change file (if any) loads, you will be asked if you want to "MODIFY ANY OF THE PLAYING RULES (Y/N)?".

If you respond Y <RETURN> at this prompt, you will be given the opportunity to change the rules used in the simulation from the default set[18] to just about any mix of conventional rules desired.

After any rules changes have been made, you will be asked if you wish to "CHANGE ANY POINT COUNT VALUE(S) (Y/N)?".

Responding Y <RETURN> at this prompt will take you to a screen that displays the current (default)[19] point-count values for the various cards in the deck.

These values should be changed, if necessary, to correspond to the count appropriate for the playing strategy used. For example, if you run the simulation using the Advanced Omega II Strategy (A OMEGA II), then the card values should be changed to those of the Omega II Count.[20]

With fixed strategies such as Basic Strategy, however, since the count is used only for betting and insurance purposes, and not for the play of the hands, you can use any count desired.

After you're happy with the card values, you will next be asked "THE NUMBER OF GAMES?"[21] you want to run in the simulation.

----

18. The Omega II Blackjack Machine defaults to the following set of rules: dealer stands on soft 17; double down on *any* two cards; split any pair (no resplits).

The effects of any minor rules changes not available in the simulation (such as late surrender or resplitting of pairs) can be estimated from Table 2.1 (Chapter Two) with an accuracy as good as, or better than, any actual simulation.

19. The Blackjack Machine assumes the following card values: Ace=-1, 2=+1, 3=+1, 4=+1, 5=+1, 6=+1, 7=0, 8=0, 9=0, 10=-1.

20. Which are, of course: Ace=0, 2=+1, 3=+1, 4=+2, 5=+2, 6=+2, 7=+1, 8=0, 9=-1, 10=-2.

21. The Blackjack Machine uses the word "games" to mean hands played *less* additional hands resulting from splits.

The important thing in simulations is to run enough hands to get an accurate result. Generally, in a mode 2 simulation, which is dealt as it would be in a casino, I run at least 1,000,000 games; this gets the standard deviation of the player's expectation down to around .1%. In a mode 1 simulation, however, since we are frequently focusing on just one facet of the game, often with a fixed player's hand and/or dealer's up card, the number of variables are greatly reduced, and it is, therefore, usually enough to run, say, 50,000 games or so.

After specifying the number of games, you will be prompted to indicate the "NUMBER OF DECKS?" to be used in the simulation. You may select anywhere from one to eight decks.

Next you will be asked to "ENTER THE MINIMUM PCI FOR INSURANCE?". PCI stands for point count index, which is just another name for the true count. If you do not want to allow insurance in the simulation, simply respond <RETURN>; otherwise enter the PCI for insurance.[22] Only whole numbers may be used; no fractions are permitted.

The next set of prompts allows you to determine what subset of the pack you wish to use for the simulation; this is accomplished by deleting cards of your choice.

For instance, in response to the message "DEL CARD:?", you can enter any card values from Ace (A) through King (K).[23]

If you were to enter J <RETURN>, for example, you would then be prompted for the number of Jacks you wanted to delete. This prompt takes the form of: "D/F(0 - 4d)?", where d is the number of decks specified for the simulation.

In a double-deck game, for example, the D/F (deletion factor) could be from 0, meaning don't delete any Jacks, to 8, meaning delete all the Jacks from the simulation.

----

22. But remember, the Blackjack Machine uses a true count based on 100 cards, not 52. The Advanced Omega II Strategy, for instance, provides for insurance at a true count of +6, but that would translate here to a PCI of +12 (100/52 x +6 = +11.54).

23. The valid entries are: A,2,3,4,5,6,7,8,9,10,J,Q,K, followed by <RETURN>.

After you enter the D/F, the updated PCI will be displayed on the right of the screen. This makes it easy to continue deleting cards until the desired PCI is achieved.

You may delete the cards in any order; that is, you do not have to delete, say, 5s before you delete 9s or Queens.

If you make a mistake or change your mind you can cancel your entries and re-enter the data, starting with "NUMBER OF GAMES?", by entering 11 <RETURN> at the "DEL CARD:?" prompt.

The quick-and-dirty way to get to any desired PCI is to merely delete or add[24] 10s until the desired count is achieved. A number of good commercial systems were developed this way. This is not, however, the optimal way to do it. The accurate way to attain a given PCI is to delete cards in proportion to their point count value. For example, in the Omega II Count, the 5 counts +2 and the 3 counts +1; therefore, any given plus deck should be depleted of twice as many 5s as 3s. The density of the zero-valued cards, such as the Ace and the 8 in the Omega II Count, should always be kept at one in 13 cards.

After all desired cards, if any, have been deleted, enter <RETURN> at the "DEL CARD:?" prompt; this will take you to the next screen, where you have the option to "fix" one or both of the player's first two cards, as well as the dealer's up card.

If you do not want to hold either of the player's first two cards or the dealer's up card constant, just respond N <RETURN> at the "FIXED PLAYER HAND OR DEALER UP CARD?" prompt.

Now the fun begins.

The next screen is a display of the actual mode 1 simulation, in realtime, as it runs.

At the top of the screen, basic information, such as playing strategy used, number of decks in play, modifications to the playing rules, cards deleted, etc., will be displayed. Beneath that, the results of the simulation, with respect to hands played, player's wins, dealer's wins, units bet, units won, player's win (or loss) percentage, etc., will be displayed and updated with each new hand played.

----

24. Tens can be "added" to the pack by deleting an equal number of all other cards *except* the 10s. For example, if I take four decks and delete four each of Ace through 9, but no 10s, I have, in effect, added 16 10s to a three-deck game.

The simulation can be interrupted at any time by pressing <RETURN>. This will result in a display of additional updated information, as well as the opportunity to resume the simulation by pressing <RETURN> again, or of returning to the opening menu by entering M <RETURN>.

When the simulation is completed, additional updated data will again be displayed, and you can choose either to run a new simulation by pressing <RETURN> or go back to the opening menu by entering M <RETURN>. At this time, you can also print out an image of the screen by using the print screen or screen dump feature of your printer or printer interface card.[25]

OK, so much for mode 1, now let's take a look at mode 2 simulation.

From the "PLEASE SPECIFY MODE DESIRED (1 OR 2):" prompt, press **2 <RETURN>**.

The high-speed mode 2 simulation program will load from diskette, and you will, as with mode 1, be asked to specify whether you want to use a fixed or variable strategy, load a revision file from disk, modify the playing rules, or change the point count values.

Refer to the above discussion on mode 1 if you have any questions on how to respond to these prompts.

In addition, as with mode 1, you will be prompted to enter the number of games to be simulated and the number of decks to be used; from here on, however, the information required differs from mode 1.

After specifying the number of decks, you will be asked the "NUMBER OF UNDEALT CARDS?". This is the shuffle point. As an example, in a double-deck game if you wanted the computer to deal three quarters of the pack before reshuffling, you would respond 26 <RETURN> at this prompt.[26]

The next prompt asks "IS BETTING TO BE BASED ON 'SPC' (Y/N)?". SPC stands for simple point count; this is just another term for the running count. If you respond Y <RETURN>, all betting decisions, including insurance, will be

----

25. See the reference manual of your printer or printer interface card for instructions on how to do this.

26. Note: You must deal at least one card, and you must leave at least one card undealt, before reshuffling. So, for example, in a four-deck game, the range of valid entries would be from 207 down to 1.

made using the running count. If you respond N <RETURN>, these decisions will be made using the PCI. Either way, the playing decisions for variable strategies will always be based on the PCI.

Next you will be asked to "ENTER MINIMUM PCI[27] FOR INSURANCE:?". Here, as with a mode 1 simulation, only whole numbers may be used; to specify no insurance, just hit <RETURN>.

Finally, you will be prompted to "ENTER NUMBER OF BET RANGES (MAX 4)?". This option allows you to determine how the Blackjack Machine handles betting. There are six valid responses: 0, 1, 2, 3, 4, and R.

If you respond 0 <RETURN>, the betting will be based strictly on the count (PCI or SPC). Upon entering 0 <RETURN>, you will be prompted to indicate "BET SIZE = PCI[28] X ?". Here you can enter in any positive or negative number you want, including fractions. Putting in a positive number is a good way to approximate proportional betting; if you choose a negative number, however, you get a sort of inverse proportional betting, where the worse the count (and player's disadvantage), the bigger the player's bet!

If you enter 1 <RETURN>, the Blackjack Machine will flat bet one unit on each hand.

Entering 2, 3, or 4 <RETURN> specifies that number of betting ranges, respectively. Additionally, you will be prompted to enter the count (PCI or SPC) and bet size, for each range.

The R option stands for "relative" betting. This is a very powerful innovation; it allows you to simulate all possible bet spreads, with just one simulation.

It works this way: When you enter R <RETURN> you will be prompted to enter the count (PCI or SPC) for three betting ranges. The bet sizes, however, will default to X and Y, instead of user values.

The beauty of this is that you assign the values of the bets (X and Y) *after* the simulation is completed.

----

27. Or SPC, if you have specified that betting is to be based on the running count.

28. See 27 above.

As the simulation runs, the amount bet at 1 unit, X units, and Y units, as well as the amount won (or lost) at 1 unit, X units, and Y units, is continuously displayed and updated.

At the conclusion of the simulation, the player's expectation for any set of X and Y values can be easily determined by dividing the total win (or loss) by the total amount bet. This is slick.

With any of the bet range options, except 0 and 1, you can go back and edit your choices for counts and bet sizes by pressing E <RETURN> at the "ENTER 'E' FOR EDIT, OR 'RETURN' FOR TEST:" prompt.

When you are satisfied with your betting choices, enter <RETURN>; the test-run screen will be displayed, and the mode 2 simulation will begin.

As with mode 1, at the top of the screen basic information, such as playing strategy used, number of decks in play, shuffle point, modifications to the playing rules, betting ranges, etc., will be displayed. Beneath that, the results of the simulation, with respect to hands played, player's wins, dealer's wins, units bet, units won, player's win (or loss) percentage, etc., will be shown and updated as each new hand is played.

And, as with mode 1, the simulation can be interrupted at any time by pressing <RETURN>. This will result in a display of additional updated information, as well as the opportunity to resume the simulation by pressing <RETURN> again, or of returning to the opening menu by entering M <RETURN>.

When the simulation is completed, additional updated data will again be displayed, and you can choose either to run a new simulation by pressing <RETURN> or go back to the opening menu by entering M <RETURN>. At this time, you can also print out an image of the screen by using the print screen or screen dump feature of your printer or printer interface card.[29]

4. RESET FIXED OR VARIABLE STRATEGY.
   OPTION - LOAD REVISIONS FROM DISK.

This option allows you to select and load additional strategies for subsequent change and review using selections 1 and 2 from the opening menu.

----

29. See the reference manual of your printer or printer interface card for instructions on how to do this.

To choose this selection enter **4 <RETURN>**.

You will first be asked whether you wish to select a "FIXED OR VARIABLE STRATEGY (F/V)?". The only valid entries here are F or V <RETURN>; any other responses will be ignored, and you will be prompted to enter again.

If you select a fixed strategy (F <RETURN>), the Blackjack Machine's strategy tables will be reinitialized with the single-deck Basic Strategy.

If you select a variable strategy (V <RETURN>), the strategy tables will be cleared and prepared to accept either a variable-strategy change file from diskette or direct user index entries from selection 1 of the opening menu.

You will then be asked, "DO YOU WANT TO LOAD A REVISION (Y/N)?". This option allows you to load a change file from diskette into the Blackjack Machine's strategy tables.

The program diskette comes with one fixed change file, called BASIC 6. This file optimizes the single-deck Basic Strategy for multiple-deck games. There are also two variable change files: A OMEGA II (the Advanced Omega II Strategy) and B OMEGA II (the Basic Omega II Strategy).

Of course, you can also create any number of additional fixed or variable change files with selection 1 from the opening menu, and then save them to diskette with selection 2.

In any case, if you respond Y <RETURN> at this prompt, you will be asked to "ENTER THE NAME OF REVISION FILE:". This prompt will accept the name of any appropriate change file on the diskette in the boot drive. If you have selected a fixed strategy (F <RETURN>), you must select a fixed change file; if you have chosen a variable strategy (V <RETURN>), you must select a variable change file. If you choose an improper filename, you will be returned to the previous prompt.

Finally, whether or not you have chosen to load a revision file, when you are ready to return to the opening menu, press <RETURN>.

5. CATALOG OR DELETE REVISION FILES.

This selection displays a catalog of all the files on the diskette in the boot drive. This includes program files as well as revision files.

To select this option, press **5 <RETURN>**.

After cataloging the diskette in the boot drive, the Blackjack Machine will ask, "DO YOU WANT TO DELETE A FILE (Y/N)?". If you respond

N <RETURN>, you will be returned to the opening menu. If you enter Y <RETURN>, however, you will be prompted to "PLEASE ENTER FILENAME:". At this prompt, you may enter the name of any revision file on diskette.[30]

After you enter the name of the file you want deleted, the Blackjack Machine will ask, "ARE YOU SURE (Y/N)?". If you respond N <RETURN>, you will be returned to the "DO YOU WANT TO DELETE A FILE (Y/N)?" prompt; if you enter Y <RETURN>, however, the Blackjack Machine will delete the file, if it exists, and return you, once again, to the "DO YOU WANT TO DELETE A FILE (Y/N)?" prompt.

When you are through deleting files, enter N <RETURN> at the "DO YOU WANT TO DELETE A FILE (Y/N)?" prompt, and you will be returned to the opening menu.

6. EXIT OMEGA II.

This selection allows you to exit the Omega II Blackjack Machine into Applesoft Basic.

To choose this option, press **6 <RETURN>**.

At the "READY TO EXIT OMEGA II (Y/N)?" prompt, enter either Y <RETURN> to exit to Applesoft Basic, or N <RETURN> to re-enter the Omega II Blackjack Machine.

SUMMARY

The Omega II Blackjack Machine is important because it takes the guesswork out of professional play.

It gives you a special edge that other players don't have in selecting games and systems. Beyond that, it provides you a standard of perfection to measure your own play against.

----

30. But be careful! Although the Omega II Blackjack Machine's program files are protected from deletion, none of the change files are. This means that you can delete BASIC 6, A OMEGA II, B OMEGA II, as well as any other revision files on the diskette.

In addition, it's just plain fun to use. I love to run simulations. There's something fascinating about watching a computer run off more hands in a few hours than I could do in a lifetime of real casino play.

So spend the time to learn to use the Blackjack Machine. Your investment will likely be repaid many times over in, well, in money that's what. After all, that *is* what this book's all about, right?

EPILOGUE

Some Final Thoughts

I did not write this book overnight, that's for sure. As a matter of fact, it's taken me several years to get it down the way I want it. But now, as I look it over, I like what I see. I don't think I'll change a thing.

The excitement of the hunt is there. The money, the adventure, the glamour, they're all there too.

But so too is the hard work, the dedication you need to get the job done, and get it done right.

It all just rings so true.

And even though the game continues to evolve as the clubs try out one new wrinkle and then the next, somehow, the more things change, the more they stay the same. One major hotel/casino in Las Vegas, for example, as of this writing is dealing several tables of single-deck Blackjack right down to the last card; and they're not afraid to gamble, either. I was there last weekend betting up to $200 a hand, and even though I hit them for a substantial win they couldn't have been nicer. Full comps, shows, the works. And they're not the only ones. There are good single- and double-deck games all over Las Vegas, all over Nevada, really. In fact, conditions are better now than they have been in years. Even Atlantic City is starting to get some decent games.

And, I guess, over time I've changed some too. I'm a little bit older, a little bit wiser, but, even here, some things never seem to change.

I'm still one of the top money winners on the pro Blackjack tour.

I still love to play.

I still feel that same rush, that same anticipation, as I turn on to the "Strip" and that first explosion of color and light transforms the night into a dazzling circus of neon delight. Las Vegas, I still love her. And I still hate her, bad.

I know that black despair. Hand after hand, hour after hour, the Blackjack gods inflicting their cruel vengeance for some unknown transgression, some forgotten sin....

But I know too the thrilling majesty of soaring wins. Blackjacks, double downs, splits and resplits. Killer hands, one after another, checks spilling across the table 'til they gut the rack.   My heart racing with excitement, my hands dripping scarlet with casino blood.

Twenty years on the pro Blackjack tour.   A long time.   Have I seen it all? Have I done it all?   Yes.   No.   I don't know.   What I do know is that I still love the action, and I still love the game.

So, let me end with this: There are lots of ways to make money; professional Blackjack just happens to be one.   But it alone offers excitement for the spirit and passion for the heart.   A rainbow of adventure anchored in gold.   So live the adventure, go for the gold, and one more thing, just in case--good luck!

GLOSSARY

The Language of Casino Twenty-One

Blackjack, like most games, has a vocabulary all its own, and your enjoyment and understanding of the game will be increased if you are familiar with the more popular terms.

Action

Your action is the sum total of all the money you bet in a session of Blackjack. As an example, if you play 100 hands at $25 per hand, your action is $2,500.

Advantage

Used in this book to mean the player's expected win/loss, expressed as a percent of his action. See Expectation.

Barring

The casino practice of excluding undesirable players. For a more complete discussion see Chapter Two, The Rules of the Game. See "86."

Basic Strategy

Basic Strategy is the proper playing strategy when the only information you consider is the dealer's up card and the cards that comprise your own hand. Depending on the number of decks in play, and the exact rules in force, Basic Strategy will result in an edge for the player of between about +.2% and -.6%.

Bee Cards

Made by the Consolidated-Dougherty Company, the famous Bee No. 92, with its dazzling diamond back design, is the most commonly used deck in the casinos. Many of the clubs use custom versions of this deck with their logos imprinted on the back.

Bet

The player's wager. Usually an amount ranging from $2 to $2,000. For a more complete discussion see Chapter Two, The Rules of the Game.

Blackjack

Another name for Twenty-One. Also used to mean a natural.

Break

To bust the hand.

Burn

After the cut, the dealer places the top card face up on the bottom of the deck or puts it in the discard tray. This is known as burning a card, and the card so placed is called the burn card.

Bust

If either the player or the dealer exceeds hard 21 in drawing to his hand, he is said to have busted the hand. If a player busts, he loses immediately; if the dealer busts, he loses to any players who have not already busted.

Cage

Casino idiom for the cashier. So called because of the metal grate that usually surrounds the cashier station.

Card Values

The Ace counts 1 or 11, as the player chooses. The 10,J,Q,K all count 10, and the other cards count their face value. For a more complete discussion see Chapter Two, The Rules of the Game.

Casino Manager

A casino employee, reporting to the casino owners, who has the overall responsibility for the successful operation of the casino.

Check

A gaming token or chip. So called because the chips are actually checks drawn on the casino.

Chip

A gaming token. See Check.

Comp

This is casinospeak for complimentary. Desirable customers are often treated to a full comp; this includes free room and board, as well as air fare to and from the casino. In return, the customer agrees to deposit a certain amount of money with the casino (usually between $4,000 and $10,000) and play for a certain number of hours per day (usually four or five) at a certain average bet (usually $50 to $100).

Free drinks are available to all players, and comps including free meals and shows are given to players whose action pleases the casino bosses.

Counter

A player who attempts to gain an advantage over the casino by counting the cards.

Customs

The traditions of the game. For a more complete discussion see Chapter Two, The Rules of the Game.

Cut

An action taken immediately after the shuffle, whereby a player divides the deck into two parts.

Deal

The process by which the dealer distributes the cards to himself and the players. For a more complete discussion see Chapter Two, The Rules of the Game.

Dealer

The casino employee who deals the cards and conducts the game.

Dealing Errors

Occasionally, a dealer will make a mistake. Mistakes that help you are called *gifts*; accept them with a smile. Mistakes that hurt you are called *errors*; accept them with a frown--and insist that they be corrected, immediately.

Deck

A standard 52-card pack, consisting of the four suits and four each of the 13 ranks.

Double Down

A playing option allowing the player to double his bet and receive one card face down. For a more complete discussion see Chapter Two, The Rules of the Game.

Draw

A hit. To take a card. Sometimes used to mean a push. For a more complete discussion see Chapter Two, The Rules of the Game.

Expectation

Used in this book to mean the player's expected win/loss, expressed as a percent of his action. See Advantage.

First Base

The playing position at the dealer's extreme left.

Hand

The cards a player receives in a round of Blackjack. Also used to mean a round of play.

Hard

A hard hand is one without an Ace, or one in which any Aces present are counted as one. Examples: (8,7) is hard 15, (6,5,Ace) is hard 12, (5,Ace,Ace) is hard 7 (or *soft* 17).

Hit

To request a card from the dealer. The card so taken is called the hit card.

Hole Card(s)

The dealer's down card. This term is also sometimes used to mean the player's initial two cards.

Hustler

A player who attempts to gain an advantage over the casino by any means available including card counting and cheating.

Insurance

If the dealer receives an Ace as his up card, the player may make a side bet equal, at most, to half his original bet. This side bet is called insurance and pays the player 2 to 1 if the dealer has a natural. For a more complete discussion see Chapter Two, The Rules of the Game.

Natural

A two-card total of 21, consisting of an Ace and a 10-value card. Another term for a blackjack. For a more complete discussion see Chapter Two, The Rules of the Game.

Over/Under

An even-money side bet allowing the player to either wager that his first two cards will total over 13, or that they will total under 13. Aces count 1; 13 always loses, and over/under bets may not exceed the amount of your original wager. For a more complete discussion see the over/under section in Chapter Seven.

Pack

The deck(s) or any undealt portion thereof. For a more complete discussion see Chapter Two, The Rules of the Game.

Pair

Any two cards of the same rank, or value; examples: (Ace,Ace), (10,10). Most casinos will consider hands comprised of unlike 10s, such as (Jack,Queen), to be a pair.

Pat

A hand totaling at least hard 17 or soft 18, but not exceeding hard 21, is said to be a pat hand.

Pit

A central casino area surrounded by a cluster of Blackjack tables.

Pit Boss

A casino employee, reporting to the shift manager, whose primary responsibilities include supervising the dealers, settling disputes, spotting counters, and handing out comps and other perks to favored customers.

Player

Generally, a casino customer. Also used to mean a high roller.

Point Count

A system of assigning values to the various card ranks, based on the effect the removal of cards of these ranks have on the player's expectation. By convention, ranks 2,3,4,5,6,7,8 are assigned positive values, and 9,10,Ace are assigned negative values.

Push

When both the player and dealer have unbusted hands of the same value, the hands are said to push, and no money changes hands. A draw.

Round

In Blackjack, a series of events beginning with the deal and ending with the settlement. Also referred to as a hand of play.

Running Count

In card-counting systems, the raw, unadjusted count. Also called the simple point count.

Settlement

After all the players and the dealer have acted on their hands, the dealer collects the bets of the losing players and pays off the winners. For a more complete discussion see Chapter Two, The Rules of the Game.

Shift

A shift is an eight-hour work day. The term is also used to mean all the employees starting work at the same time.

Shift Manager

A casino employee supervising the pit bosses, and reporting to the casino manager. The shift manager's primary responsibilities include scheduling personnel, processing accounting paperwork, and pampering high rollers.

Shill

A casino employee hired to stimulate action at the table games by engaging in simulated play.

Shills usually play by fixed "shill rules," and generally use non-redeemable chips, as well.

Shoe

A dealing box used to hold the cards. Although normally only used in multiple-deck games, the Nevada State Gaming Control Board requires very small casinos to deal one- and two-deck games from a shoe as well.

Shuffling

The random mixing of the cards done by the dealer between hands. For a more complete discussion see Chapter Two, The Rules of the Game.

Soft

A soft hand contains an Ace valued as 11. Examples: (Ace,6) is soft 17, (Ace,Ace,6) is soft 18. The lowest soft hand is 12, the highest soft hand is 21.

Split

A playing option allowing the player to treat each card of a pair as the first card of two separate hands. For a more complete discussion see Chapter Two, The Rules of the Game.

Stand

When a player is satisfied with his unbusted hand and takes no additional cards, he is said to stand. The dealer stands when his total reaches 17 or more (some casinos have modified this rule for soft hands and stand on soft 18 or more).

Stiff

A hand that totals hard 12 through 16. A stiff may be busted by a one card draw.

Surrender

A playing option allowing the player to give up his hand and forfeit half his bet. There are three versions of this option, late surrender, Asian surrender, and early surrender.

For a more complete discussion see Chapter Two, The Rules of the Game.

Third Base

The playing position at the dealer's extreme right.

Toke

Casinospeak for a tip or gratuity.

True Count

The running count adjusted for the proportion of the pack remaining to be dealt. Also called the count per deck or point count index.

Twenty-One

Another name for the game of Blackjack.

Up card

The dealer's face up card.

10

Commonly used in this book to denote a 10-valued card, specifically a 10, Jack, Queen or King.

86

The casino practice of excluding undesirable patrons and players. See Barring.

REFERENCES

Andersen, Ian. Turning the Tables on Las Vegas. New York: Vanguard Press, 1976.

Archer, John. The Archer Method of Winning at 21. Chicago: Henry Regnery Co., 1973.

Baldwin, Roger, Wilbert Cantey, Herbert Maisel, James McDermott. "The Optimum Strategy in Blackjack." Journal of the American Statistical Association 51 (1956).

Baldwin, Roger, Wilbert Cantey, Herbert Maisel, James McDermott. Playing Blackjack to Win. New York: M. Barrows & Co., 1957.

Braun, Julian H. The Development and Analysis of Winning Strategies for the Casino Game of Blackjack. Chicago, 1974; rev. ed., 1975.

Braun, Julian H. How to Play Winning Blackjack. Chicago: Data House Publishing Co., 1980.

Einstein, Charles. How to Win at Blackjack. Las Vegas: Gambler's Book Club, 1968.

Epstein, Richard A. The Theory of Gambling and Statistical Logic. New York: Academic Press, 1977.

Feller, William. An Introduction to Probability Theory and its Applications. New York: John Wiley & Sons, Inc., 1957.

Griffin, Peter A. The Theory of Blackjack. Las Vegas: GBC Press, 1979; rev. ed., Davis: Faculty Publishing, 1986.

Humble, Lance. Blackjack Gold. Toronto: International Gaming, 1976; rev. ed., Blackjack Super/Gold. Toronto, 1979.

Kelly, J. L. "A New Interpretation of Information Rate" IRE Transactions on Information Theory IT-2 (September, 1956). Bell System Technical Journal 35 (1956), 917-926.

REFERENCES

Livingston, A. D. Dealing with Cheats. Philadelphia: J. B. Lippincott Company, 1973.

Revere, Lawrence. Playing Blackjack as a Business. New Jersey: Lyle Stuart, 1969; rev. ed., New Jersey: Lyle Stuart, 1980.

Schlesinger, Don. Blackjack Attack: Playing the Pros' Way. Oakland: RGE Publishing, 1997.

Snyder, Arnold. Blackbelt in Blackjack. Berkeley: RGE Publishing, 1983.

Snyder, Arnold. Blackjack Forum. Oakland: RGE Publishing, 1981-.

Thorp, Edward O. Beat the Dealer. New York: Random House, 1962; rev. ed., New York: Vintage Books, 1966.

Uston, Ken. Million Dollar Blackjack. Hollywood: Gambling Times, 1981.

Uston, Ken. The Big Player. New York: Holt, Rinehart and Winston, 1977.

Vancura, Olaf, Ken Fuchs. Knock-Out Blackjack. Las Vegas: Isochoric Publishing, 1996.

Wilson, Allan N. The Casino Gambler's Guide. New York: Harper & Row, 1966.

Wong, Stanford. Professional Blackjack. La Jolla: Pi Yee Press, 1975; rev. ed., New York: William Morrow and Co., 1980, 1981.

Wong, Stanford. Winning Without Counting. La Jolla: Pi Yee Press, 1978.

Wong, Stanford. Current Blackjack News. La Jolla: Pi Yee Press, 1979-.

LIST OF TABLES

LIST OF FIGURES

LIST OF PRACTICE CHARTS

Index

PUBLICATIONS BY STANFORD WONG

BOOKS

Professional Blackjack. This 350-page book has a complete and accurate presentation of the *high-low,* the counting system used by more card counters than any other because of its combination of simplicity and power. If you want a more advanced counting system, *Professional Blackjack* also contains the *halves.*

Blackjack Secrets. This 250-page book explains how to get away with playing a winning game of blackjack in casinos. (You can't win money just by playing your cards well; you also must avoid drawing attention to your card-counting ability.) It also contains an introduction to the high-low card counting system.

Basic Blackjack. This 250-page book is a comprehensive presentation of basic strategy and win rates for all common rules and most exotic rules for the game of blackjack. It also explains methods of getting an edge that do not involve counting cards.

Casino Tournament Strategy. This is the book that explains how to get an edge over the other players in tournaments. In 350 pages it covers blackjack, craps, baccarat, keno, and horses. The strategies required for success in a blackjack tournament are completely different from the strategies that are appropriate for blackjack away from tournaments.

Professional Video Poker. This is the book that shows how to get an edge on video poker at both Nevada and Atlantic City casinos. The material was developed with the aid of two video-poker pros. (Yes, there are people who support themselves playing video poker.)

Optimal Strategy For Pai Gow Poker. This is the book that shows how to get an edge at pai gow poker. Mike Caro, author of *Professional Pai Gow Poker Report,* says "Those serious players seeking to make a living at pai gow poker will find Wong's *Optimal Strategy for Pai Gow Poker* an almost perfect path to profit."

NEWSLETTER

Current Blackjack News is a monthly newsletter for blackjack players. It is available electronically, and the entire content is posted on the bj21.com Internet site. *Current Blackjack News* is also available by regular mail.

The entire content of *Current Blackjack News* is descriptions of rules and playing conditions in casinos in Las Vegas and elsewhere in the United States. Every month reporters visit hundreds of casinos and email their findings to Pi Yee Press, and those reports are compiled into the newsletter.

INTERNET WEB SITE

Green chip is a private club for card counters. It is a place for serious blackjack players to exchange information and socialize with one another. Green chip is a membership group on BJ21, an Internet web site. Green chippers post messages for each other to read, and hook up electronically to chat every evening.

Besides exchanging messages and chatting, green chippers meet other green chippers in casinos. There are get-togethers involving small numbers of green chippers in casino cities every weekend, and larger green-chip parties from time to time.

Every month one green-chip post is selected as "Post of the Month." Each person who wins Post of the Month receives the acclaim of his or her peers and a check. All Posts of the Month are preserved in the Archives of BJ21.

Access to the green-chip pages of BJ21 requires a password, but you can get an idea of what is on the green-chip pages by visiting the free pages of BJ21. The BJ21 Internet site is interactive; anyone can read messages or post messages instantly. Just get on the Internet and go to:

http://www.bj21.com

There are four categories of pages on BJ21: green chip, black chip, CBJN, and free. The CBJN page is the electronic version of the monthly *Current Blackjack News*.

The top-of-the-line blackjack information source is the black chip. Black-chip membership includes a password that opens black chip, green chip, and CBJN pages of BJ21.

SOFTWARE

Blackjack Count Analyzer (BCA). This is a DOS program for playing blackjack. Besides playing blackjack, *BCA* generates tables of strategy indexes and runs high-speed simulations. It handles all common and uncommon rules variations, and also some rules variations that have never been offered in any casino.

A Windows version is also available: *Professional Blackjack Analyzer (PBA)* by David Smith. *PBA* does everything *BCA* does, and more.

A simplified version of *BCA*, *Blackjack Analyzer*, also is available; *Blackjack Analyzer* uses basic strategy only, whereas *BCA* and *PBA* support card counting.

Also available: *Omega II Blackjack Casino* by Bryce Carlson. This is the MS-DOS version of the *Omega II Blackjack Machine* described in Chapter Eleven. (The *Omega II Blackjack Machine* is no longer available; it was written for Apple II computers, and they no longer are being sold by Apple.

Tournament Blackjack. This is a Windows program for playing blackjack tournaments. It can be used to analyze tournament situations by simulation.

Stanford Wong Video Poker (SWVP). This program, like its predecessor *Video Poker Analyzer*, is a computer program for playing and analyzing video poker. *SWVP* is a DOS program that supports use of a mouse.

Also available is *VPEXACT*, a DOS program whose only function is to cycle through all possible hands of video poker to calculate the payback to the customer.

ORDERING INFORMATION

Write to Pi Yee Press, 7910 Ivanhoe Ave, PMB #34, La Jolla, CA 92037-4511 for prices and an order form. Or email piyeepress@bj21.com. Or call (858) 456-4080. Or fax (858) 456-8076.